Permanent M

ST/PLS/SER.A/305

Protocol and Liaison Service

Permanent Missions

to the United Nations

Nº 305

April 2015

United Nations, New York

Note: This publication is prepared by the Protocol and Liaison Service for information purposes only.

The listings relating to the permanent missions are based on information communicated to the Protocol and Liaison Service by the permanent missions, and their publication is intended for the use of delegations and the Secretariat. They do not include all diplomatic and administrative staff exercising official functions in connection with the United Nations.

Further information concerning names of members of permanent missions entitled to diplomatic privileges and immunities and other mission members registered with the United Nations can be obtained from:

Protocol and Liaison Service
Room S-0209
United Nations
New York, N.Y., 10017

Telephone: (212) 963-2938
Telefax: (212) 963-1921

website: **http://www.un.int/protocol**

All changes and additions to this publication should be communicated to the above Service.

Language: **English**
Sales No.: **E.15.1.6**
ISBN:.**978-92-1-101319-1**
e-ISBN: **978-92-1-057401-3**

Contents

I. Member States maintaining permanent missions at Headquarters

II. Non-member States having received a standing invitation to participate as observer in the sessions and the work of the General Assembly and maintaining permanent observer missions at Headquarters

III. Intergovernmental organizations having received a standing invitation to participate as observers in the sessions and the work of the General Assembly and maintaining permanent offices at Headquarters*

* For IGOs not maintaining permanent offices in New York, see p. 310

IV. Other entities having received a standing invitation to participate as observers in the sessions and the work of the General Assembly and maintaining permanent offices at Headquarters

V. Specialized agencies and related organizations maintaining liaison offices at Headquarters

Annexes

1. Members of the principal organs of the United Nations

2. Members of other standing organs at Headquarters

I. Member States maintaining permanent missions at Headquarters

Afghanistan

Member State since 19 November 1946

Address: Permanent Mission of Afghanistan
to the United Nations
633 Third Avenue, 27th Floor
New York, N.Y. 10017

Telephone: (212) 972-1212

Telefax: (212) 972-1216

e-mail: info@afghanistan-un.org

Correspondence: English

National holiday: 19 August
Independence Day

H.E. Mr. Zahir **Tanin**
Ambassador Extraordinary and Plenipotentiary
Permanent Representative (DPC: 19 December 2006)*
Mrs. Zarghoona Sediq Tanin

Ms. Asila **Wardak**
Minister Counsellor

Mr. Naseer Ahmad **Faiq**
Counsellor

Mr. Obaid Khan **Noori**
Counsellor
Mrs. Afshan Gul Noori

Mr. Mohd. Hassan **Faizee**
First Secretary
Mrs. Afsana Faizee

Mr. Rafiullah **Naseri**
Second Secretary
Mrs. Yalda Naseri

Mrs. Anisa Akbary **Omid**
Second Secretary

Mr. Mustafa **Masoudi**
Second Secretary

Mr. Wahdat **Safiullah**
Second Secretary

Mr. Lutfullah **Lutfi**
Second Secretary

Mr. Mohammad Fahim **Rahimi**
Third Secretary

* Date of presentation of credentials to the Secretary-General.

Albania

Member State since 14 December 1955

Address: Permanent Mission of the Republic of Albania to the United Nations
320 East 79th Street
New York, N.Y. 10075

Telephone: (212) 249-2059, -5654

Telefax: (212) 535-2917

e-mail: mission.newyork@mfa.gov.al
albania.un@albania-un.org

Correspondence: English

National holiday: 28 November
Independence Day

H.E. Mr. Ferit **Hoxha**
Ambassador Extraordinary and Plenipotentiary
Permanent Representative (DPC: 5 August 2009)
Mrs. Armelle Suzanne Montenot-Hoxha

Mr. Ervin **Nina**
Minister Counsellor
Deputy Permanent Representative
Mrs. Merilda Nina

Ms. Ingrit **Prizreni**
First Secretary

Ms. Olisa **Cifligu**
Second Secretary

Mrs. Brizida **Nina**
Second Secretary

Algeria

Member State since 8 October 1962

Address:	Permanent Mission of Algeria to the United Nations 326 East 48th Street New York, N.Y. 10017
Telephone:	(212) 750-1960, -1962, -1965, -1966
Telefax:	(212) 759-9538, -5274
e-mail:	mission@algeria-un.org
website:	www.algeria-un.org
Correspondence:	French
National holiday:	1 November

H.E. Mr. Sabri **Boukadoum**
Ambassador Extraordinary and Plenipotentiary
Permanent Representative (DPC: 14 March 2014)
Mrs. Sabria Boukadoum

H.E. Mr. Mohameed **Bessedik**
Ambassador
Deputy Permanent Representative

Mr. Larbi **Djacta**
Minister Counsellor
Mrs. Souad Djacta

Mr. Abdelhakim **Mihoubi**
Counsellor

Mr. Mourad **Mebarki**
Counsellor
Mrs. Nacima Mebarki

Mr. Kamel **Chir**
First Secretary
Mrs. Baya Chir

Mr. Fethi **Metref**
First Secretary
Mrs. Amel Metref

Mr. Mohamed Salah Eddine **Belaid**
First Secretary
Mrs. Rafika Belaid

Mr. Khaled **Benamadi**
First Secretary
Mrs. Rym Benamadi

Mr. Mohand Tahar **Mokhtari**
First Secretary
Mrs. Nouara Mokhtari

Mr. Mustapha **Abbani**
First Secretary
Mrs. Houria Abbani

Mr. Abdelghani **Merabet**
First Secretary
Mrs. Lynda Merabet

Mr. Idris **Latreche**
Third Secretary
Mrs. Zakia Latreche

Ms. Bakhta Selma **Mansouri**
Third Secretary

Mr. Abdelkarim **Ait Abdeslam**
Third Secretary
Mrs. Soumia Ait Abdeslam

Ms. Zaina **Benhabouche**
Third Secretary

Mr. Khireddine **Chouiref**
Attaché
Mrs. Aicha Chouiref

Mr. Younes **Mahiout**
Attaché

Mr. Kamel **Edjekouane**
Attaché
Mrs. Radia Edjekouane

Andorra

Address: Permanent Mission of the Principality of Andorra to the United Nations
Two United Nations Plaza, 27th Floor
New York, N.Y. 10017

Telephone: (212) 750-8064, -8065

Telefax: (212) 750-6630

e-mail: contact@andorraun.org

website: www.mae.ad

Correspondence: English

National holiday: 8 September

H.E. ...
Ambassador Extraordinary and Plenipotentiary
Permanent Representative (DPC: ...)

Ms. Gemma **Raduan Corrius**
Third Secretary
Deputy Permanent Representative

Address:	Permanent Mission of the Republic of Angola to the United Nations 820 Second Avenue, 12th Floor New York, N.Y. 10017
Telephone:	(212) 861-5656, -5787, -5789
Telefax:	(212) 861-9295
e-mail:	themission@angolaun.org
website:	www.angolamissionun.org
Correspondence:	English
National holiday:	11 November Independence Day

Ext. 222 H.E. Mr. Ismael Abraão **Gaspar Martins**
Ambassador Extraordinary and Plenipotentiary
Permanent Representative (DPC: 23 May 2001)
Mrs. Luzia de Jesus Gaspar Martins

H.E. Mr. Julio Helder Moura **Lucas**
Ambassador
Deputy Permanent Representative

Mr. João Iambeno **Gimolieca**
Minister Counsellor

Ext. 234 Mr. Manuel Vieira da **Fonseca**
Counsellor
Mrs. Janete de Jesus Fonseca

Ext. 238 Ms. Sara Maria de Assunção **Silva**
Counsellor

Mr. Mário Domingos **Simão**
Counsellor
Military Adviser
Mrs. Maria Imaculada Torres Baptista Simão

Ext. 239 Mr. Miguel **Dialamicua**
Counsellor
Mrs. Makumbo Moreno Nfinda

Mr. Fidel **Casimiro**
Counsellor

Ext. 235 Mr. Mateus Pedro **Luemba**
First Secretary
Mrs. Paula Ferreira Luemba

Mrs. Cesaltina Dias **Ferreira**
First Secretary
Mr. Augusto Joaqim Dias Ferreira

Ms. Jackie Hetungamena **Ndombasi**
First Secretary

Ms. Efigénia Perpetua dos Prazeres **Jorge**
First Secretary

Mr. Aguinaldo Patrice Rosário **Baptista**
First Secretary

Ms. Vezua Bula Diogo de **Paiva**
Second Secretary

Ext. 250 Mrs. Virginia Eleazar Diogo Fernandes **Bayonne**
Third Secretary
Mr. Guy Gilbert Bayonne

Ext. 237 Mr. Marcio Sandro Aleixo Pereira **Burity**
Third Secretary
Mrs. Jasminea Isabel M. Narciso Burity

Mr. Domingos César **Correia**
Third Secretary

Ext. 246 Mr. Xavier **Santa Rosa**
Attaché (Press)
Mrs. Maria Isabel Carlos Santa Rosa

Mr. Osvaldo José Seabra **Roque**
Attaché (Finance)
Mrs. Domingas Germano João Roque

Mr. Domingos **Mesquita Sapalo**
Assistant Attaché
Military Adviser
Mrs. Alice Mónica da C. de C. Sapalo

Address:	Permanent Mission of Antigua and Barbuda to the United Nations 305 East 47th Street, 6th Floor New York, N.Y. 10017
Telephone:	(212) 541-4117
Telefax:	(212) 757-1607
e-mail:	unmission@abgov.org
website:	www.abgov.org
Correspondence:	English
National holiday:	1 November Independence Day

---

(646) 215-6013	H.E. Mr. Walton Alfonso **Webson** Ambassador Extraordinary and Plenipotentiary Permanent Representative (DPC: 17 December 2014)
(646) 215-6021	Mr. Glentis **Thomas** Counsellor Mrs. Kerryann Jamella Thomas
(646) 215-6023	Mr. Tumasie **Blair** Counsellor
(646) 215-6013	Mrs. Jackley **Peters** Attaché Mr. Rupert Peters

Argentina

Member State since 24 October 1945

Address:	Permanent Mission of Argentina to the United Nations One United Nations Plaza, 25th Floor New York, N.Y. 10017
Telephone:	(212) 688-6300
Telefax:	(212) 980-8395 (General number)
e-mail:	enaun@mrecic.gov.ar
website:	enaun.mrecic.gov.ar
Correspondence:	Spanish
National holiday:	25 May

Ext. 203	H.E. Mrs. María Cristina **Perceval** Ambassador Extraordinary and Plenipotentiary Permanent Representative (23 November 2012) Mr. Pablo Martín
Ext. 201	Mr. Mateo **Estreme** Minister Plenipotentiary Deputy Permanent Representative Mrs. Gabriela Martinic
Ext. 238	Mr. Mario **Oyarzábal** Minister Plenipotentiary Deputy Permanent Representative
	Mrs. Gabriela **Martinic** Minister Plenipotentiary Mr. Mateo Estreme
Ext. 231	Ms. Fernanda **Millicay** Minister Plenipotentiary
Ext. 228	Mr. José Luis **Fernandez Valoni** Counsellor Mrs. María Eugenia Mahiques
Ext. 226	Mr. Rafael Héctor **Dalo** Counsellor
Ext. 237	Mr. Francisco Javier **de Antueno** First Secretary Mrs. María Magdalena Sostaric
Ext. 219	Ms. Pía **Poroli** First Secretary
Ext. 235	Mr. Marcos **Stancanelli** Second Secretary Mrs. Belén Sorzana de Stancanelli
Ext. 236	Mr. Sebastián **Di Luca** Second Secretary

	Mr. Tomás **Pico** Second Secretary
Ext. 207	Mr. Juan Carlos **Ganam** Attaché Mrs. Laura Conti de Ganam
	Ms. Paula Elena **Valenza** Attaché
Ext. 212	Mrs. Gabriela Mabel **Nieva** Attaché Mr. Federico Cesar Reynoso
Ext. 207	Mr. Jonathan Javier **Lescano** Attaché Mrs. María Victoria Campanino

Address:	Permanent Mission of the Republic of Armenia to the United Nations 119 East 36th Street New York, N.Y. 10016
Telephone:	(212) 686-9079, -3871
Telefax:	(212) 686-3934
e-mail:	armenia@un.int
website:	www.un.mfa.am
Correspondence:	English
National holiday:	21 September

Ext. 102 H.E. Mr. Zohrab **Mnatsakanyan**
Ambassador Extraordinary and Plenipotentiary
Permanent Representative (DPC: 10 June 2014)
Mrs. Irina Igitkhanyan

Ext. 111 Mr. Tigran **Samvelian**
Counsellor
Deputy Permanent Representative
Mrs. Inna Torgomyan

Mr. Mikaeyl **Sarukhanyan**
Counsellor
Mrs. Silva Sargsyan

Ext. 114 Mr. Sahak **Sargsyan**
First Secretary

Mrs. Sofya **Simonyan**
Attaché
Mr. Suren Sargsyan

Colonel Mesrop **Nazaryan**
Counsellor
Military Adviser
Mrs. Roza Tovmasyan

Address:	Permanent Mission of Australia to the United Nations 150 East 42nd Street, 33rd Floor New York, N.Y. 10017-5612
Telephone:	(212) 351-6600
Telefax:	(212) 351-6610
e-mail:	australia@un.int
Correspondence:	English
National holiday:	26 January Australia Day

351-6611	H.E. Ms. Gillian **Bird** Ambassador Extraordinary and Plenipotentiary Permanent Representative (DPC: 17 February 2015) Mr. Henri Ergas
351-6638	H.E. Ms. Caitlin **Wilson** Ambassador Deputy Permanent Representative
351-6657	Mr. Peter Lloyd **Versegi** Minister Counsellor (Development) Mrs. Catherine Versegi
351-6655	Ms. Amy **Haddad** Counsellor (Development) Mr. Joshua Milthorpe
351-6673	Ms. Susan **King** Counsellor Police Adviser Ms. Melissa Ryan
351-6698	Ms. Rosemary **Driscoll** Counsellor Mr. Brett De Longville
351-6684	Mr. Gareth **Williams** Counsellor
351-6626	Ms. Penelope **Morton** First Secretary
351-6639	Mr. Jared **Potter** First Secretary
351-6623	Ms. Julia **O'Brien** First Secretary Mr. Fraser Drummond

351-6652	Cmdr. Simon **Andrews** First Secretary Deputy Military Adviser Mrs. Anne Andrews
	Mr. Darren **Hansen** First Secretary Mrs. Waka Hansen
351-6624	Mr. Scott-Marshall **Harper** Second Secretary Ms. Madeleine Patricia Oliver
	Mr. Gregory **Nichols** Second Secretary Mrs. Song Yi Pak
351-6628	Mr. Ryan **Neelam** Second Secretary
	Mr. Nathan **Henderson** Second Secretary Ms. Ashlynn Stewart
351-6641	Ms. Peta **McDougall** Second Secretary
351-6615	Mr. Peter **Stone** Attaché (Election Officer) Ms. Renée Grigson
351-6619	Ms. Sally **Weston** Attaché (Legal and Sanctions Officer)
351-6656	Mr. Christopher John **Stokes** Attaché (Development)
351-6632	Mr. John **Olenich** Attaché (Media and Public Affairs)
351-6672	Ms. Phillipa Lucy **Walker** Attaché (Police)
	Mr. Kevin **Murray** Attaché (Defence) Mrs. Namoi Murphy

Address:	Permanent Mission of Austria to the United Nations 600 Third Avenue, 31st Floor New York, N.Y. 10016
Telephone:	(917) 542-8400
Telefax:	(212) 949-1840
e-mail:	new-york-ov@bmeia.gv.at
website:	www.un.int/austria
Correspondence:	English
National holiday:	26 October

---

(917) 542-8402	H.E. Mr. Martin **Sajdik** Ambassador Extraordinary and Plenipotentiary Permanent Representative (DPC: 4 January 2012) Mrs. Tamara Otounbaeva
(917) 542-8403	Mr. Andreas **Riecken** Minister Plenipotentiary Deputy Permanent Representative Mrs. Elisabeth Riecken
(917) 542-8414	Mr. Fritz **Pokorny** Counsellor (Administrative Affairs) Mrs. Gabriele Marie-Luise Pokorny
(917) 542-8432	Mr. Hannes **Machor** Counsellor
(917) 542-8405	Mr. Gerold Thilo **Vollmer** Counsellor Mr. Mika Sakari Salovaara
(917) 542-8436	Ms. Maria Angela **Holzmann** First Secretary
(917) 542-8434	Ms. Nadia Alexandra **Kalb** First Secretary
	Mr. George Wilhelm **Gallhofer** First Secretary Mrs. Christina Anne Gallhofer Hawley
(917) 542-8406	Mr. Stefan **Pretterhofer** First Secretary
(917) 542-8407	Mr. Joško **Emrich** Second Secretary
(917) 542-8435	Mr. Stephen Matthias **Koppanyi** Attaché
(917) 542-8429	Mr. Christian **Bolzer** Assistant Attaché

(917) 542-8424	Ms. Marina **Mailänder** Assistant Attaché
(917) 542-8420	Ms. Sonia **Szydelko** Assistant Attaché Mr. Thiago Bastos Mello Pereira
(917) 542-8439	Brigadier General Franz **Berndorfer** Counsellor Military Adviser Mrs. Gabriele Berndorfer
(917) 542-8438	Colonel Helmut **Breitfuss** Counsellor Mrs. Christine Breitfuss

Address:	Permanent Mission of the Republic of Azerbaijan to the United Nations 866 United Nations Plaza, Suite 560 New York, N.Y. 10017
Telephone:	(212) 371-2559; 2832
Telefax:	(212) 371-2784; (646) 738-6143
e-mail:	azerbaijan@un.int
Correspondence:	English
National holiday:	28 May Republic Day

H.E. Mr. Yashar T. **Aliyev**
Ambassador Extraordinary and Plenipotentiary
Permanent Representative (DPC: 10 June 2014)

Mrs. Khanim **Ibrahimova**
Counsellor

Ms. Husniyya **Mammadova**
Counsellor

Mr. Elnur **Iskandarov**
First Secretary

646-738-6244 Mr. Farid **Jabrayilov**
First Secretary
Mrs. Mehriban Jabrayilova

646-738-6246 Mr. Mukhtar **Abduyev**
First Secretary
Mrs. Laman Gurbanova

Ms. Gunay **Rahimova**
Second Secretary

646-738-6265 Mr. Fakhri **Aliyev**
Third Secretary
Mrs. Fatima Aliyeva

Mr. Elman **Azizov**
Attaché
Mrs. Fargana Azizova

Mrs. Firuza **Valikhanli**
Attaché

Mr. Murad **Balajayev**
Attaché
Mrs. Ulviyya Balajayeva

Address:	Permanent Mission of the Commonwealth of the Bahamas to the United Nations 231 East 46th Street New York, N.Y. 10017
Telephone:	(212) 421-6925
Telefax:	(212) 759-2135
e-mail:	mission@bahamasny.com
Social Media:	Facebook: https://www.facebook.com/bmissionny
Correspondence:	English
National holiday:	10 July Independence Day

Ext. 840	H.E. Mr. Elliston **Rahming** Ambassador Extraordinary and Plenipotentiary Permanent Representative (DPC: 13 September 2013) Mrs. Arthurlouise Rahming
Ext. 845	Ms. Allison P. **Booker** Counsellor
Ext. 842	Ms. Tishka H. **Francis** First Secretary
Ext. 836	Mrs. Christie **Cargill** First Secretary Mr. Adrian Cargill
Ext. 838	Ms. Joy A. **Newbold** Second Secretary
Ext. 867	Mr. Craig **Powell** Third Secretary
Ext. 841	Ms. Sasha **Dixon** Third Secretary
Ext. 844	Ms. Mashanna L. **Russell** Third Secretary
Ext. 869	Mrs. Michelle L. **Stubbs** Attaché Mr. Keith Garnet Stubbs
Ext. 828	Mr. Chanarve A. **McBride** Attaché

Bahrain

Member State since 21 September 1971

Address: Permanent Mission of the Kingdom of Bahrain to the United Nations
866 Second Avenue, 14th and 15th Floors
New York, N.Y. 10017

Telephone: (212) 223-6200

Telefax: (212) 319-0687, 223-6206

e-mail: bahrain1@un.int

Correspondence: English

National holiday: 16 December

H.E. Mr. Jamal Fares **Alrowaiei**
Ambassador Extraordinary and Plenipotentiary
Permanent Representative (DPC: 14 September 2011)
Mrs. Sara Khabar

Ms. Shaikha Aysha Ahmed Saquer **Alkhalifa**
Counsellor
Deputy Permanent Representative

Mr. Fahad Hamad Ahmed Abdulaziz **Alaamer**
Counsellor
Mrs. Munira Khalifa Hamad Alkaabi

Mr. Hamad Fareed Ahmed **Hasan**
Third Secretary
Mrs. Lamya Husain Mohamed Hasan AlHasan

Ms. Fatema Rasheed Mohamed **Ali**
Attaché

Mr. Fahad Ahmed **Aldoseri**
Attaché

Address:	Permanent Mission of the People's Republic of Bangladesh to the United Nations 820 Second Avenue, 4th Floor New York, N.Y. 10017
Telephone:	(212) 867-3434, -3437
Telefax:	(212) 972-4038
e-mail:	bangladesh@un.int; bdpmny@gmail.com
website:	www.un.int/bangladesh
Correspondence:	English
National holiday:	26 March Independence and National Day

Ext. 111

H.E. Mr. Abulkalam Abdul **Momen**
Ambassador Extraordinary and Plenipotentiary
Permanent Representative (DPC: 27 August 2009)
Mrs. Selina Momen

Ext. 105

Mr. Md. Mustafizur **Rahman**
Minister
Deputy Permanent Representative
Mrs. Tanzina Binte Alamgir

Ms. Sadia **Faizunnesa**
Counsellor
Deputy Permanent Representative
Mr. Quasem Azam

Mr. Andalib **Elias**
Counsellor
Mrs. Sohani Huq Elias

Ext. 115

Ms. Samia **Anjum**
Counsellor
Mr. Sayeel Kawsar

Mr. Mohammad **Mahmuduzzaman**
Counsellor
Mrs. Shorna Hamid

Mr. ATM Rakebul **Haque**
Counsellor
Mrs. Shehnaz Afrin Rakeb

Mr. Bijan Lal **Dev**
First Secretary (Press)

Mr. Jamal Uddin **Ahmed**
Second Secretary
Ms. Abida Sultana Sumy

	Mr. Mohamad Mamun Or **Rashid** First Secretary (Press)
Ext. 106	Mr. Barun Dev **Mitra** Minister (Economic Affairs) Ms. Rakhee Mitra Chowdhury
Ext. 108	Mr. Akm **Akhtaruzzaman** Minister Defence Adviser Mrs. Rehana Sultana

Barbados

Member State since 9 December 1966

Address: Permanent Mission of Barbados to the United Nations
820 Second Avenue, 9th Floor
New York, N.Y. 10017

Telephone: (212) 551-4300

Telefax: (212) 986-1030

e-mail: prun@foreign.gov.bb; barbados@un.int

Correspondence: English

National holiday: 30 November

H.E. Mr. Keith Hamilton Llewellyn **Marshall**
Ambassador Extraordinary and Plenipotentiary
Permanent Representative (DPC: 22 April 2015)

Ms. Juliette Rosita **Riley**
Minister Counsellor
Deputy Permanent Representative

Ms. Kereeta Nicole **Whyte**
First Secretary

Ms. Rosalind Gail **Riley**
First Secretary

Ms. Lynda Cecilia **Waithe**
Attaché

Address:	Permanent Mission of the Republic of Belarus to the United Nations 136 East 67th Street, 4th Floor New York, N.Y. 10065
Telephone:	(212) 535-3420
Telefax:	(212) 734-4810
e-mail:	usaun@mfa.gov.by
website:	www.un.int/belarus
Correspondence:	English
National holiday:	3 July Independence Day

535-3420 H.E. Mr. Andrei **Dapkiunas**
Ambassador Extraordinary and Plenipotentiary
Permanent Representative (DPC: 4 January 2012)

734-1689 Mr. Evgeny **Lazarev**
Minister Counsellor
Deputy Permanent Representative

772-2354 Ms. Larysa **Belskaya**
Counsellor

734-4354 Mr. Vitaly **Mackay**
Counsellor
Mrs. Margarita Mackay

734-3997 Mr. Alexander **Shpakovsky**
Counsellor

734-2326 Mr. Sergei **Zaikov**
Counsellor
Mrs. Elena Zaikova

734-3997 Mr. Aleksei **Kolesov**
First Secretary
Mrs. Ekaterina Kolesova

734-3997 Mr. Ilya **Adamov**
Second Secretary
Mrs. Elena Adamova

772-2354 Ms. Oksana **Melnikovich**
Second Secretary

Mr. Nikolai **Khramtsov**
Attaché
Mrs. Zhanna Khramtsova

Address:	Permanent Mission of Belgium to the United Nations One Dag Hammarskjöld Plaza 885 Second Avenue, 41st Floor New York, N.Y. 10017
Telephone:	(212) 378-6300
Telefax:	(212) 681-7618
e-mail:	newyorkun@diplobel.fed.be
web-site:	www.diplomatie.be/newyorkun
Correspondence:	French
National holiday:	21 July National Day

378-6361	H.E. Ms. Bénédicte **Frankinet** Ambassador Extraordinary and Plenipotentiary Permanent Representative (DPC: 13 March 2013) Mr. Jacques Hasday
378-6366	Mr. Pascal **Buffin** Minister Counsellor Deputy Permanent Representative Mr. Marcus Lopes
378-6337	Mr. Guy **Rayée** Minister Counsellor Mrs. Véronique Van Bilsen
378-6353	Mr. Jean-Jacques **Bastien** Counsellor Mrs. Nadine Mollers
378-6351	Mr. Peter **Verbrugghe** First Secretary
378-6373	Mr. Vincent **Willekens** First Secretary
378-6354	Mr. Antoine **Misonne** First Secretary Mrs. Agata Strzelecka-Missone
378-6342	Mr. Wim **Schaerlaekens** First Secretary
378-6336	Mr. Wouter **Poels** First Secretary
378-6374	Mr. Frédéric **Henrard** First Secretary Mr. Stephen Berson

378-6389	Ms. Marie **Cherchari** First Secretary Mr. Benoit Romijn
378-6368	Mr. Dominiek **Dutoo** Attaché

378-6383	Colonel BEM Lutgardis **Claes** Counsellor Military Adviser
378-6377	Mr. Yves **Haquenne** Attaché Assistant Military Adviser Mrs. Fabienne Promelle

Belize

Member State since 25 September 1981

Address:	Permanent Mission of Belize to the United Nations 675 Third Avenue, Suite 1911 New York, N.Y. 10017
Telephone:	(212) 986-1240
Telefax:	(212) 593-0932
e-mail:	blzun@belizemission.com blzun@aol.com
Correspondence:	English
National holiday:	21 September Independence Day

Ext. 202	H.E. Ms. Lois Michele **Young** Ambassador Extraordinary and Plenipotentiary Permanent Representative (DPC: 19 September 2012)
Ext. 206	H.E. Mrs. Janine Elizabeth **Coye-Felson** Ambassador Deputy Permanent Representative Mr. Alexander Jacob Felson
Ext. 205	Mr. Wen Tou **Wu** Minister Counsellor
Ext. 203	Ms. Paulette Vanessa **Elrington** Counsellor Mr. Maxime Cyrille
Ext. 204	Ms. Tasha **Young** First Secretary
Ext. 202	Ms. Sharleen Claudette **Henderson** Attaché

Address:	Permanent Mission of the Republic of Benin to the United Nations 125 East 38th Street New York, N.Y. 10016
Telephone:	(212) 684-1339
Telefax:	(646) 790-3556 (General number)
e-mail:	beninewyork@gmail.com
Correspondence:	French
National holiday:	1 August

Ext. 318 — H.E. Mr. Jean-Francis Régis **Zinsou**
Ambassador Extraordinary and Plenipotentiar
Permanent Representative (DPC: 7 January 2010)
Mrs. Colette Fatimabay-Zinsou

Ext. 329 — H.E. Mr. Thomas **Adoumasse**
Ambassador
Deputy Permanent Representative
Mrs. Angèle Prospère Avagbo-Adoumasse

Ext. 305 — Mr. Thierry **Alia**
Minister Counsellor
Mrs. Euphrasie Georgine Todedjarapou-Alia

Ext. 310 — Mr. Jonas **Djebou**
Minister Counsellor
Mrs. Léocadie Fassinou-Djebou

Ext. 309 — Mr. Yves Eric **Ahoussougbemey**
Second Counsellor
Mrs. Edwige Roseline Gilberte Ekoundayo Agossou-Ahoussougbemey

Ext. 328 — Mr. Hervé D. **Djokpe**
Counsellor
Mrs. Sandrine Sehou-Djokpe

Ext. 311 — Mr. Eric Jean-Marie **Zinsou**
Counsellor
Mrs. Adelaide K.V.S. Ninon Houndekon-Zinsou

Ext. 326 — Mrs. Edwige Roseline Gilberte Ekoundayo **Agossou-Ahoussougbemey**
Counsellor
Mr. Yves Eric Ahoussougbemey

Mr. Marius Akpe Cocou **Loko**
Counsellor
Mrs. Ahode Diane Sotindjo-Loko

Mr. Yassea N. Ems Eddy **Houndeffo**
First Secretary
Head of Chancery
Mrs. Nadia Lolita A. Pofagi-Houndeffo

Mrs. Ahode Diane **Sotindjo Loko**
Attaché
Mr. Marius Akpe Cocou Loko

Ext. 327 Mr. Innocent **Tchegnon**
Attaché
Mrs. Adèle Emma Sabine Agbo-Tchegnon

Mr. Patrick Jean-Baptiste **Aho**
Attaché (Defence)
Mrs. Janine Michèle Edwige Aplogan-Aho

Mr. Cyrille **Gainyo**
Assistant Attaché (Defense)
Mrs. Louisette Didavi-Gainyo

Bhutan

Address:	Permanent Mission of the Kingdom of Bhutan to the United Nations 343 East 43rd Street New York, N.Y. 10017
Telephone:	(212) 682-2268, -2312, -2371, -2752
Telefax:	(212) 661-0551
e-mail:	bhutanmission@pmbny.bt
Correspondence:	English
National holiday:	17 December National Day

Ext. 210 — H.E. Mrs. Kunzang C. **Namgyel**
Ambassador Extraordinary and Plenipotentiary
Permanent Representative (DPC: 25 February 2014)
Mr. Tseyring Namgyel

Ext. 208 — Mr. Tshering Gyaltshen **Penjor**
Minister
Deputy Permanent Representative

Ext. 202 — Colonel Sonam **Tobgye**
Minister
Military Adviser

Ext. 203 — Mr. Pema L. **Dorji**
Minister
Deputy Permanent Representative
Mrs. Deki Y. Dorji

Ext. 206 — Mr. Thinley **Dorji**
Minister Counsellor
Deputy Permanent Representative
Mrs. Rinzin Lham

Ext. 205 — Mr. Karma **Choeda**
Counsellor

Ext. 206 — Mrs. Sonam **Yangchen**
Counsellor
Mr. Tashi Dorji

Mr. **Kinzang**
Counsellor
Head of Chancery
Mrs. Karma Lhadon

Bolivia (Plurinational State of)

Member State since 14 November 1945

Address: Permanent Mission of the Plurinational State of Bolivia to the United Nations
801 Second Avenue, 4th Floor, Suite 402
New York, N.Y. 10017

Telephone: (212) 682-8132, -8133, -4113

Telefax: (212) 687-4642

e-mail: missionboliviaun@gmail.com

Correspondence: Spanish

National holiday: 6 August
Independence Day

H.E. Mr. Sacha Sergio **Llorentty Solíz**
Ambassador Extraordinary and Plenipotentiary
Permanent Representative (DPC: 19 September 2012)

Mrs. Ingrid **Sabja**
First Secretary

Ms. Adriana **Pacheco**
First Secretary
Mr. Alexandro Nicolas Valenzuela Martinic

Mr. Luis Mauricio **Arancibia Fernández**
Second Secretary

Mr. Gilbert Zacarias **Mamani Paco**
Second Secretary

Mrs. Brenda Nelly **Medina Mita**
Second Secretary

Bosnia and Herzegovina

Member State since 22 May 1992

Address: Permanent Mission of Bosnia and Herzegovina
to the United Nations
420 Lexington Avenue, Suites 607 & 608
New York, N.Y. 10170

Telephone: (212) 751-9015

Telefax: (212) 751-9019

e-mail: bihun@mfa.gov.ba

website: www.bhmisijaun.org

National holiday:

H.E. Ms. Mirsada **Čolaković**
Ambassador Extraordinary and Plenipotentiary
Permanent Representative (DPC: 6 July 2012)

Ms. Valentina **Marinčić**
Minister Counsellor
Deputy Permanent Representative

Mr. Mirza **Pašić**
Counsellor
Mrs. Aida Pašić

Ms. Šejla **Đurbuzović**
Counsellor

Mr. Željko **Vukobratović**
Counsellor

Mrs. Ljilja **Grgić-Stojanović**
First Secretary

Mrs. Dina **Fejzić Ismirlija**
Second Secretary

Address:	Permanent Mission of Botswana to the United Nations 154 East 46th Street New York, N.Y. 10017
Telephone:	(212) 889-2277, -2331, -2491, -2772
Telefax:	(212) 725-5061
e-mail:	botswana@un.int
Correspondence:	English
National holiday:	30 September

Ext. 124	H.E. Mr. Charles Thembani **Ntwaagae** Ambassador Extraordinary and Plenipotentiary Permanent Representative (DPC: 31 July 2008) Mrs. Elizabeth Mmasello Ntwaagae
Ext. 110	Mr. Nkoloi **Nkoloi** Minister Plenipotentiary Deputy Permanent Representative
Ext. 120	Ms. Mpho Michelle **Mogobe** Minister Counsellor
Ext. 115	Mr. Tlhalefo Batsile **Madisa** First Secretary Mrs. Kealeboga Madisa
Ext. 114	Ms. Ketshidile Gloria **Bafetanye** First Secretary
Ext. 108	Mr. Pako **Moremi** Second Secretary Mrs. Morobi Evelyn Moremi
Ext. 116	Mr. Katlego Boase **Mmalane** Second Secretary
Ext. 107	Mrs. Hellen Emang **Jack** Attaché (Administrative Affairs) Mr. Christopher Bashi Jack

Address:	Permanent Mission of Brazil to the United Nations 747 Third Avenue, 9th Floor New York, N.Y. 10017-2803
Telephone:	(212) 372-2600, 832-6868
Telefax:	(212) 371-5716
e-mail:	Distri.delbrasonu@itamaraty.gov.br
website:	www.un.int/brazil
Correspondence:	English
National holiday:	7 September Independence Day

372-2604	H.E. Mr. Antonio **de Aguiar Patriota** Ambassador Extraordinary and Plenipotentiary Permanent Representative (DPC: 24 October 2013)
372-2607	H.E. Mr. Guilherme **de Aguiar Patriota** Ambassador Deputy Permanent Representative Mrs. Erika Almeida Watanabe Patriota
372-2648	Ms. Fatima Keiko **Ishitani** Minister Plenipotentiary
372-2644	Mr. Leonardo Luís **Gorgulho Nogueira Fernandes** Minister Plenipotentiary Mrs. Daniella Köhnen Abramovay Fernandes
372-2611	Mr. Sérgio **Rodrigues dos Santos** Minister Plenipotentiary Mrs. Josiane Da Luz Dias
372-2651	Mr. Mauricio Fernando **Dias Favero** Counsellor Mrs. Kelly Chung
372-2647	Mr. João Paulo **Soares Alsina Jr.** Counsellor Mrs. Amelia Cristina Cherulli Alsina
372-2621	Mrs. Erika **Almeida Watanabe Patriota** Counsellor Mr. Guilherme de Aguiar Patriota
	Mr. Fernando **de Oliveira Sena** Counsellor Mrs. Karen Lock
372-2660	Mrs. Juliana **Gaspar Ruas** Second Secretary Mr. Daniel Scandeleri

372-2661	Ms. Adriana **Telles Ribeiro** Second Secretary
372-2643	Mr. Gustavo **dos Santos Pereira** Second Secretary Mr. Vinicius Luis Fraga
372-2662	Mr. Fernando **Sardenberg Zelner Gonçalves** Second Secretary Mrs. Maria Maciel Zelner Gonçalves
372-2652	Mr. Aloisio **Barbosa de Sousa Neto** Second Secretary Mrs. Larissa Yuri Ushizima
372-2645	Mr. João Francisco **Campos da Silva Pereira** Second Secretary Mrs. Marina Massote de Moura e Sousa
372-2633	Mr. Vicente **Amaral Bezerra** Second Secretary Mrs. María Soledad Maroca de Castro
372-2609	Mrs. Marina **Moreira Costa Pittella** Second Secretary Mr. Fabio Pittella Silva
372-2654	Mr. Eduardo **Alcebíades Lopes** Second Secretary Mrs. Maria Zmitrowicz Lopes
372-2670	Ms. Amena **Martins Yassine** Second Secretary Ms. Daniele Leite Soares
372-2657	Mr. Vicente **de Azevedo Araujo Filho** Second Secretary Mrs. Freya Christobel Mary Seath de Azevedo Araujo
372-2675	Mr. Daniel **Cristiano Guimarães** Third Secretary Mr. Inácio Domingos Freitas de Medeiros
372-2614	Mr. Thomaz Alexandre **Mayer Napoleão** Third Secretary
372-2603	Mrs. Larissa **Schneider Calza** Third Secretary Mr. Patrick Luna
372-2606	Mr. Patrick **Luna** Third Secretary Mrs. Larissa Schneider Calza
372-2623	Mr. Thiago **Tavares Vidal** Third Secretary

372-2635	Mrs. Ricedla Maria **Filgueira Dias** Attaché Mr. Hailhi Lauriano Dias
372-2663	Mr. Rafael **Lourenço Beleboni** Attaché
372-2608	Mr. José Vicente **Moreira Mello** Attaché
372-2629	Mr. Érico **Calixto de Sousa Lima** Attaché Mrs. Patricia Edwirges Lara dos Reis
372-2604	Ms. Candida **Cavanelas Mares** Attaché
372-2664	Mr. Jucilton **Salazar Pereira** Attaché Mrs. Maria Das Gracas Alexandre Pereira
372-2626	Ms. Nercina **da Cruz Valadares** Attaché
372-2626	Mr. João **Teixeira Burlamaqui** Attaché Mrs. Marcela Cristina de Barros Silva Burlamaqui
372-2636	Mr. Kleber **Silva Santos** Attaché Mr. Everton Edward de Moura

---

372-2620	Admiral (Navy) Fernando Eduardo **Studart Wiemer** Minister Counsellor Military Adviser Mrs. Helena Barthem Wiemer
372-2618	Colonel (Air Force) Ricardo **Rodrígues Rangel** Counsellor Deputy Military Adviser Mrs. Simone Marcia de Souza Rangel
372-2638	Colonel (Army) Carlos Augusto **Ramires Teixeira** Counsellor Deputy Military Adviser Mrs. Kennedy Beirian Ladeira Ramires Teixeira
372-2639	Commander (Navy) Sebastião **Simões de Oliveira** First Secretary Deputy Military Adviser Mrs. Danielle Fernandes Martins de Oliveira
372-2663	Commander (Navy) Ana Paula **Alves de Souza** Second Secretary Deputy Military Adviser

Brunei Darussalam

Member State since 21 September 1984

Address: Permanent Mission of Brunei Darussalam
to the United Nations
771 United Nations Plaza
New York, N.Y. 10017

Telephone: (212) 697-3465

Telefax: (212) 697-9889

e-mail: brunei@un.int

Correspondence: English

National holiday: 23 February
National Day

Ext. 224 H.E. Dato Abdul Ghafar **Ismail**
Ambassador Extraordinary and Plenipotentiary
Permanent Representative (DPC: 28 March 2013)
Datin Aishah Husain

Ext. 241 Ms. Norazlianah **Ibrahim**
Minister Counsellor
Deputy Permanent Representative

Ext. 236 Mr. Abdul Mateen **Mohamed Deli**
Second Secretary
Mrs. Kartizan Kapli

Ext. 237 Mr. Mohd Aizul Hakim Pehin Dato Haji **Suyoi**
Second Secretary
Mrs. Hamizah Mohd Yunos

Ext. 225 Ms. Muna Masera **Masri**
Second Secretary
Mr. Syarif Ihsan Rasani

Ext. 228 Mr. Haji Roslan bin **PDISD Haji Johari**
Third Secretary
Mrs. Hajah Selailah Haji Ajiman

Ext. 247 Ms. Norhasalinda **Mohd Salleh**
Third Secretary
Mr. Pg Md Amirul Zaman Pg Hj Mohammed

Ext. 243 Ms. Maryani binti **Haji Lamit**
Attaché

Ext. 226 Mr. Haji Mohd Ibrahim **Haji Mohd Kassim**
Attaché
Mrs. Nuratiqah Jaafar

Bulgaria

Address: Permanent Mission of the Republic
of Bulgaria to the United Nations
11 East 84th Street
New York, N.Y. 10028

Telephone: (212) 737-4790, -4791

Telefax: (212) 472-9865

e-mail: bulgaria@un.int , mission.newyork@mfa.bg

website: www.mfa.bg/embassies/usapr

Correspondence: English, French

National holiday: 3 March
Liberation Day

H.E. Mr. Stephan **Tafrov**
Ambassador Extraordinary and Plenipotentiary
Permanent Representative (DPC: 6 June 2012)

Mr. Boyan Nedialkov **Belev**
Minister Plenipotentiary
Deputy Permanent Representative

Ms. Lachezara **Stoeva**
Counsellor

Mr. Nikolay **Vanchev**
First Secretary
Mrs. Julia Vancheva

Mrs. Yuliana **Angelova**
Second Secretary
Mr. Angel Angelov

Ms. Asya **Tsvetanova**
Second Secretary

Mr. Angel **Angelov**
Second Secretary
Mrs. Yuliana Angelova

Mr. Yanko **Yordanov**
Second Secretary

Mr. Anton **Angelov**
Attaché
Mrs. Nadezhda Velikova-Angelova

Ms. Anni **Bozhilska-Nedelcheva**
Attaché
Mr. Emil Yordanov Nedelchev

Address: Permanent Mission of Burkina Faso
to the United Nations
633 Third Avenue, Suite 31A, 31st Floor
New York, N.Y. 10017

Telephone: (212) 308-4720, -4721

Telefax: (212) 308-4690

e-mail: bfapm@un.int

Correspondence: French

National holiday: 11 December

H.E. ...
Ambassador Extraordinary and Plenipotentiary
Permanent Representative (DPC:)

H.E. Mr. Simplice Honoré **Guibila**
Ambassador
Deputy Permanent Representative
Mrs. Marie Florence Guibila/Ouedraogo

Mr. Mamadou **Coulibaly**
Second Counsellor
Mrs. Janice Murielle Coulibaly/Ouédraogo

Mr. Dominique **Kaboré**
Second Counsellor

Mr. Ouinibani **Konate**
Second Counsellor
Mrs. Wemitiagha Alice Abem

Ms. Myriam Aman **Soulama**
Second Counsellor

Mr. Filateni **Coulibaly**
Second Counsellor
Mrs. Zoda Brigitte Coulibaly/Ouaattra

Mr. Pambary Cyrille Pascal **Bonzi**
Third Secrteary
Mrs. Tey Gwladys Bonzi/Sanou

Mr. Ernest **Kaboré**
Attaché (Financial Affairs)
Mrs. Raniguitale Diane Madeleine Kabore/Ouédraogo

Mrs. Marie Florence **Guibila/Ouedraogo**
Attaché
H.E. Mr. Simplice Honoré Guibilia

Mrs. Zoda Brigitte **Coulibaly/Ouaattra**
Attaché
Mr. Filateni Coulibaly

Mrs. Marie Lydie **Ouedraogo Sawadogo**
Attaché
Mr. Noaga Edouard Ouédraogo

Mr. Dominique **Yameogo**
Attaché (Financial Affairs)

Mr. Noaga Edouard **Ouedraogo**
Attaché (Defence)
Mrs. Marie Lydie Ouedraogo Sawadogo

Mr. Ouaongo Karim Aristide **Ouedraogo**
Attaché
Mrs. Witibyanda Agathe Ouedraogo Compaore

Burundi

Member State since 18 September 1962

Address: Permanent Mission of the Republic
of Burundi to the United Nations
336 East 45th Street, 12th Floor
New York, N.Y. 10017

Telephone: (212) 499-0001, -0002

Telefax: (212) 499-0006

e-mail: ambabunewyork@yahoo.fr

Website: www.burundimission.org

Correspondence: French

National holiday: 1 July
Independence Day

H.E. Mr. Albert **Shingiro**
Ambassador Extraordinary and Plenipotentiary
Permanent Representative (DPC: 4 September 2014)

Mrs. Anésie **Ndayishimiye**
First Counsellor

Mr. Evariste **Ngendankengera**
Second Counsellor

Mr. Delphin **Ndayemeye**
Second Counsellor
Mrs. Charlotte Ndayishimiye

Mr. Athanas Joshua **Ndaye**
Attaché

Cabo Verde

Member State since 16 September 1975

Address: Permanent Mission of the Republic
of Cabo Verde to the United Nations
27 East 69th Street
New York, N.Y. 10021

Telephone: (212) 472-0333; -0334

Telefax: (212) 794-1398

e-mail: capeverde@un.int

Correspondence: French

National holiday: 5 July

H.E. Mr. Fernando Jorge Wahnon **Ferreira**
Ambassador Extraordinary and Plenipotentiary
Permanent Representative (DPC: 28 February 2014)

Ms. Edna Filomena Alves **Barreto**
Minister Plenipotentiary

Mr. José Carlos **Mendonça**
First Secretary
Mrs. Angela Helena Mendonça

Mrs. Miryam Djamila Sena **Vieira**
Second Secretary
Mr. Tito Olavo Da Lomba Rocha Gonçalves

Address: Permanent Mission of the Kingdom of Cambodia to the United Nations
327 East 58th Street
New York, N.Y. 10022

Telephone: (212) 336-0777

Telefax: (212) 759-7672

e-mail: cambodia@un.int

Correspondence: English

National holiday: 9 November
Independence Day

H.E. Mr. Ry **Tuy**
Ambassador Extraordinary and Plenipotentiary
Permanent Representative (DPC: 28 February 2014)
Mrs. Reno Him

Mr. Sophea **Yaung Chan**
Counsellor
Mrs. Pichchandany Phorn

Mr. Samnang **Tho**
First Secretary
Mrs. Sovannary Kimsour

Mr. Chanveasna **Rath**
First Secretary
Mrs. Chhayheang Moa

Mr. Saroeun **Korm**
Second Secretary
Mrs. Sakim Ngy

Mr. Visoth **Prum**
Third Secretary

Lt. Colonel Dara **Him**
Military Attaché
Mrs. Veasna Chap

Cameroon

Address: Permanent Mission of the Republic
of Cameroon to the United Nations
22 East 73rd Street
New York, N.Y. 10021

Telephone: (212) 794-2295, -2299

Telefax: (212) 249-0533

website: cameroon.mission@yahoo.com

Correspondence: French/English

National holiday: 20 May

H.E. Mr. Michel **Tommo Monthe**
Ambassador Extraordinary and Plenipotentiary
Permanent Representative (DPC: 8 September 2008)
Mrs. Thérèse Tommo

Mr. Ferdinand **Ngoh Ngoh**
Minister Counsellor
Mrs. Céline Ngoh Ngoh

Mr. Mamoudou **Mana**
First Counsellor
Mrs. Djenabou Mana

Mr. Victor **Tchatchouwo**
Second Counsellor
Mrs. Alice Tchatchouwo

Mr. Nganje Kinge **Ewumbe-Monono**
Second Counsellor
Mrs. Jemea Nganje Kinge

Mr. Henri Léopold **Meboe Otele**
Second Counsellor
Mrs. Agnès Antoinette Meboe

Mr. Joseph **Mvomo**
Counsellor (Military)

Ms. Cécile **Mballa Eyenga**
First Secretary

Mr. Alain Wilfried **Biya**
Second Secretary
Mrs. Estelle Diane Ngono-Chartier

Address:	Permanent Mission of Canada to the United Nations One Dag Hammarskjöld Plaza 885 Second Avenue, 14th Floor New York, N.Y. 10017
Telephone:	(212) 848-1100
Telefax:	(212) 848-1195
e-mail:	canada.un@international.gc.ca
website:	www.un.int/canada
Social Media:	Twitter: @CanadaUN (English), @CanadaONU (French)
Correspondence:	English/French
National holiday:	1 July Canada Day

848-1150 H.E. Mr. Guillermo **Rishchynski**
Ambassador Extraordinary and Plenipotentiary
Permanent Representative (DPC: 14 September 2011)
Mrs. Jeannette Rishchynski

848-1165 H.E. Mr. Michael Douglas **Grant**
Ambassador Extratordinary and Plenipotentiary
Deputy Permanent Representative
Ms. Heidi Lorraine Kutz

848-1152 Mr. Michael **Bonser**
Minister Counsellor (Political Affairs)
Mrs. Vicky Lynn Edgecombe

848-1119 Mr. Roger **Chen**
Counsellor (Management)

848-1160 Mr. Giles Andrew **Norman**
Counsellor (Legal, Social Affairs, and Human Rights)
Ms. Valerie Elizabeth Lane

848-1162 Ms. Caterina **Ventura**
Counsellor (Political Affairs)

848-1185 Mr. Conrad Lamont **Sheck**
Counsellor (Finance and Management)

848-1114 C/Supt. Barbara Ann Suzon **Fleury**
Counsellor (Police Adviser)

848-1167 Ms. Anar **Mamdani**
Counsellor (Development)

848-1168 Mr. Jonathan Paul **Quinn**
Counsellor (Defence and Security)
Ms. Teresa Christine Petch

848-1156	Colonel René **Melançon** Counsellor (Military Adviser) Ms. Joan Mary Wright
848-1182	Ms. Isabelle **Hentic** First Secretary (Development)
848-1155	Ms. Katrina **Burgess** First Secretary (Human Rights and Humanitarian Affairs)
848-1157	Major James Kent **Stewart** First Secretary (Deputy Military Adviser) Mrs. Leslie Ann Stewart
848-1172	Mr. Simon Marc-Emmanuel **Collard-Wexler** First Secretary (Political Affairs) Mrs. Siobhan O'Neil
848-1176	Mr. Gregory Keith **Dempsey** Second Secretary (Human Rights and Social Affairs)
848-1154	Ms. Karen Kwen Yee **Hung** Second Secretary (Political Affairs) Mr. Gregory Ronald Lawrie
848-1109	Mr. Erich **Cripton** Second Secretary
848-1151	Ms. Barbara **Koop** Attaché
848-1116	Mr. John Andrew **d'Entremont** Attaché Mrs. Gina Monique d'Entremont
848-1158	Ms. Cristina Magdallena **Mosneagu** Attaché

Central African Republic

Member State since 20 September 1960

Address: Permanent Mission of the Central African Republic
to the United Nations
866 United Nations Plaza, Suite 444
New York, N.Y. 10017

Telephone: (646) 415-9122, 9281

Telefax: (646) 415-9149

e-mail: repercaf.ny@gmail.com

website: www.pmcar.org

Correspondence: French

National holiday: 1 December

H.E. Ms. Ambroisine **Kpongo**
Ambassador Extraordinary and Plenipotentiary
Permanent Representative (DPC: 19 September 2014)

Mr. Larry Marcel **Koyma**
First Counsellor
Mrs. Bernadette Koyma

Mr. Marcien Aubin **Kpatamango**
Counsellor (Legal)

Mr. Mesmin **Dembassa Worogagoi**
Counsellor (Economics)
Mrs. Arlette Dembassa Worogagoi Mbazoa

Ms. Mélanie Corine Nina **Goliatha**
Counsellor (Cultural Affairs)

Mr. Pierre **Dalin-Kpana**
Counsellor (Chief of Protocol)

Mr. Francis Patrick **Loungoulah**
Second Secretary

Mr. Yannick Michel **Lenanguy Brinz**
Attaché

Mr. Mario de Gonzales **Bengabo-Gomo**
Attaché

Address:	Permanent Mission of the Republic of Chad to the United Nations 801 2nd Avenue, 13th Floor New York, NY 10017
Telephone:	(212) 986-0980, -0262
Telefax:	(212) 986-0152
e-mail:	chadmission@gmail.com
Correspondence:	French
National holiday:	11 August

H.E. Mr. Mahamat Zene **Cherif**
Ambassador Extraordinary and Plenipotentiary
Permanent Representative (DPC: 13 September 2013)
Mrs. Mahamoud Mahamat Darassalam

Mr. Bante **Mangaral**
Minister Counsellor
Deputy Permanent Representative

Mr. Papouri **Tchingonbé Patchanné**
First Counsellor
Mrs. Paden Thingonbé

Mr. Eric **Miangar**
Second Counsellor

Mr. Ahmat **Ali Adoum**
Counsellor (Legal)

Mr. Adoum Koulbou **Mahamat**
Counsellor

Mr. Letinan **Makadjibeye**
Counsellor

Mrs. Madeleine Andebeng Labeu **Alingue**
Counsellor

Mr. Idriss Abderamane **Amir**
Counsellor

Mr. Bachar Bong **Abdallah**
Counsellor (Economic)

Mr. Nourène Abderaman **Mahamat**
First Secretary
Mrs. Tahir Abderaman Seide

Mr. Ali **Mahamat Zene**
First Secretary
Mrs. Issa Mahamat Achta

Mr. Kachallah Kasser **Mohamed Mohamed**
Second Secretary

Mr. Oumar Seidou **Hissein**
Attaché
Mrs. Khadidja Ahmat Garmaradine

Mr. Boukar **Doungous**
Attaché (Press)
Mrs. Amina Mamadou Kane

Mr. Absakine Yerima **Ahmat**
Attaché (Press)

Mr. Kagne Christophe **Doubane**
Attaché (Defense)
Mrs. Brigitte Reingham Boyalkaya

Address:	Permanent Mission of Chile to the United Nations One Dag Hammarskjöld Plaza 885 Second Avenue, 40th Floor New York, N.Y. 10017
Telephone:	(917) 322-6800
Telefax:	(917) 322-6890, -6891
e-mail:	chile.un@minrel.gov.cl
website:	chileabroad.gov.cl/onu/en
Correspondence:	Spanish
National holiday:	18 September National Day

---

(917) 322-6844	H.E. Mr. Cristián **Barros Melet** Ambassador Extraordinary and Plenipotentiary Permanent Representative (DPC: 16 April 2014) Mrs. Mary Florence Michelle Nielsen
	H.E. Mr. Carlos **Olguín Cigarroa** Ambassdor Deputy Permanent Representative Mrs. Josefina Garcia Pandiello
(917) 322-6810	Mr. Ignacio **Llanos** Minister Counsellor Mrs. Paulina Angela Echeverria Valenzuela
(917) 322-6803	Mr. Fidel **Coloma** Counsellor
(917) 322-6804	Mr. René Alfonso **Ruidiaz** Counsellor
(917) 322-6818	Ms. Belen **Sapag Muñoz de la Peña** Counsellor
(917) 322-6811	Ms. Gloria **Cid Carreño** Counsellor
(917) 322-6823	Mr. Jorge Andres **Iglesias Mori** First Secretary Mrs. Laura Carolina Umbert Ureta
(917) 322-6811	Mr. Sergio **Toro** First Secretary Mrs. Claudia Contreras
(917) 322-6822	Mr. Patricio **Aguirre Vacchieri** First Secretary

	Mr. Claudio **Garrido** First Secretary Mrs. Lina Maria Fajardo Vallejo
(917) 322-6802	Mr. Juan Pablo **Espinoza** First Secretary Mrs. María Liz Vera
(917) 322-6839	Mr. Javier **Gorostegui** Second Secretary
(917) 322-6808	Mr. Diego **Araya Cisternas** Second Secretary Mrs. Javiera Hurtado
(917) 322-6809	Mr. Fernando **Cabezas** Third Secretary Mrs. Francisca Jurgensen

(917) 322-6809	Colonel Máximo **Venegas** Attaché (Defence) Mrs. Ximena Ugarte
	Colonel Gustav **Meyerholz** Attaché (Defence) Mrs. Elena Maria Salazar Wildner
(917) 322-6841	Ms. María Elena Moraga **Quintanilla** Attaché

Address:	Permanent Mission of the People's Republic of China to the United Nations 350 East 35th Street New York, N.Y. 10016
Telephone:	(212) 655-6100
Telefax:	(212) 634-7626 (General) (212) 634-0042 (Permanent Representative's Office) (212) 634-7625 (Political Section) (212) 220-6543 (Press Section)
e-mail:	chinesemission@yahoo.com
website:	www.china-un.org
Correspondence:	English
National holiday:	1 October National Day

655-6191	H.E. Mr. **Liu** Jieyi Ambassador Extraordinary and Plenipotentiary Permanent Representative (DPC: 3 September 2013) Ms. Zhang Qiyue
655-6123	H.E. Mr. **Wang** Min Ambassador Extraordinary and Plenipotentiary Deputy Permanent Representative Ms. Ren Hui
655-6194	Ms. **Zhang** Qiyue Minister Mr. Liu Jieyi
655-6177	Mr. **Zhou** Ming Minister Ms. Ding Yajun
655-6185	Mr. **Xie** Xiaowu Minister Counsellor Ms. Liu Jie
655-6154	Ms. **Wang** Hongbo Minister Counsellor
655-6160	Mr. **Zhou** Jian Counsellor Ms. Zhang Xi
655-6159	Mr. **Liu** Jun Counsellor Ms. Zhou Jing

655-6175	Ms. **He** Yi Counsellor Mr. Xu Bin
655-6127	Ms. **Zhang** Xi Counsellor Mr. Zhou Jian
655-6100	Mr. **Xia** Yuming Counsellor
655-6164	Ms. **Lu** Mei Counsellor Mr. Ma Jianhua
655-6148	Mr. **Shen** Bo Counsellor
655-6147	Mr. **Yao** Shaojun Counsellor Ms. Zhao Jinming
655-6189	Mr. **Li** Yongsheng Counsellor (Legal Adviser)
655-6183	Mr. **Sun** Lei Counsellor Ms. Yang Yi
655-6171	Mr. **Guo** Xuejun Counsellor
655-6181	Mr. **Zhao** Yong Counsellor
655-6165	Ms. **Li** Jijuan Counsellor
655-6174	Mr. **Yin** Zhongliang Counsellor Ms. Yang Hua
655-6176	Mr. **Yu** Tian Counsellor
655-6180	Mr. **Chen** Quingsong Counsellor Ms. Guo Yanyan
655-6137	Mr. **Sun** Xudong Counsellor Ms. Zhang Qiaozhi
655-6172	Mr. **Feng** Bo Counsellor Ms. Jiang Yeye
655-6104	Mr. **Yang** Li Counsellor

655-6167	Mr. **Ma** Xin Counsellor Ms. Zhu Ping
655-6194	Mr. **Cai** Weiming Counsellor Ms. Yue Li
655-6111	Mr. **Zheng** Huiyu Counsellor
655-6182	Ms. **Li** Weng Counsellor
655-6184	Ms. **Wang** Yanning First Secretary
655-6142	Ms. **Hu** Changfu First Secretary Ms. Zan Sulan
655-6101	Mr. **Wang** Dawei First Secretary
655-6101	Ms. **Liu** Xing First Secretary
655-6168	Mr. **Li** Dongsong First Secretary
655-6100	Ms. **Chen** Fang First Secretary Mr. Wang Dawei
655-6173	Mr. **Wang** Zhiquan First Secretary Ms. Zhao Lin
655-6142	Mr. **Li** Weihua First Secretary Ms. Liu Qiong
655-6117	Mr. **Zeng** Xiaohua First Secretary Ms. Pan Lei
655-6132	Mr. **Wei** Zonglei First Secretary Ms. Zhang Jianhua
655-6193	Mr. **Xiang** Xin First Secretary Ms. Li Ling
655-6192	Mr. **Xu** Zhongsheng First Secretary Ms. Wang Xiaolan

655-6170	Ms. **Guo** Zhiqi First Secretary Mr. Li Shuangqing
655-6199	Ms. **Yang** Yi First Secretary Mr. Sun Lei
655-6166	Mr. **Wang** Gang Second Secretary
655-6179	Ms. **Hua** Ye Second Secretary
655-6109	Mr. **Luo** Cheng Second Secretary Ms. Yin Lanlan
655-6145	Mr. **Chu** Guang Second Secretary
655-6102	Mr. **Mi** Tao Second Secretary Ms. Lou Yue
655-6126	Ms. **Ren** Hui Second Secretary Mr. Wang Min
655-6197	Ms. **Cai** Yue Second Secretary
655-6142	Mr. **Cui** Hongwei Second Secretary Ms. He Yanfang
655-6153	Ms. **Wu** Jingjing Second Secretary Mr. Qian Fang
655-6119	Mr. **Liu** Song Second Secretary
655-6191	Ms. **Sun** Qing Second Secretary
655-6142	Ms. **Ye** Dongmei Second Secretary
655-6123	Ms. **Li** Liming Second Secretary
634-7624	Ms. **Chi** Yuxin Second Secretary
655-6130	Mr. **Gong** Guoxi Second Secretary Mrs. Yao Ximeng

655-6163	Mr. **Wang** Rui Third Secretary Ms. Gao Shan
655-6199	Mr. **Yang** Zhiyu Third Secretary Ms. Dong Jin
655-6152	Ms. **Wang** Yifei Third Secretary
655-6141	Mr. **Zhu** Yanwei Third Secretary
655-6178	Mr. **Guo** Dongliang Third Secretary Mrs. Zhan Linlin
655-6105	Mr. **Wang** Liang Third Secretary Mrs. Xu Wen
655-6109	Mr. **Duan** Ning Third Secretary Ms. Sun Xiaoxiao
655-6155	Mr. **Wang** Dazhong Third Secretary Ms. Fei Jie
634-7624	Ms. **Wang** Yilin Third Secretary
655-6158	Mr. **Wang** Yu Third Secretary
655-6129	Mr. **Lu** Yuhui Third Secretary Ms. Zhou Wanlu
655-6100	Mr. **Yang** Hui Attaché Ms. Xiang Yang
655-6144	Ms. **Xiao** Yue Attaché
655-6122	Mr. **Wang** Zhenning Attaché
655-6100	Ms. **Zhu** Li Attaché Mr. Zhang Yanhua
655-6196	Ms. **Chen** Qingru Attaché
655-6141	Mr. **Zhu** Shuai Attaché

655-6129	Mr. **Cao** Zhiyong Attaché
655-6100	Mr. **Ruan** Dashan Attaché Ms. Law Tuo
481-2013	Ms. **Lin** Hui Attaché

Address:	Permanent Mission of Colombia to the United Nations 140 East 57th Street, 5th Floor New York, N.Y. 10022
Telephone:	(212) 355-7776
Telefax:	(212) 371-2813
e-mail:	colombia@colombiaun.org
website:	www.colombiaun.org/
Correspondence:	Spanish
National holiday:	20 July Independence Day

Ext. 223 H.E. Ms. María Emma **Mejía Vélez**
Ambassador Extraordinary and Plenipotentiary
Permanent Representative (DPC: 25 February 2014)
Mr. Alberto Casas Santamaria

Ext. 229 H.E. Mr. Miguel Camilo **Ruiz Blanco**
Ambassador Extraordinary and Plenipotentiary
Deputy Permanent Representative
Mrs. María Elena Botero de Ruiz

H.E. Mr. Isaac **Gilinski Sragowicz**
Ambassador Extraordinary and Plenipotentiary
Deputy Permanent Representative
Mrs. Perla Bacal de Gilinski

Ext. 251 H.E. Mr. Carlos Arturo **Morales López**
Ambassador Extraordinary and Plenipotentiary
Deputy Permanent Representative
Mrs. Betty León Ossa

Ext. 232 Ms. Marcela **Ordoñez Fernández**
Minister Plenipotentiary

Ext. 230 Ms. María Paulina **Dávila Dávila**
Minister Counsellor

Ext. 224 Mr. David Orlando **Rodríguez Escandón**
First Secretary

Ext. 240 Mr. Luis Fernando **Orozco Barrera**
First Secretary

Ext. 234 Mr. Germán **Calderón Velásquez**
Second Secretary
Mr. Antonio Sánchez

Ext. 238 Ms. Diana Lucía **Rengifo Vargas**
Second Secretary

Ext. 228	Ms. Diana Carolina **Moya Mancipe** Second Secretary
Ext. 231	Mr. Ricardo **Garzón Torres** Second Secretary
Ext. 225	Mr. Fabio Esteban **Pedraza Torres** Second Secretary
Ext. 227	Mr. Juan Camilo **Díaz Reina** Second Secretary Mrs. Maria Carolina Valbuena Carrasquilla
Ext. 226	Colonel Gonzalo **Carrero Pérez** Attaché Police Adviser Mrs. Mary Julieth Uribe Isaza
Ext. 241	Ms. Sandra **Ochoa Verdeza** Attaché

Address:	Permanent Mission of the Union of the Comoros to the United Nations 866 United Nations Plaza, Suite 418 New York, N.Y. 10017
Telephone:	(212) 750-1637
Telefax:	...
e-mail:	comoros@un.int
Website:	www.un.int/comoros
Correspondence:	French
National holiday:	6 July Independence Day

H.E. Mr. Mohamed Soilihi **Soilih**
Ambassador Extraordinary and Plenipotentiary
Permanent Representative (DPC: 5 November 2014)

H.E. Mr. Ahmed **Abdallah**
Ambassador
Deputy Permanent Representative
Mrs. Muhammad Aboud Biubwa

Mr. Mohamed **El Marouf**
Minister Counsellor
Mrs. Fahlun Al Betty

Mrs. Fatima **Alfeine**
Counsellor

Mr. Kadim **Oussein**
First Secretary

Mr. Salah Edine **Djimbanaou**
Attaché

Mr. Youssouf **Mbaé**
Attaché

Congo

Member State since 20 September 1960

Address: Permanent Mission of the Republic of the Congo to the United Nations
14 East 65th Street
New York, N.Y. 10065

Telephone: (212) 744-7840, -7841

Telefax: (212) 744-7975

e-mail: congo@un.int; mpcongo_onu@hotmail.com

Correspondence: French

National holiday: 15 August
National Day

H.E. Mr. Raymond Serge **Balé**
Ambassador Extraordinary and Plenipotentiary
Permanent Representative (DPC: 11 November 2008)
Mrs. Christine Isabelle Balé

Mr. Paul **Maloukou**
Minister Counsellor
Mrs. Henriette Edith Maloukou Makoumbou

Mr. Gaston **Kimpolo**
Minister Counsellor

Mr. Appolinaire **Dingha**
Counsellor
Mrs. Apendi Nelie Natacha Dingha

Mr. Maurice Gatien **Makiza**
Counsellor
Mrs. Albertine Ghislaine Makiza

Mr. Jean Didier Clovis **Ngoulou**
Counsellor

Mr. Camille **Mbinzi**
First Secretary
Mrs. Roseline Peggy Mbinzi Missilou

Mrs. Lauria **Nguele Makouelet**
Second Secretary

Ms. Claude Josiane **Oba**
Second Secretary

Address:	Permanent Mission of Costa Rica to the United Nations 211 East 43rd Street, Room 1002 New York, N.Y. 10017
Telephone:	(212) 986-6373
Telefax:	(212) 986-6842
e-mail:	contact@missioncrun.org
Correspondence:	Spanish
National holiday:	15 September Independence Day

Ext. 111	H.E. Mr. Juan Carlos **Mendoza-García** Ambassador Extraordinary and Plenipotentiary Permanent Representative (DPC: 4 September 2014) Mrs. Sofia Herrera Cubillo
Ext. 117	Ms. Adriana **Murillo** Minister Counsellor
Ext. 119	Ms. Maritza **Chan** Minister Counsellor
Ext. 113	Ms. Georgina **Guillén-Grillo** Minister Counsellor
Ext. 114	Mrs. Carol Viviana **Arce Echeverría** Minister Counsellor Mr. Erick Ulate
Ext. 122	Mrs. Paula **Coto-Ramírez** Minister Counsellor Mr. Luis Roberto José de la Rosa-Martínez
Ext. 116	Mr. William José **Calvo Calvo** Minister Counsellor

Côte d'Ivoire

Address:	Permanent Mission of Côte d'Ivoire to the United Nations 800 2nd Avenue, 5th Floor New York, N.Y. 10017
Telephone:	(646) 649-5061; -5986; -781-9572; 9523; 861 3145
Telefax:	(646) 781-9974
e-mail:	cotedivoiremission@yahoo.com
Correspondence:	French
National holiday:	7 August

---

(646) 861-3751	H.E. Mr. Claude Stanislas **Bouah-Kamon** Ambassador Extraordinary and Plenipotentiary Permanent Representative (DPC: 11 May 2015)
Ext. 143	H.E. Mr. Bafétigué **Ouattara** Ambassador Deputy Permanent Representative
Ext. 114	Mr. Feh Moussa **Gone** Counsellor Mrs. Christelle Ahou N'Gatta Gone
Ext. 113	Mr. Nestor **Koko** Counsellor Mrs. Amoin Felicite Koko-Amon
Ext. 117	Mr. François Xavier **Zabavy** Counsellor
Ext. 144	Mr. Joseph **Gbrou** Counsellor Mrs. Claudine Gbrou-Tieffi
Ext. 147	Mrs. Nanzeguela **Kone-Fofana** Counsellor
Ext. 123	Mrs. Flora Christiane **Seka-Fouah** Counsellor
Ext. 129	Mr. Koffi Narcisse **Daté** Counsellor
	Mr. N'Cho Virgile **Akiapo** First Secretary Mrs. Berthe Odile Akiapo Boli
	Colonel-Major Ouattara **Karim** Attaché Military Adviser

Ext. 122	Mr. Dogoba **Bakayoko** Attaché (Financial Affairs) Mrs. Mahoua Bakayoko
Ext. 142	Mrs. Solange **Kattie** Attaché Mr. Aimé Kattie

Address:	Permanent Mission of the Republic of Croatia to the United Nations 820 Second Avenue, 19th Floor New York, N.Y. 10017
Telephone:	(212) 986-1585
Telefax:	(212) 986-2011
e-mail:	cromiss.un@mvep.hr
website:	un.mfa.hr
Correspondence:	English
National holiday:	25 June

Ext. 200	H.E. Mr. Vladimir **Drobnjak** Ambassador Extraordinary and Plenipotentiary Permanent Representative (DPC: 5 August 2013) Mrs. Marija Drobnjak
	Mr. Danijel **Medan** Minister Counsellor Deputy Permanent Representative
Ext. 203	Ms. Vesna **Baus** Minister Counsellor
Ext. 216	Ms. Jadranka **Bošnjak** Minister Counsellor
	Mr. Sebastian **Rogač** First Secretary
Ext. 204	Ms. Martina **Težak Budišić** Second Secretary Mr. Hrvoje Budišić
	Ms. Maja **Simunic** Attaché

Address:	Permanent Mission of Cuba to the United Nations 315 Lexington Avenue New York, N.Y. 10016
Telephone:	(212) 689-7215, -7216, -7217
Telefax:	(212) 779-1697, (212) 689-9073
e-mail:	cuba_onu@cubanmission.com
Website:	www.cubadiplomatica.cu/onu
Correspondence:	Spanish
National holiday:	1 January Anniversary of the Revolution

---

(212) 689-9308 Ext. 361, 362	H.E. Mr. Rodolfo **Reyes Rodríguez** Ambassador Extraordinary and Plenipotentiary Permanent Representative (DPC: 4 February 2013)

Ext. 340	H.E. Mr. Oscar **León González** Ambassador Extraordinary and Plenipotentiary Deputy Permanent Representative Mrs. Sullén Carrero Cedrón
Ext. 364	Mr. Guillermo **Suarez Borges** Counsellor Mrs. Massiel Rivero Baeza
	Mr. Omar **Rodríguez Montero** Counsellor Mrs. Mariska Calañas Sabina
Ext. 345	Mrs. Nadieska **Navarro Barro** First Secretary
Ext. 357	Mr. Ovidio **Roque Pedrera** First Secretary Mrs. Zudelis Cosano Zayas
	Mr. Luis Javier **Baro Baez** First Secretary Mrs. Sandra Oliva Orrantía
	Mr. Ariel **Hernández Hernández** First Secretary Mrs. Nina Almeida Paramonova
	Mr. Jorge Antonio **González Sánchez** First Secretary Mrs. Maricela Urrutia Villavicencio
	Mr. Alexis **Fernández Abraham** Second Secretary Mrs. Niurka Arriete Hernández

	Mrs. Jitka **Betancourt Cuesta** Second Secretary
Ext. 345	Mr. Emilio **González Soca** Third Secretary Mrs. Daylenis Moreno Guerra
	Mrs. Tanieris **Dieguez Lao** Third Secretary
Ext. 346	Mrs. Daylenis **Moreno Guerra** Third Secretary Mr. Emilio González Soca
	Mrs. Ivian **Del Sol Dominguez** Third Secretary Mr. David Forés Rodríguez
	Mr. Iraset **Brooks Moreno** Attaché
	Mr. Damián **Galvañy Taborda** Attaché Mrs. Beatriz Cordovez González
	Mrs. Beatriz **Cordovez González** Attaché Mr. Damián Galvañy Taborda
	Mr. Carlos Enrique **Puentes Malagón** Attaché
	Mr. Ariel **Parra Mieres** Attaché
	Mr. Andrés **Villareal Crespo** Attaché Mrs. Yolanda Guerra Rodríguez
	Mrs. Yolanda **Guerra Rodríguez** Attaché Mr. Andrés Villareal Crespo
Ext. 340	Mrs. Sullen **Carrero Cedrón** Attaché Mr. Oscar León González
	Mr. José Maria **Vives Pérez** Attaché
Ext. 341	Mr. Tomás **Ramírez Cabrera** Attaché
	Mr. Jorge **Alfonso Sotolongo** Attaché
	Mrs. Zudelis **Cosano Zayas** Attaché

Mr. Alexander **Rodríguez Olivarez**
Attaché

Mr. Alberto José **Marro González**
Attaché

Mr. Andro **González Arbella**
Attaché

Mr. Javier **Marrero Alvares**
Attaché

Mr. David **Forés Rodríguez**
Attaché
Mrs. Ivian Del Sol Dominguez

Mr. Armando Cristóbal **Menéndez Pulido**
Attaché

Mr. Leonar **Aguilar Hechavarria**
Attaché

Mr. Carlos **Quesada Bengochea**
Attaché

Mr. Alexis **Muchuly Beltrán**
Attaché

Mr. José Luis **Licea Rodríguez**
Attaché

Mrs. Sisi **Rosario Rouco**
Attaché

Mr. Reynel **Hernández Socarra**
Attaché

Address:	Permanent Mission of the Republic of Cyprus to the United Nations 13 East 40th Street New York, N.Y. 10016
Telephone:	(212) 481-6023, -6024, -6025
Telefax:	(212) 685-7316
e-mail:	mission@cyprusun.org
website:	www.cyprusun.org
Correspondence:	English
National holiday:	1 October Independence Day

Ext. 21 — H.E. Mr. Nicholas **Emiliou**
Ambassador Extraordinary and Plenipotentiary
Permanent Representative (DPC: 9 April 2012)
Mrs. Astero Constantinou

Ext. 31 — Mr. Menelaos **Menelaou**
Counsellor
Deputy Permanent Representative
Mrs. Panagiota Dimitriou

Ext. 32 — Mr. Nektarios **Soteriou**
Attaché

Ext. 36 — Ms. Constantina **Constantinidou**
Attaché

Ext. 27 — Ms. Monika **Pachoumi**
Attaché

Ext. 30 — Ms. Vasiliki **Krasa**
Attaché

Ext. 24 — Mrs. Maria G. **Zoupaniotis**
Counsellor (Press)
Mr. Apostolis Zoupaniotis

Ext. 23 — Mrs. Ioanna **Shiatou Agathocleous**
Attaché (Press)

Address:	Permanent Mission of the Czech Republic to the United Nations 1109-1111 Madison Avenue New York, N.Y. 10028
Telephone:	(646) 981-4001
Telefax:	(646) 981-4099
e-mail:	un.newyork@embassy.mzv.cz
website:	www.mfa.cz
Correspondence:	English
National holiday:	28 October

---

(646) 981-4001 H.E. Mrs. Edita **Hrdá**
Ambassador Extraordinary and Plenipotentiary
Permanent Representative (DPC: 24 January 2011)
Mr. Jozef Šepetka

---

(646) 981-4007 Mr. Jiri **Ellinger**
Minister Counsellor
Deputy Permanent Representative
Mrs. Libuse Ellingerová

(646) 981-4035 Mr. Peter **Urbánek**
Counsellor
Mrs. Jana Urbanková

(646) 981-4018 Col. Zdeněk **Kugler**
Counsellor
Military Adviser
Mrs. Zdeňka Kuglerová

Ms. Monika **Studená**
First Secretary

Mr. Rene **Zeleny**
First Secretary
Mrs. Lucie Zelena

(646) 981-4057 Ms. Petra **Benešová**
Third Secretary
Head of Chancery

(646) 981-4058 Mrs. Barbora **Skácelová**
Third Secretary
Mr. Jan Skácel

Mr. Milan **Konrád**
Third Secretary
Mrs. Hana Kondrádová

Mr. Miroslav **Porosz**
Attaché
Mrs. Pavlína Porosz

Mr. Jan **Polcr**
Attaché
Military Staff Assistant to the Military Adviser
Mrs. Denisa Polcrová

Democratic People's Republic of Korea

Member State since 17 September 1991

Address: Permanent Mission of the Democratic People's Republic of Korea to the United Nations
820 Second Avenue, 13th Floor
New York, N.Y. 10017

Telephone: (212) 972-3105, -3106, -3128

Telefax: (212) 972-3154

e-mail: dpr.korea@verizon.net

Correspondence: English

National holiday: 9 September
Founding of the Democratic People's Republic of Korea

H.E. Mr. **Ja** Song Nam
Ambassador Extraordinary and Plenipotentiary
Permanent Representative (DPC: 28 February 2014)
Mrs. Jang Hye Gyong

H.E. Mr. **An** Myong Hun
Ambassador
Deputy Permanent Representative
Ms. Jang Ryong Hui

H.E. Mr. **Jang** Il Hun
Ambassador
Mrs. Kim Tong Suk

Mr. **Pak** Chol
Counsellor
Mrs. Ri Yong Ran

Mr. **Kim** Jin Song
Counsellor
Mrs. Kim Hui Yong

Mr. **Kim** Song
Counsellor
Mrs. An Yong Ok

Mr. **Kwon** Jong Gun
Counsellor
Mrs. Kim Myong Hui

Mr. **Ri** Song Chol
Counsellor
Mrs. Ji Un Sil

Mr. **Jo** Jong Chol
First Secretary

Mr. **Kim** Un Chol
Second Secretary
Mrs. Kim Kum Hui

Mr. **Ri** Ji Song
Attaché
Mrs. Cha Yong Hui

Democratic Republic of the Congo

Member State since 20 September 1960

Address:	Permanent Mission of the Democratic Republic of the Congo to the United Nations 866 United Nations Plaza, Suite 511 New York, N.Y. 10017
Telephone:	(212) 319-8061
Telefax:	(212) 319-8232
e-mail:	missiondrc@gmail.com
Website:	www.un.int/drcongo
Correspondence:	French
National holiday:	30 June Independence Day

H.E. Mr. Ignace **Gata Mavita wa Lufuta**
Ambassador Extraordinary and Plenipotentiary
Permanent Representative (DPC: 5 September 2012)
Mrs. Celine Marie Laetitia Nemena Bukele

Mrs. Charlotte Omoy **Malenga**
Minister Counsellor

Mr. Zénon **Mukongo Ngay**
Minister Counsellor
Mrs. Myriam Mukongo

Mr. Paul Losoko Efambe **Empole**
First Counsellor
Mrs. Mamie-Yvette Mandekene Nsuka

Denmark

Member State since 24 October 1945

Address:	Permanent Mission of Denmark to the United Nations One Dag Hammarskjöld Plaza 885 Second Avenue, 18th Floor New York, N.Y. 10017-2201
Telephone:	(212) 308-7009
Telefax:	(212) 308-3384
e-mail:	nycmis@um.dk
website:	www.fnnewyork.um.dk/en
Correspondence:	English
National holiday:	16 April Birthday of the Queen

705-4968

H.E. Mr. Ib **Petersen**
Ambassador Extraordinary and Plenipotentiary
Permanent Representative (DPC: 5 August 2013)
Mrs. Annie Bakke Jensen

705-4928

H.E. Mr. Erik **Laursen**
Ambassador
Deputy Permanent Representative
Mrs. Mette Hald

Mr. Peter Martin Lehmann **Nielsen**
Counsellor
Mrs. Nisha Lykke Sethi Nielsen

Ms. Kit **Clausen**
Counsellor

Mr. Christian Ejby Stroem **Karstensen**
Counsellor

Mr. Jens Ole Bach **Hansen**
Counsellor
Mrs. Siham Faidoli Hansen

Ms. Karen Gorenlund **Nielsen**
First Secretary

705-4930

Colonel Michael Wiggers **Hyldgaard**
Minister Counsellor
Military Adviser
Mrs. Anne Cecilie Jang Lim Max Hyldgaard

Mr. Mads **Juul-Nyholm**
Counsellor
Assistant Military Adviser

Djibouti

Member State since 20 September 1977

Address: Permanent Mission of the Republic
of Djibouti to the United Nations
866 United Nations Plaza, Suite 4011
New York, N.Y. 10017

Telephone: (212) 753-3163

Telefax: (212) 223-1276, (212) 758-1056

e-mail: djibouti@nyct.net

Correspondence: French

National holiday: 27 June

H.E. Mr. Roble **Olhaye***
Ambassador Extraordinary and Plenipotentiary
Permanent Representative (DPC: 18 January 1988)
Mrs. Olhaye

Miss Kadra Ahmed **Hassan**
First Counsellor

Mrs. Saada Daher **Hassan**
Counsellor
Mr. Cheikh Omar Aden

Mr. Youssouf Aden **Moussa**
First Secretary

Mrs. Vera **Sakha**
Attaché
Mr. Elias Sakha

* Ambassador Extraordinary and Plenipotentiary to the United States of America.

Dominica

Member State since 18 December 1978

Address:	Permanent Mission of the Commonwealth of Dominica to the United Nations 800 Second Avenue, Suite 400H New York, N.Y. 10017
Telephone:	(212) 949-0853
Telefax:	(212) 808-4975, 661-0979
e-mail:	domun@onecommonwealth.org; dominicaun@gmail.com
Correspondence:	English
National holiday:	3 November

H.E. Mr. Vince **Henderson**
Ambassador Extraordinary and Plenipotentiary
Permanent Representative (DPC: 15 March 2010)
Mrs. Brhane Haile-Henderson

H.E. Mr. Paolo **Zampolli**
Ambassador
Mrs. Amanda Ungaro

Address:	Permanent Mission of the Dominican Republic to the United Nations 144 East 44th Street, 4th Floor New York, N.Y. 10017
Telephone:	(212) 867-0833, -0834, 661-2432
Telefax:	(212) 986-4694
e-mail:	drun@un.int
Correspondence:	Spanish
National holiday:	27 February Independence Day

Ext. 1811	H.E. Mr. Francisco Antonio **Cortorreal** Ambassador Extraordinary and Plenipotentiary Permanent Representative (DPC: 16 April 2014) Mrs. Minerva Cortorreal
Ext. 1836	H.E. Mr. Marcos **Montilla** Ambassador Deputy Permanent Representative Mrs. Margarita Montilla
Ext. 1812	H.E. Mr. Enriquillo A. **del Rosario Ceballos** Ambassador Mrs. Audrey Z. del Rosario
Ext. 1812	H.E. Mr. Juan **Ávila** Ambassador
Ext. 1847	H.E. Mr. Carlos **Michelen** Ambassador Mrs. Juana Sánchez de Michelen
Ext. 1831	H.E. Mr. José **Blanco Conde** Ambassador Mrs. María Gabriela Cáceres de Blanco
	H.E. Mr. Francis **Lorenzo** Ambassador
Ext. 1838	H.E. Mrs. Mildred **Guzmán Madera** Ambassador
Ext. 1816	Mr. Francisco **Tovar Morillo** Minister Counsellor Mrs. Ruth Elizabeth Vargas de Tovar
Ext. 1833	Mrs. María de Jesús **Díaz de Córdova** Minister Counsellor Mr. Emilio Manuel Córdova Roca

Ext. 1817	Mr. Sully **Saneaux** Minister Counsellor Mrs. Roxana Tejada
Ext. 1834	Mrs. Alexandra **Arias Orlowska** Minister Counsellor Mr. Hany Youhana
Ext. 1835	Ms. Mariela **Sánchez de Cruz** Minister Counsellor
Ext. 1815	Mr. Olivio **Fermín** Minister Counsellor Mrs. María Fermín
Ext. 1832	Ms. Joan Margarita **Cedano** Minister Counsellor Mr. Óscar Madera
Ext. 1846	Mr. Darío **Medina** Minister Counsellor Mrs. Jocelin Muñoz de Medina
Ext. 1848	Ms. Elda **Cepeda** Minister Counsellor
Ext. 1813	Mrs. Ana Cecilia **Helena Pimentel** Minister Counsellor
Ext. 1829	Mr. Gustavo **Rodríguez** Minister Counsellor
Ext. 1844	Mr. Juan Manuel **Mercedes Graciano** Minister Counsellor Mrs. Claridania Altagracia Jackson de Mercedes
Ext. 1819	Mr. Julio Bienvenido **Pujols** Counsellor Mrs. Kirsten Ann Kupetz de Pujols
Ext. 1818	Mrs. Marlene A. **Boves Arroyo** Counsellor Mr. José L. Arroyo
Ext. 1838	Mr. Francisco **Álvarez Sosa** Counsellor Mrs. Gladys Álvarez
Ext. 1850	Ms. María Eugenia **del Castillo** Counsellor
Ext. 1836	Ms. Meira **Rijo** Counsellor
Ext. 1841	Ms. Luz del Carmen **Andujar** Counsellor
Ext. 1822	Mrs. Moira **Francisco** Counsellor

Ext. 1845	Ms. Ana Desiré **Romero Prince** Counsellor
Ext. 1837	Ms. Maduisca **Batista Díaz** First Secretary
Ext. 1814	Mrs. Claudia M. **LaRue** First Secretary
Ext. 1848	Ms. Melanie **Hidalgo** First Secretary
Ext. 1830	Ms. Maria **Bello** First Secretary
Ext. 1848	Mr. Juan **Pepén Quezada** Third Secretary Ms. Yrene Vicioso de Pepén
	Brigadier General Julio E. **Florián** Attaché Military Adviser

Address:	Permanent Mission of Ecuador to the United Nations 866 United Nations Plaza, Room 516 New York, N.Y. 10017
Telephone:	(212) 935-1680, -1681
Telefax:	(212) 935-1835
e-mail:	ecuador@un.int
website:	www.ecuadoronu.com
Correspondence:	Spanish
National holiday:	10 August Independence Day

Ext. 300 H.E. Mr. Xavier **Lasso Mendoza**
Ambassador Extraordinary and Plenipotentiary
Permanent Representative (DPC: 20 December 2012)
Mrs. Martha Eguiguren de Lasso

Ext. 300 H.E. Ms. Verónica **Bustamante**
Ambassador Extraordinary and Plenipotentiary
Deputy Permanent Representative
Mr. Samuel Arriagada

Ext. 301 Mr. Agustín **Fornell**
Minister Plenipotentiary

Ext. 303 Mr. Fernando **Luque Márquez**
Counsellor

Ext. 315 Mr. José Eduardo **Proaño**
Counsellor

Ext. 312 Mr. Esteban **Cadena**
First Secretary
Mrs. Andrea Montalvo de Cadena

Ext. 313 Mr. Andrés **Fiallo**
Second Secretary
Mrs. Alondra Moncayo de Fiallo

Ext. 302 Mr. Jonathan **Viera**
Second Secretary

Ext. 313 Mr. Diego Alonso **Tituaña Matango**
Third Secretary
Mrs. Ana Amaguaña de Tituaña

Ext. 309 Mr. Sergio **Shcherbakov**
Third Secretary

Ext. 304 Mr. Luis Xavier **Oña Garcés**
Third Secretary
Mrs. Marta Agudelo de Oña

Ext. 306	Mrs. Maritza **Piedrahita** Attaché Mr. Mario Silva
Ext. 316	Colonel José Alfonso **Gallardo Carmona** Defence Attaché Mrs. Carmita Rosalba Beltran Serrano

Address:	Permanent Mission of the Arab Republic of Egypt to the United Nations 304 East 44th Street New York, N.Y. 10017
Telephone:	(212) 503-0300
Telefax:	(212) 949-5999
e-mail:	egypt@un.int; pr.egypt@un.int (Ambassador's Office)
Correspondence:	English
National holiday:	23 July National Day

503-0338	H.E. Mr. Amr Abdellatif **Aboulatta** Ambassador Extraordinary and Plenipotentiary Permanent Representative (DPC: 4 September 2014) Mrs. Faika Zaki
503-0336	Mr. Osama Abdelkhalek **Mahmoud** Minister Plenipotentiary Deputy Permanent Representative Mrs. Randa Mohamed Ahmed
503-0341	Mr. Amr Fathi **Aljowaily** Minister Plenipotentiary Mrs. Hanan Mohamed Galal Dowidar
503-0310	Mr. Seif Alla Youssef **Kandeel** Counsellor Mrs. Sahar Elsherbini
503-0315	Mr. Amr **Elhamamy** Counsellor Mrs. Lamia Baraka
503-0351	Mr. Tamer **Mostafa** Counsellor Mrs. Nancy Elsohafy
503-0322	Mr. Ahmed **Elshandawily** First Secretary
503-0320	Mr. Mohamed Diaaeldin **Abdrabbo** First Secretary Mrs. Sara Mohamed Mostafa
503-0317	Mr. Emad Morcos **Mattar** First Secretary
503-0314	Mr. Mohamed Badr **Mohamed** First Secretary Mrs. Noha Mousalem

503-0324 Ms. Fatmaalzahraa Hassan Abdelaziz **Abdelkawy**
Second Secretary

503-0346 Mr. Karim Samir Ismail **Alsayed**
Second Secretary

503-0308 Mr. Mohammad Helmy Ahmad **Aboulwafa**
Third Secretary

503-0331 Mr. Mohammed S. **Halima**
Attaché
Mrs. Sarah Khaled Ali Ahmed

503-0327 Mr. Khaled Mahmoud **Haggag**
Attaché (Administrative Affairs)
Mrs. Manal Ragab Mohamed Kadry

503-0325 Mr. Khaled Mohamed Ahmed **Flifel**
Attaché (Administrative Affairs)
Mrs. Dalal Mansour Mohamed Flifel

503-0326 Mr. Hussein Abdelfattah **Shabana**
Attaché (Administrative Affairs)
Mrs. Yassmin Salah Eldin Fouad

503-0381 Mr. Mohamed Youssef **Abdallah**
Attaché (Administrative Affairs)
Mrs. Dalia Elsayed Fahmy Mohamed

503-0340 Mr. Mostafa Elsyed Mostafa **Elnajjar**
Administrative Attaché
Mrs. Khlood Mohamed Abdelkader Fathlla

503-0370 Col. Yasser Mohamed Salah Aly **Hassan**
Counsellor
Military Adviser
Mrs. Marwa Alhussieny Ahmed Allam

503-0371 Major Haisam **Badawy**
Counsellor
Assistant Military Adviser
Mrs. Dena Magdy Abdelhammed Abdelaziz

503-0345 Mr. Ahmed Sharaf **Morsy**
Counsellor (Press and Information)
Mrs. Alyaa Mamoon Ahmed Elbaz

Address:	Permanent Mission of El Salvador to the United Nations 46 Park Avenue New York, N.Y. 10016
Telephone:	(212) 679-1616, -1617
Telefax:	(212) 725-3467
e-mail:	elsalvador@un.int
Correspondence:	Spanish
National holiday:	15 September Independence Day

Ext.3042	H.E. Mr. Rubén Ignacio **Zamora Rivas** Ambassador Extraordinary and Plenipotentiary Permanent Representative (DPC: 13 August 2014) Mrs. Maria Ester Chamorro de Zamora
Ext.3043	H.E. Mr. Rubén Armando **Escalante Hasbún** Ambassador Deputy Permanent Representative
Ext.3045	Mr. Carlos Alejandro **Funes Henríquez** Minister Counsellor
Ext.3054	Mr. Hector Enrique **Jaime Calderón** Minister Counsellor Mrs. Gabriela María Cuéllar de Jaime
Ext.3046	Ms. Carla Esperanza **Rivera Sánchez** Minister Counsellor
	Ms. Fatima Geraldina **Calderon de Flores** Minister Counsellor Mr. Jaime Flores
	Mr. Dagoberto Alcides **Torres Peña** Minister Counsellor Mrs. Sonia Veronica Merino de Torres
	Ms. Egriselda Arecely **González López** Counsellor
Ext.3049	Ms. Ana Leticia **Artiga** Third Secretary
Ext.3047	Mrs. Beatriz Clará de **Vassil** Third Secretary Mr. Peter Vassil
	Mr. Luis E. **Alvarado Ramírez** Third Secretary (Administrative Affairs) Mrs. Vicenta de Alvarado

Ext.3056	Colonel Hugo Arístides **Angulo Rogel** Minister Counsellor Defence Attaché Mrs. Maria de Lourdes Jarquin de Angulo
Ext.3055	Major Luís Alfredo **Maída Leíva** Counsellor Deputy Defence Attaché
	Colonel Pablo Alberto **Soriano Cruz** Counsellor Deputy Defence Attaché

Equatorial Guinea

Member State since 12 November 1968

Address:	Permanent Mission of Equatorial Guinea to the United Nations 800 Second Avenue, Suite 305 New York, N.Y. 10017
Telephone:	(212) 223-2324
Telefax:	(212) 223-2366
e-mail:	equatorialguineamission@yahoo.com
Correspondence:	Spanish
National holiday:	12 October Independence Day

H.E. Mr. Anatolio **Ndong Mba**
Ambassador Extraordinary and Plenipotentiary
Permanent Representative (DPC: 7 January 2010)
Mrs. Maria Teresa Chele Iyanga

Mr. Juan Mbomio **Ndong Mangue**
First Secretary
Mrs. Natividad Mangue Obiang Mayene

Mrs. Lourdes **Oyono Angue**
Second Secretary

Ms. María Jesús **Diallo Besari**
Third Secrteary

Mr. Marcial **Edu Mbasogo**
Third Secrteary
Mrs. Estela Ana Andeme Nguema

Ms. Isabel **Avomo Sima**
Third Secretary

Mrs. Inés **Olo Lima**
Attaché

Eritrea

Member State since 28 May 1993

Address: Permanent Mission of Eritrea
to the United Nations
800 Second Avenue, 18th Floor
New York, N.Y. 10017

Telephone: (212) 687-3390

Telefax: (212) 687-3138

e-mail: general@eritrea-unmission.org

website: www.eritrea-unmission.org

Correspondence: English

National holiday: 24 May
Independence Day

H.E. Mr. Girma Asmerom **Tesfay**
Ambassador Extraordinary and Plenipotentiary
Permanent Representative (DPC: 23 April 2014)

Mr. Amanuel **Giorgio**
Counsellor
Deputy Permanent Representative
Mrs. Adhanet Tsegay

Mr. Nebil Said **Idris**
First Secretary

Address: Permanent Mission of the Republic of Estonia to the United Nations
3 Dag Hammarskjöld Plaza
305 East 47th Street, Unit 6B
New York, N.Y. 10017

Telephone: (212) 883-0640

Telefax: (646) 514-0099

e-mail: mission.newyork@mfa.ee

Correspondence: English

National holiday: 24 February
Independence Day

H.E. Mr. Margus **Kolga**
Ambassador Extraordinary and Plenipotentiary
Permanent Representative (DPC: 16 December 2010)
Mrs. Maarja Maasikas

Ms. Minna-Liina **Lind**
First Secretary
Deputy Permanent Representative

Mr. Gert **Auväärt**
First Secretary
Ms. Kristel Auväärt

Ms. Kristel **Lõuk**
First Secretary
Mr. Tarmo Lillsoo

Ms. Pille **Kesler**
Second Secretary
Mr. Jan Kesler

Ms. Terje **Raadik**
Second Secretary

Address: Permanent Mission of the Federal Democratic Republic of Ethiopia to the United Nations
866 Second Avenue, 3rd Floor
New York, N.Y. 10017

Telephone: (212) 421-1830

Telefax: (646) 756-4690

e-mail: ethiopia@un.int

Correspondence: English

National holiday: 28 May

H.E. Mr. Tekeda **Alemu**
Ambassador Extraordinary and Plenipotentiary
Permanent Representative (DPC: 24 January 2011)
Mrs. Lakech Goitom Habtetsion

H.E. Mr. Aman Hassen **Bame**
Ambassador
Deputy Permanent Representative
Mrs. Mekuria Adanech Mekonnen

H.E. Mr. Dawit **Yohannes**
Ambassador
Mrs. Haimanot Kebede Woldemichael

Mr. Degife Bedi **Doggaya**
Minister
Military Adviser

Mrs. Fortuna Dibaco **Cizare**
Minister Counsellor

Mrs. Nuria Mohammed **Ferej**
Minister Counsellor

Mr. Dawit Yirga **Woldegerima**
Minister Counsellor

Mr. Abrham Engida **Mekonen**
Minister Counsellor

Mr. Abate Madebo **Duguno**
Minister Counsellor

Mr. Belachew Gujubo **Gutulo**
Counsellor
Mrs. Tesfanesh Leka Lencha

Mr. Yidnekachew G/Meskel **Zewdu**
Counsellor
Mrs. Woldemariam Mahlet Gebreyesus

Mr. Tegegne Getahun **Zerihun**
Counsellor
Mrs. Zenebech Markos Tsehay

Mrs. Alganesh Melese **Meshesha**
First Secretary

Mrs. Kebebush Abiche **Jelamo**
First Secretary

Mr. Kidanemariam Gidey **Weldeyohannes**
First Secretary
Mrs. Lemlem Tadesse Kidane

Ms. Almaz Tesfahunegn **Hailu**
Second Secretary

Ms. Soboke Derara **Gossa**
Second Secretary

Address: Permanent Mission of the Republic of Fiji
to the United Nations
801 Second Avenue, 10th Floor
New York, N.Y. 10017

Telephone: (212) 687-4130

Telefax: (212) 687-3963

e-mail: mission@fijiprun.org

Correspondence: English

National holiday: 10 October

H.E. Mr. Peter **Thomson**
Ambassador Extraordinary and Plenipotentiary
Permanent Representative (DPC: 4 March 2010)
Mrs. Marijcke Anne Thomson

Ms. Namita **Khatri**
Counsellor
Deputy Permanent Representative

Mr. Gene **Bai**
First Secretary
Mrs. Marica Rokolutu Bai

Mr. Peni B. **Suveinakama**
Second Secretary
Mrs. Adi Koula Suveinakama

Finland

Member State since 14 December 1955

Address:	Permanent Mission of Finland to the United Nations 866 United Nations Plaza, Suite 222 New York, N.Y. 10017
Telephone:	(212) 355-2100
Telefax:	(212) 759-6156
e-mail:	sanomat.yke@formin.fi
Correspondence:	English
National holiday:	6 December Independence Day

821-0246	H.E. Mr. Kai **Sauer** Ambassador Extraordinary and Plenipotentiary Permanent Representative (DPC: 19 August 2014) Ms. Erika Sauer
821-0244	H.E. Mr. Janne **Taalas** Ambassador Deputy Permanent Representative Ms. Mervi Taalas
821-0248	Ms. Theresa **Zitting** Minister Counsellor (Political Affairs) Mr. Richard Zitting
821-0278	Mr. Lasse **Keisalo** Minister Counsellor (Economic and Social Affairs) Ms. Rocio Acosta
821-0229	Ms. Sari **Mäkelä** Counsellor (Legal Adviser) Mr. Vesa Koivisto
821-0241	Mr. Pasi **Pöysäri** Counsellor (Human Rights) Ms. Sandra Pöysäri
821-0251	Ms. Anna **Salovaara** Counsellor (Political Affairs) Mr. Perttu Salovaara
821-0243	Mr. Mika **Ruotsalainen** Counsellor (Political Affairs)
821-0276	Ms. Petra **Yliportimo** First Secretary (Economic and Social Affaires)
821-0255	Ms. Pilvi **Taipale** First Secretary (Political Affairs) Mr. Joonas Luotonen

821-0272	Ms. Emilia **van Veen** First Secretary (Sustainable Development) Mr. Bert van Veen
821-0249	Ms. Elina **Lemmetty-Hartoneva** First Secretary (Financial and Budgetary Affairs)
821-0250	Ms. Sole **Abrahamsen** Attaché (Election Officer) Mr. Clifford Abrahamsen
821-0267	Colonel Matti **Lampinen** Counsellor Military Adviser Ms. Diana Lampinen

Address:	Permanent Mission of France to the United Nations One Dag Hammarskjöld Plaza 245 East 47th Street, 44th Floor New York, N.Y. 10017
Telephone:	(212) 702-4900
Telefax:	(212) 702-3190
e-mail:	france@franceonu.org
Correspondence:	French
National holiday:	14 July National Day

702-4949	H.E. Mr. François **Delattre** Ambassador Extraordinary and Plenipotentiary Permanent Representative (DPC: 4 September 2014) Mrs. Sophie L'Helias-Delattre
702-4982	Mr. Alexis **Lamek** First Counsellor Deputy Permanent Representative Mrs. Sara Dolatabadi Lamek
702-4970	Mr. Philippe **Bertoux** First Counsellor Mrs. Isabelle Bertoux
	Mr. Tanguy **Stehelin** First Counsellor
702-4938	Brigadier General Christian **Beau** First Counsellor Head of Military Mission Mrs. Gaêlle Beau
702-4958	Mrs. Vanessa **Gouret Verschueren** Counsellor (Economic and Financial Affairs) Mr. Yves Verschueren
702-4927	Mrs. Fabienne **Bartoli** Counsellor (Social Affairs) Mr. Michel Blanchard
702-4950	Mr. François **Gave** Counsellor (Development Affairs)
702-4976	Mr. Thierry **Caboche** Counsellor (Press) Mrs. Tamara Kummer

702-4985	Colonel Christophe **Deherre** Counsellor Military Adviser Mrs. Lidiya Kozlova Deherre
702-4984	Mr. Christophe **Morchoine** Counsellor
	Mrs. Camille **Petit** Second Counsellor Mr. David Chekroun
(646) 839-6652	Mr. Arnaud **Pescheux** First Secretary
702-4966	Mr. Adrien **Pinelli** First Secretary
702-4968	Mr. Teymouraz **Gorjestani** First Secretary
702-4976	Mrs. Vanessa **Selk** First Secretary
702-4918	Mr. Gabriel **Normand** First Secretary Mrs. Clémentine Deniel
702-4907	Mr. Emmanuel **Suquet** First Secretary Mrs. Violaine Pattée
702-4986	Mr. Jean-Noël **Bonnieu** First Secretary
702-4993	Mrs. Marie **Audouard** First Secretary
702-4962	Ms. Ahlem **Gharbi** First Secretary
702-4974	Mr. Jean-Luc **Alméras** First Secretary (Head of Administration) Mrs. Chen Wei
702-4920	Mr. Guillaume **Dabouis** First Secretary Mrs. Roxane Revon
702-4963	Mr. Benjamin **Cabouat** First Secretary Mrs. Agathe Cabouat
702-4919	Ms. Isis **Jaraud-Darnault** First Secretary
702-4975	Mr. Tomas **Napolitano Martinez** First Secretary Mrs. Jessica Gourdon

	Mr. Alexis **Berthier** First Secretary
702-4995	Ms. Bettina **Boughani** First Secretary
702-4930	Mrs. Marianne **Oudet Vincent** First Secretary Mr. Jean-François Oudet
702-4929	Mr. Eudes **Ramadier** First Secretary Mrs. Nadia Blanc
	Ms. Anne-Laure **Jeanvoine** First Secretary
702-4942	Mr. Morgan **Larhant** First Secretary
702-4997	Mr. Franck **Busson** Second Secretary Ms. Nathalie Poensin-Busson
702-4911	Mr. Laurent **Grison** Third Secretary Mrs. Paldon Tsering-Grison
702-4994	Mrs. Olivia **Gravillon** Third Secretary Mr. Cyrille Soret
702-4932	Mr. Michaël **Belmonte** Attaché Mrs. Audrey Fournel

Gabon

Member State since 20 September 1960

Address: Permanent Mission of the Gabonese Republic
to the United Nations
18 East 41st Street, 9th Floor
New York, N.Y. 10017

Telephone: (212) 686-9720; -9721; -1705

Telefax: (212) 689-5769

e-mail: info@gabonmission.com

Correspondence: French

National holiday: 17 August

H.E. ...
Ambassador Extraordinary and Plenipotentiary
Permanent Representative (DPC...)

H.E. Mrs. Marianne Odette **Bibalou**
Ambassador
Deputy Permanent Representative

H.E. Mr. Franklin Joachim **Makanga**
Ambassador
Deputy Permanent Representative

Mr. Michel Régis **Onanga Ndiaye**
Minister Counsellor
Mrs. Christiane Onanga Ndiaye

Mr. Charles **Lembouma**
First Counsellor
Mrs. Manuela Armelle Lembouma

Ms. Lilly Stella **Ngyema Ndong**
First Counsellor

Mrs. Annette Andrée **Onanga**
Counsellor
Mr. Parfait Anyanga-Onanga

Mrs. Allegra Pamela Romance **Bongo**
Counsellor

Mr. William Rodrigue **Nyama**
Counsellor

Mr. Pierre **Oniane Nguema**
Counsellor

Mr. Christophe **Nanga**
Counsellor

Mrs. Rolande **Mengue Bekale**
Counsellor

Mr. Jean-Pierre-Hemery **Doumbeneny Ndzigna**
Counsellor

Mr. Hans Martien **Diaba**
Counsellor (Protocol)

Mr. Gervais **Ngyema Ndong**
Counsellor

Address: Permanent Mission of the Gambia
to the United Nations
336 East 45th Street, 7th Floor
New York, N.Y. 10017

Telephone: (212) 949-6640

Telefax: (212) 856-9820

e-mail: gambia_un@hotmail.com

website: gambia.un.int

Correspondence: English

National holiday: 18 February

H.E. Mr. Mamadou **Tangara**
Ambassador Extraordinary and Plenipotentiary
Permanent Representative (DPC: 18 September 2013)
Mrs. Saffiatou Tangara Samba

Mr. Yakuba A. **Drammeh**
Counsellor
Deputy Permanent Representative
Mrs. Maimuna Ndong Drammeh

Mr. Habib Tamasa Baba **Jarra**
Counsellor

Mr. Alieu Badou B. Y. **Samba**
Attaché
Mrs. Haddy Jallow-Samba

Georgia

Member State since 31 July 1992

Address:	Permanent Mission of Georgia to the United Nations One United Nations Plaza, 26th Floor New York, N.Y. 10017
Telephone:	(212) 759-1949
Telefax:	(212) 759-1832
e-mail	geomission.un@mfa.gov.ge
website:	www.un.int/georgia
Correspondence:	English
National holiday:	26 May Independence Day

Ext. 201	H.E. Mr. Kaha **Imnadze** Ambassador Extraordinary and Plenipotentiary Permanent Representative (DPC: 23 July 2013) Mrs. Lika Elene Paliashvili Imnadze
Ext. 203	Mr. Vakhtang **Makharoblishvili** Minister Plenipotentiary Deputy Permanent Representative
Ext. 208	Mr. Giorgi **Kvelashvili** Minister Plenipotentiary Mrs. Irma Kirkitadze
Ext. 205	Mrs. Inga **Kanchaveli** Counsellor Mr. Richard Kamladze
Ext. 204	Ms. Tamta **Kupradze** Counsellor
Ext. 207	Ms. Nino **Shekriladze** Counsellor Mr. Shalva Tskhakaya
Ext. 210	Mr. Merab **Manjgaladze** Counsellor Mrs. Ekaterine Dapkviashvili

Address:	Permanent Mission of Germany to the United Nations 871 United Nations Plaza New York, N.Y. 10017
Telephone:	(212) 940-0400
Telefax:	(212) 940-0402 (General) (212) 940-0403 (Political Section) (212) 940-0404 (Economic Section) (212) 610-9709 (Administration)
e-mail:	info@new-york-un.diplo.de
Correspondence:	English
National holiday:	3 October

940-0410	H.E. Mr. Harald **Braun** Ambassador Extraordinary and Plenipotentiary Permanent Representative (DPC: 14 March 2014) Mrs. Ute Braun
940-0414	H.E. Mr. Heiko **Thoms** Ambassador Extraordinary and Plenipotentiary Deputy Permanent Representative Mrs. Anahita Thoms
940-0494	Mr. Thomas **Schieb** Minister Mrs. Claudia Schieb
940-0446	Mr. Reinhard Josef **Krapp** Minister Mrs. Beatrice Emilie Krapp
940-0490	Mr. Dietrich **Lingenthal** Minister Counsellor Mrs. Constanze Fitz Lingenthal
940-0437	Mr. Friedrich-Alexander **Hoppe** First Counsellor Mrs. Victoria Hoppe
940-0436	Mr. Andreas **Stoebe** First Counsellor Mrs. Meike Reinhard
940-0454	Mrs. Stephanie **Kage** Counsellor Mr. Elmar Juchem

940-0430	Lt. Colonel Klaus **Merkel** Counsellor Deputy Military Adviser Mrs. Ilona Merkel
940-0426	Mr. Florian **Reindel** Counsellor
940-0456	Mr. Christian **Nell** Counsellor Mrs. Alix Sophia Studnitz Nell
940-0445	Mr. Ralph **Kohlen** Counsellor Mrs. Christine Kohlen
940-0420	Mr. Till **Knorn** Counsellor Mrs. Kristen Elizabeth Knorn
940-0457	Mrs. Sabine **Mondorf** Counsellor Mr. Hans-Joerg Baumgartner
940-0448	Mr. Jan **Kantorczyk** Counsellor Mrs. Elena Kantorczyk
940-0427	Mrs. Christiane **Hullman** Counsellor Mrs. Valeriya Golovina
940-0458	Mr. Andreas **Pfeil** Counsellor Mrs. Christina Janssen
940-0498	Mr. Rudolf Christof **Ernst** Counsellor
940-0470	Mr. Frieder **Schnitzler** Counsellor Mrs. Annie Schnitzler
940-0423	Mr. Hendrik **Selle** First Secretary
940-0442	Mr. Jan **Helmig** First Secretary Mrs. Vanessa Helmig
940-0429	Mr. Peter **Winkler** First Secretary Mrs. Eun-Ji Yi
940-0421	Mr. Heiko **Nitzschke** First Secretary Mrs. Tanja Bernstein

940-0416	Mr. Benedikt **Zanker** First Secretary Mrs. Anna Zanker
940-0416	Mr. Christian **Doktor** First Secretary Mr. Dirk Oliver Eggert-Doktor
940-0422	Mr. Thomas **Seidel** First Secretary
940-0461	Ms. Ursula Caroline **Kern** First Secretary
940-0476	Mrs. Anne Pia **Mannweiler** Second Secretary Mr. Udo Mannweiler
940-0451	Ms. Carolin Denise **Pohlmann** Second Secretary
940-0441	Mr. Daniel Johannes **Schemske** Second Secretary Mrs. Lisa Christine Schemske
940-0425	Mrs. Janina **Hasse-Mohsine** Second Secretary Mr. Omar Mohsine
940-0543	Mr. Sebastian **Baumann** Second Secretary Mrs. Christin Petra Baumann
940-0452	Mrs. Julia Mascha **Nuessen** Second Secretary Mr. Oliver Scharf
610-9819	Mr. Michael **Spill** Third Secretary Mrs. Maricel Altavano Alapan-Spill
940-0418	Mrs. Katja Omnia **Dingens** Third Secretary Mr. Peter Claus Dingens
940-0473	Ms. Nadine **Skale** Third Secretary
610-9811	Ms. Patricia **Karsten** Third Secretary
940-0467	Mrs. Silke **Majuru** Third Secretary
610-9812	Mr. Frank **Toeller** Third Secretary Mrs. Irene Toeller

940-0487	Mr. Bernd **Jennert** Third Secretary Mrs. Taina Jaervinen
940-0499	Mr. Reiner **Wilhus** Third Secretary
940-0434	Mr. Lawrence Vincent **Walker** Attaché Mrs. Gabriele Walker
940-0431	Ms. Ina Maria **Vogel** Attaché
940-0534	Mr. Sammy **Duesdieker** Attaché
940-9825	Mr. Mike **Velten** Attaché Ms. Anke Velten
610-9779	Ms. Christine Maria **Haimerl** Attaché
940-0499	Mr. Stefan **Priemel** Attaché
940-0443	Mr. Hans-Georg **Gress** Assistant Attaché Mrs. Jana Gress-Arensmeier
610-9481	Mr. Lutz **Gebhardt** Assistant Attaché Mrs. Cynthia E. Gebhardt
940-0480	Mr. Volker **Haberlandt** Assistant Attaché Mrs. Susan Haberlandt-Nevisi
940-0424	Mrs. Gabriele **Sippel-Moignard** Assistant Attaché Mr. Jean-Pierre Louis Moignard
940-0447	Ms. Alexandra **Kloppe** Assistant Attaché
610-9492	Mr. Andreas Marcus **Rocznik** Assistant Attaché Mrs. Maria Lourdes Bonifacio
610-9813	Mr. Hendrik Martin **Kim-Wolf** Assistant Attaché Mrs. Vivian Kim-Wolf
940-0771	Mr. Michael **Studt** Assistant Attaché Mrs. Christine Studt

940-0479	Mr. Mike Lothar **Schamotzki** Assistant Attaché Mrs. Manuela Baur
940-0415	Ms. Erna **Stamp** Assistant Attaché
940-0483	Mr. Christophe **Goehre** Assistant Attaché
940-0438	Ms. Svenja **Strobel** Assistant Attaché
940-0469	Mrs. Diana **Sporer** Assistant Attaché Mr. Guido Cristancho
940-0419	Mrs. Amalie **Harrison** Assistant Attaché Mr. John Robert Harrison
940-0468	Ms. Sybille **Pontow** Assistant Attaché
940-0497	Mr. Alexander **Albach** Assistant Attaché Mrs. Irina Albach
940-0435	Ms. Isabel **Haring** Assistant Attaché
940-0444	Mrs. Tanja **Doerfler** Assistant Attaché Mr. Marco Doerfler
940-0455	Mr. Wolfgang **Kotulla** Assistant Attaché Mrs. Andrea Kotulla
940-0488	Ms. Carolin Sofia **Kullmann** Assistant Attaché
940-0488	Mr. Murat **Civan** Assistant Attaché
940-0459	Ms. Judith **Billionnière** Assistant Attaché Mr. Frédéric Billionnière
940-0499	Mr. Eckard **Meyer** Assistant Attaché
940-0499	Ms. Denise **Kunze** Assistant Attaché
940-0413	Ms. Christa **Koerber** Assistant Attaché

Address:	Permanent Mission of Ghana to the United Nations 19 East 47th Street New York, N.Y. 10017
Telephone:	(212) 832-1300
Telefax:	(212) 751-6743
e-mail:	ghanaperm@aol.com
Correspondence:	English
National holiday:	6 March Independence Day

Ext. 299	H.E. ... Ambassador Extraordinary and Plenipotentiary Permanent Representative (DPC: .) .
Ext. 326	Mr. Philbert **Johnson** Minister Deputy Permanent Representative Mrs. Sophia Johnson
Ext. 105	Mr. Jedidiah Reuben **Adogla** Minister Counsellor Ms. Shantini Selvarajah
Ext. 291	Mrs. Audrey Naana **Abayena** Minister Counsellor Mr. Johannes Everet Abayena
Ext. 245	Mr. John Agyin **Eshun** Counsellor Mrs. Abena Eshun
Ext. 329	Mr. Emmanuel Kwaku **Dade** Counsellor
Ext. 293	Mrs. Christiana Nana Ofosua **Tenkorang** Counsellor Mr. Kwame Asamoah Tenkorang
Ext. 327	Ms. Aba **Ayebi-Arthur** First Secretary
Ext. 286	Mr. Fawaz **Aliu** First Secretary
Ext. 268	Mr. Michael **Addofoly** First Secretary
Ext. 271	Mr. Isaac Owusu **Djin** Second Secretary Mrs. Janet Gyamfiwaa Djin

Ext. 299	Mrs. Georgina **Blankson** Second Secretary Mr. Stanley Blankson
Ext. 246	Brigadier General Samuel **Yanyi-Akofur** Minister Military Adviser Mrs. Ignatia Ashelley Quaye-Akofur
Ext. 221	Colonel Constance Emefa **Edjeani-Afenu** Minister Counsellor Deputy Military Adviser
Ext. 280	Mr. Francis Mawunyo **Tsetse** Minister Counsellor Mrs. Victoria Tsetse
Ext. 265	Mr. Raymond Harry **Reynolds** Counsellor (Information) Mrs. Rita Ama Reynolds

Address:	Permanent Mission of Greece to the United Nations 866 Second Avenue, 13th Floor New York, N.Y. 10017-2905
Telephone:	(212) 888-6900 (212) 479-1300
Telefax:	(212) 888-4440
e-mail:	grdel.un@mfa.gr
website:	www.mfa.gr/un
Correspondence:	English
National holiday:	25 March Independence Day

479-1350 479-1322	H.E. Mrs. Catherine **Boura** Ambassador Extraordinary and Plenipotentiary Permanent Representative (DPC: 10 March 2015)

479-1349	Ms. Nafsika Nancy Eva **Vraila** Minister Plenipotentiary Deputy Permanent Representative
479-1318	Ms. Ekaterini **Fountoulaki** First Counsellor
479-1326	Mr. Dimitrios **Gioldassis** First Counsellor
479-1333	Lieutenant Colonel Angelos **Kalligaridis** Counsellor Military Adviser Mrs. Anysia Kokkinopoulou
479-1333	Major Vasileios **Trimmis** Counsellor Deputy Military Adviser Mrs. Georgia Koutrafouri
751-8788	Mr. Nikolaos **Papaconstantinou** Counsellor (Press) Mrs. Marina Papaconstantinou
479-1369	Mr. Georgios **Pouleas** First Secretary Mrs. Efrossini Polyzoidou
479-1354	Mrs. Efrossini **Polyzoidou** First Secretary Mr. Georgios Pouleas
479-1313	Mr. Konstantinos **Kodellas** First Secretary

479-1329	Mrs. Aikaterini **Tzima** Second Secretary Mr. Anastasios Bartzokis
479-1321	Mrs. Konstantina **Diakogianni** Attaché Mr. Samouil Zisis
479-1347	Ms. Despina **Boubalos** Attaché
479-1367	Mr. Nicolaos-Enrique **Ramirez-Chatsios** Attaché
479-1356	Mr. Stavros **Spanos** Attaché
479-1360	Mr. Georgios **Stavrou** Attaché Mrs. Aimilia Oikonomou
479-1360	Mr. Petros **Alexakos** Attaché
479-1350	Mrs. Vasiliki **Petridou** Attaché Mr. Fotios Eleftheriadis
479-1337	Mr. Fotios **Eleftheriadis** Attaché Mrs. Vasiliki Petridou
479-1349	Mrs. Aimilia **Oikonomou** Attaché Mr. Georgios Stavrou

---

Mr. Lampros **Kazis**
Second Secretary (Press)

Grenada

Member State since 17 September 1974

Address: Permanent Mission of Grenada to the United Nations
800 Second Avenue, Suite 400K
New York, N.Y. 10017

Telephone: (212) 599-0301, -0302

Telefax: (212) 599-1540

e-mail: grenada@un.int

Correspondence: English

National holiday: 7 February
Independence Day

H.E. Mr. Denis G. **Antoine**
Ambassador Extraordinary and Plenipotentiary
Permanent Representative (DPC: 13 September 2013)

H.E. Mr. Derrick **James**
Ambassador

H.E. Ms. Amanda **Ungaro**
Ambassador
Mr. Paolo Zampolli

Ms. Marguerite Y. **St. John-Sebastian**
Counsellor
Mr. Smith J. Sebastian

Mrs. Celia **Thomas**
First Secretary
Mr. Anthony Thomas

Address:	Permanent Mission of Guatemala to the United Nations 57 Park Avenue New York, N.Y. 10016
Telephone:	(212) 679-4760
Telefax:	(212) 685-8741
e-mail:	guatemala@un.int; onupnud@minex.gob.gt
website:	www.guatemalaun.org
Correspondence:	Spanish
National holiday:	15 September Independence Day

Ext. 210	H.E. Mr. Fernando **Carrera Castro** Ambassador Extraordinary and Plenipotentiary Permanent Representative (DPC: 19 September 2014)
Ext. 216	Ms. Mónica **Bolaños Pérez** Minister Plenipotentiary Deputy Permanent Representative
Ext. 224	Ms. Ana Cristina **Rodríguez Pineda** Minister Counsellor
Ext. 227	Mr. Omar **Castañeda Solares** Minister Counsellor
	Ms. María Concepción **Castro Mazariegos** Minister Counsellor
Ext. 215	Ms. María Soledad **Urruela Arenales** Counsellor
Ext. 218	Mr. Gabriel **Orellana Zabalza** First Secretary
Ext. 222	Ms. María José **del Águila Castillo** First Secretary
Ext. 220	Ms. María Belén **Portillo** Second Secretary
Ext. 219	Ms. Magaly **Masaya Ruiz de Flores** Third Secretary Mr. Jorge Javier Flores Sandoval
Ext. 225	Colonel Edwin Rafael **Cosio-Melara** Attaché Military Adviser

Guinea

Member State since 12 December 1958

Address: Permanent Mission of the Republic of Guinea to the United Nations
140 East 39th Street
New York, N.Y. 10016

Telephone: (212) 687-8115

Telefax: (212) 687-8248

e-mail: missionofguinea@aol.com

Correspondence: French

National holiday: 2 October
Independence Day

H.E. Mr. Mamadi **Touré**
Ambassador Extraordinary and Plenipotentiary
Permanent Representative (DPC: 14 September 2011)

Mr. Mohamed Cherif **Diallo**
Minister Counsellor
Mrs. Mariam Diallo

Mr. Alassane **Conte**
Counsellor

Mr. Abou **Sakho**
First Secretary

Mrs. Haby **Barry**
Second Secretary

Mrs. Fanta **Doumbouya**
Attaché

Guinea-Bissau

Member State since 17 September 1974

Address: Permanent Mission of the Republic
of Guinea-Bissau to the United Nations
336 East 45th Street, 13th Floor
New York, N.Y. 10017

Telephone: (212) 896-8311

Telefax: (212) 896-8313

e-mail: guinea-bissau@un.int; guinebissauonu@gmail.com

Correspondence: French

National holiday: 24 September

H.E. Mr. João Soares **Da Gama**
Ambassador Extraordinary and Plenipotentiary
Permanent Representative (DPC: 13 August 2010)
Mrs. Julia A.R.S. Da Gama

Mr. Ernestino Jorge **Mango**
Second Secretary
Mrs. Babilé Baticam Mafra Mango

Mrs. Maria Antonieta **P. D'Alva**
Second Secretary

Guyana

Member State since 20 September 1966

Address: Permanent Mission of the Republic of Guyana to the United Nations
801 Second Avenue, 5th Floor
New York, N.Y. 10017

Telephone: (212) 573-5828, -5829

Telefax: (212) 573-6225

e-mail: guyana@un.int

Correspondence: English

National holiday: 23 February

H.E. Mr. George Wilfred **Talbot**
Ambassador Extraordinary and Plenipotentiary
Permanent Representative (DPC: 18 January 2012)
Mrs. Grace Angela Talbot

Mr. Troy **Torrington**
Minister Counsellor

Ms. Bibi Sheliza **Ally**
Counsellor

Mr. Shiraz Arif **Mohamed**
First Secretary

Address: Permanent Mission of Haiti to the United Nations
815 Second Avenue, 6th Floor
New York, N.Y. 10017

Telephone: (212) 370-4840

Telefax: (212) 661-8698

e-mail: mphonu.newyork@diplomatie.ht

Correspondence: French

National holiday: 1 January
Independence Day

H.E. Mr. Denis **Régis**
Ambassador Extraordinary and Plenipotentiary
Permanent Representative (DPC: 23 July 2013)

Mr. Jean Baptiste Reynold **Leroy**
Minister Counsellor
Deputy Permanent Representative

Ext. 136 Mrs. Astride **Nazaire**
Minister Counsellor
Mr. Jean Sébastien Riché

Ext. 130 Mrs. Nicole **Romulus**
Counsellor

Ext. 124 Mr. Willy **Louis**
Counsellor

Ext. 132 Mrs. Marie Françoise **Bernadel**
Counsellor

Ext. 129 Mr. Paul **Alliance**
Counsellor

Ext. 135 Ms. Dayna Mirlene **Hyppolite**
First Secretary

Ext. 128 Ms. Daphné **Lafontant**
First Secretary

Ext. 120 Mrs. Marie Bernadette **Narcisse-Salomon**
Second Secretary

Mrs. Marjorie **Cosmey**
Second Secretary

Ms. Tafna Anne Dominique **Regis**
Second Secretary

Ext. 134 Ms. Jessica Nédie **Bordes**
Attaché

Honduras

Member State since 17 December 1945

Address:	Permanent Mission of Honduras to the United Nations 866 United Nations Plaza, Suite 417 New York, N.Y. 10017
Telephone:	(212) 752-3370, -3371
Telefax:	(212) 223-0498
e-mail:	honduras_un@hotmail.com
website:	www.un.int/honduras
Correspondence:	Spanish
National holiday:	15 September Independence Day

H.E. Ms. Mary Elizabeth **Flores**
Ambassador Extraordinary and Plenipotentiary
Permanent Representative (DPC: 29 April 2010)

H.E. Mr. Marco A. **Suazo**
Ambassador
Deputy Permanent Representative

Ms. Dulce **Sánchez**
Minister Counsellor

Ms. Vivian **Lezama**
Minister Counsellor

Ms. Dessy **Reyes**
Counsellor

Ms. Karla **García López**
Counsellor

Ms. Suyapa **Carías**
Counsellor

Ms. Rosa Elena **Lobo Juarez**
First Secretary

Ms. Flor Idalma **Mejía**
Attaché

Mr. Neftali **Mendoza**
Attaché
Mrs. Nury Galindo

Mrs. Rosa Elena **Lobo Juárez**
Attaché (Press)

Address:	Permanent Mission of Hungary to the United Nations 227 East 52nd Street New York, N.Y. 10022-6301
Telephone:	(212) 752-0209
Telefax:	(212) 755-5395
e-mail:	hungary@un.int
Website:	www.mfa.gov.hu/kulkepviselet/New_York_ENSZ/en
Correspondence:	English
National holiday:	20 August

660-7932	H.E. Ms. Katalin Annamária **Bogyay** Ambassador Extraordinary and Plenipotentiary Permanent Representative (DPC: 20 January 2015) Mr. Tamás Lőrinczy
660-7932	H.E. Mr. Zsolt **Hetesy** Ambassador Deputy Permanent Representative Mrs. Katalin Hetesy
660-7939	Mr. Tamás **Tóth** First Secretary Mrs. Nikolett Szepes Tóthné
	Mr. Zoltán **Turbék** Second Secretary Ms. Eszter Nagy
	Ms. Anna **Szénási** Second Secretary
660-7937	Mrs. Éva Henriett **Schäfer** Third Secretary Mr. Ákos Lósz
660-7941	Ms. Rita **Herencsár** Third Secretary
	Mr. Balázs **Dobrosi** Third Secretary

Iceland

Member State since 19 November 1946

Address:	Permanent Mission of Iceland to the United Nations 800 Third Avenue, 36th Floor New York, N.Y. 10022
Telephone:	(212) 593-2700, (646) 282-9370
Telefax:	(212) 593-6269
e-mail:	unmission@mfa.is
Correspondence:	English
National holiday:	17 June Anniversary of the Establishment of the Republic

---

(646) 282-9382	H.E. Mr. Einar **Gunnarsson** Ambassador Extraordinary and Plenipotentiary Permanent Representative (DPC: 20 January 2015) Mrs. Elisabet Thordardottir
(646) 282-9374	Mr. Nikulas Peter John **Hannigan** Minister Counsellor Deputy Permanent Representative Mrs. Ran Tryggvadottir
(646) 282-9379	Mr. Thorvardur Atli **Thórsson** First Secretary Ms. Sandra Lyngdorf
(646) 282-9385	Ms. Maria Mjoll **Jonsdottir** First Secretary Mr. Brynjolfur Stefansson
(646) 282-9383	Ms. Kristín Eva **Jansson** Attaché (Head of Administration) Mr. Karl Ove Lennart Jansson

Address:	Permanent Mission of India to the United Nations 235 East 43rd Street New York, N.Y. 10017
Telephone:	(212) 490-9660, -9661
Telefax:	(212) 490-9656
e-mail:	india@un.int indiaun@prodigy.net
Correspondence:	English
National holiday:	26 January Anniversary of the Proclamation of the Republic

---

490-9670	H.E. Mr. Asoke Kumar **Mukerji** Ambassador Extraordinary and Plenipotentiary Permanent Representative (DPC: 16 April 2013) Mrs. Vanita Singh **Mukerji**
490-0327	H.E. Mr. Bhagwant Singh **Bishnoi** Ambassador Deputy Permanent Representative Mrs. Rupa Bishnoi
	Mr. Suryanarayan Srinivas **Prasad** Minister Mrs. Poornima Prasad
490-9681	Mr. Amit **Narang** Counsellor Mrs. Divya Narang
490-0327	Mr. Alok **Kumar** Counsellor Mrs. Rashmi Kumar
	Mr. Koteswara Rao **Madimi** Counsellor Mrs. Rajya Lakshmi Madimi
490-9682	Mr. Vishnu Dutt **Sharma** Counsellor Mrs. Pinki Sharma
490-9679	Mr. Prakash **Gupta** Counsellor Mrs. Neha Gupta
490-9679	Col. Divya Gaurav **Misra** First Secretary Military Adviser Mrs. Minnie Misra

	Mr. Mayank **Joshi** First Secretary Mrs. Isha Joshi
(646) 292-7180	Mr. Abhishek **Singh** First Secretary Mrs. Meghna Singh
661-1803	Mr. Devesh **Uttam** First Secretary Mrs. Ruchi Uttam
490-9676	Mr. Manjunath Denkanikotta **Chenneerappa** First Secretary Mrs. Arpana Manjunath
490-9671	Mr. Suresh **Kumar** Second Secretary Mrs. Asha Chauhan
490-9677	Mr. Ravi **Arora** Second Secretary Mrs. Babita Arora
661-1803	Mr. Anil **Kumar** Attaché Mrs. Suman Bala
	Mr. Girish Chandra **Pujari** Attaché Mrs. Yamuna Pujari
490-9660	Mr. Durga **Dass** Attaché Mrs. Deepa Dass
	Mr. Fnu **Hemraj** Attaché
	Mrs. Uma **Dhyani** Attaché Mr. Sudhir K. Dhyani
	Mr. Venkata Sri Rama Krishna **Vishnubhotla** Attaché Mrs. Purnima Ramakrishna
	Mr. Sudhir Kumar **Dhyani** Attaché Mrs. Uma Dhyani
490-9670	Mr. Arun **Bahuguna** Attaché Mrs. Ruchita Bahuguna
490-9660	Mr. Vinod **Kumar** Attaché Mrs. Suman Yadav

600-2570 Mr. Thomas Kokken **Thomas**
Attaché
Mrs. Gini Thomas

Mr. Ashish Ukandrao **Kolhe**
Attaché
Mrs. Gita Ashish Kolhe

Mrs. Promila **Sharma**
Attaché
Mr. Ashok Kumar Sharma

Indonesia

Member State since 28 September 1950

Address: Permanent Mission of the Republic of Indonesia
to the United Nations
325 East 38th Street
New York, N.Y. 10016

Telephone: (212) 972-8333

Telefax: (212) 972-9780

e-mail: ptri@indonesiamission-ny.org

Correspondence: English

National holiday: 17 August
Independence Day

H.E. Mr. Desra **Percaya**
Ambassador Extraordinary and Plenipotentiary
Permanent Representative (DPC: 10 February 2012)
Mrs. Diana Mawarsari Percaya

H.E. Muhammad **Anshor**
Ambassador
Deputy Permanent Representative
Mrs. Tantri Rukimini Dewi

Mr. Purnomo Ahmad **Chandra**
Minister Counsellor
Mrs. Susi Daruni

Mr. Kamapradipta **Isnomo**
Minister Counsellor (Political Affairs)
Mrs. Ria Rafika Sari Isnomo

Mr. Masni **Eriza**
Counsellor
Mrs. Ismarlinda Eriza

Mrs. Reshanty **Bowoleksono**
Counsellor (Political Affairs)
Mr. Budi Bowoleksono

Ms. Yuliana **Bahar**
First Secretary

Mr. Harry Rusmana **Irawan**
First Secretary (Economic Affairs)
Mrs. Chitra Juniasyahri

Ms. Rima **Cempaka**
First Secretary (Economic Affairs)

Mr. Ary **Aprianto**
First Secretary (Political Affairs)
Mrs. Dieny Maya Sari

Mrs. Indah Nuria **Savitri**
First Secretary (Political Affairs)
Mr. Rudi Frakarsa

Mrs. Yvonne Elizabeth **Mewengkang**
Second Secretary (Political Affairs)
Mr. Simon Fernando Hutasoid

Mr. Danny **Rahdiansyah**
Second Secretary (Political Affairs)
Mrs. Seira Wallentina

Ms. Nona **Gae Luna**
Third Secretary (Political Affairs)

Ms. Nara Masista **Rakhmatia**
Third Secretary (Economic Affairs)

Mr. Agustinus Aninditуo Adi **Primasto**
Third Secretary (Political Affairs)
Mrs. Lydia Widiaty

Mr. Mohammad David **Arslan**
Third Secretary (Economic and Social Affairs)
Mrs. Risma Muthia Mohammad

Mr. Denny Marthin **Kaurow**
Attaché
Mrs. Erni Kartini

Mr. Chandra **Setiawan**
Attaché (Administrative Affairs)
Mrs. Desi Anggraeni

Address: Permanent Mission of the Islamic Republic
of Iran to the United Nations
622 Third Avenue, 34th Floor
New York, N.Y. 10017

Telephone: (212) 687-2020

Telefax: (212) 867-7086

e-mail: iran@un.int

Website: www.iran-un.org

Correspondence: English

National holiday: 11 February

H.E. Mr. Gholamali **Khoshroo**
Ambassador Extraordinary and Plenipotentiary
Permanent Representative (DPC: 17 February 2015)
Mrs. Fatemeh Rahmati Khoshroo

H.E. Mr. Gholamhossein **Dehghani**
Ambassador
Deputy Permanent Representative
Mrs. Mansoureh Dehghani

Ext. 214 Mr. Mohammad Reza **Mofatteh**
First Counsellor
Mrs. Ozra Mofatteh

Ext. 256 Mr. Kourosh **Ahmadi**
First Counsellor
Mrs. Tahereh Ahmadi

Ext. 254 Mr. Javad **Safaei**
First Counsellor
Mrs. Afsaneh Safaei

Ext. 217 Mr. Hossein **Maleki**
First Counsellor
Mrs. Fouzieh Maleki

Ext. 245 Mrs. Forouzandeh **Vadiati**
Second Counsellor
Mr. Mohsen Karimi

Ext. 253 Mr. Hossein **Gharibi**
Second Counsellor
Mrs. Safieh Gharibi

Ext. 215 Mr. Javad **Momeni**
Second Counsellor
Mrs. Azar Momeni

Ext. 223	Mr. Eisa **Kameli** Second Counsellor Mrs. Maryam Kameli
Ext. 246	Mr. Mesbah **Ansari Dogaheh** Third Counsellor Mrs. Sedigheh Ansari Dogaheh
Ext. 247	Mr. Seyed Mehdi **Hosseini Matin** Third Counsellor Mrs. Zakieh Hosseini Matin
Ext. 203	Mr. Kiumars **Javidnia** Third Counsellor Mrs. Leila Javidnia
Ext. 257	Mr. Hamid **Babaei** Third Counsellor Mrs. Giti Babaei
Ext. 219	Mr. Mohammad Reza **Mohammadi** Third Counsellor Mrs. Maryam Mohammadi
Ext. 222	Mr. Seyed Mohammad Ali **Robatjazi** First Secretary Mrs. Vajihe Robatjazi
Ext. 232	Mr. Ali Asghar **Mohebbi Rezazadeh** First Secretary Mrs. Akram Mohebbi Rezazadeh
Ext. 231	Mr. Abbas **Yazdani** First Secretary Mrs. Seyedeh Laya Yazdani
Ext. 221	Mr. Ebrahim **Alikhani** First Secretary Mrs. Fereshteh Alikhani
Ext. 216	Mr. Mostafa **Chaman Zad** First Secretary Mrs. Mansoureh Chaman Zad
Ext. 220	Mr. Mahmoud **Dibaei** Second Secretary Mrs. Sima Dibaei
Ext. 230	Mr. Jamal **Taleb Pour Ardekani** Second Secretary Mrs. Molouke Taleb Pour Ardekani
Ext. 228	Mr. Mostafa **Ghafouri** Third Secretary Mrs. Maliheh Ghafouri

Address: Permanent Mission of Iraq to the United Nations
14 East 79th Street
New York, N.Y. 10075

Telephone: (212) 737-4433

Telefax: (212) 772-1794, -737-6265

e-mail: iraqny@un.int

Correspondence: English

National holiday:

H.E. Mr. Mohamed Ali **Alhakim**
Ambassador Extraordinary and Plenipotentiary
Permanent Representative (DPC: 3 May 2013)

Mrs. Mayadah Abdullah Yaseen **Al-Adhammi**
Minister Plenipotentiary

Mr. Salwan Rasheed Anjo **Anjo**
Minister Plenipotentiary
Mrs. Marwah Hikmat Mahmood Mahmood

Mr. Sarhad Sardar Abdulrahman **Fatah**
Counsellor
Mrs. Mayan Talat Mohammed Gilly

Mr. Mohammed Husham Malik **Al-Fityan**
Counsellor
Mrs. Sura Ismaeil Abdullaziz

Ms. Bushra Abbas Hasan **Al-Nussairy**
Counsellor

Mr. Sarmad Muwafaq Mohammed **Al-Taie**
Counsellor
Mrs. Asmaa Mohammed Taha Al-Mashhadani

Mr. Razaq Salman **Mashkoor**
Councellor
Mrs. Amel Tahir Lamloom Al-Rikabi

Mr. Ali Mohameed Faeq Abdalaziz **Al-Dabag**
First Secretary
Mrs. Noor Faeq Abdulateef Abdulateef

Mr. Mohammed Samir Ezzat Sami **Alnaqshabandi**
First Secretary
Mrs. Zina Hadi Ahmed Alubaidy

Mr. Ammar Sabah Mustafa **Al-Durra**
First Secretary

Mr. Mohamad A. **Shaboot**
First Secretary
Mrs. Aysar Y. Al-Najjar

Ms. Zaytoon Faraj Abdullah **Abdullah**
First Secretary

Mr. Lawen Sherdil Abdullah **Hawezy**
Second Secretary

Mr. Bander Fawzi **Al-Bander**
Second Secretary

Mr. Ahmed Kamil Rahif **Albu-Mohammed**
Second Secretary
Mrs. Basma Nazar Hasan Al-Shabandar

Ms. Khabat Ahmed Najib **Al-Barwari**
Third Secretary

Address:	Permanent Mission of Ireland to the United Nations One Dag Hammarskjöld Plaza 885 Second Avenue, 19th Floor New York, N.Y. 10017
Telephone:	(212) 421-6934
Telefax:	(212) 752-4726
e-mail:	newyorkpmun@dfa.ie
website:	www.dfa.ie/pmun/newyork/
Correspondence:	English
National holiday:	17 March St. Patrick's Day

204-7145	H.E. Mr. David **Donoghue** Ambassador Extraordinary and Plenipotentiary Permanent Representative (DPC: 13 September 2013) Mrs. Jill Donoghue
204-7143	Mr. Tim **Mawe** Counsellor Deputy Permanent Representative Mrs. Patricia Anne Mc Carthy
204-7152	Colonel Conor **Fitzsimons** Counsellor Military Adviser Mrs. Margaret Fitzsimons
204-7144	Mr. Vincent **Herlihy** First Secretary Mrs. Catherine Laure Herlihy
204-7148	Mr. Michael **O'Toole** First Secretary Mrs. Ciara O'Toole
204-7146	Mr. Colm **Ó Conaill** First Secretary
204-7160	Mr. John **Gilroy** First Secretary Ms. Patricia Mary Daly
204-7163	Ms. Julie **O'Brien** Second Secretary Mr. Colum Higgins
204-7153	Ms. Edel **Dwyer** Second Secretary
204-7147	Ms. Orla **McMahon** Attaché (Administration)

Address:	Permanent Mission of Israel to the United Nations 800 Second Avenue New York, N.Y. 10017
Telephone:	(212) 499-5510
Telefax:	(212) 499-5515
e-mail:	Info-un@newyork.mfa.gov.il
website:	www.israel-un.org
Correspondence:	English
National holiday:	23 April (2015) Independence Day

499-5510	H.E. Mr. Ron **Prosor** Ambassador Extraordinary and Plenipotentiary Permanent Representative (DPC: 23 June 2011) Mrs. Hadas Prosor
499-5520	H.E. Mr. David Yitshak **Roet** Ambassador Deputy Permanent Representative
499-5519	H.E. Mr. Mordehai **Amihai Bivas** Ambassador Mrs. Ayalah Shapiro Bivas
	H.E. Mr. David-Tomas **Ran-Radnitz** Ambassador
499-5464	Ms. Sigal **Yavets** Minister Counsellor Mr. Iftah Yavets
499-5570	Mr. Israel **Nitzan** Minister Counsellor Mrs. Hadassa Hinda Nitzan
499-5579	Ms. Hadas Ester **Meitzad** Counsellor (Second Committee)
499-5517	Ms. Nelly **Shilo** Counsellor (Third Committee)
499-5350	Mr. Hagay **Avimor** Counsellor Mrs. Ilana Shira Avimor
499-5573	Mr. Yotam **Goren** First Secretary (Fifth Committee)
499-5574	Mr. Amit **Heumann** First Secretary, Legal Adviser Mrs. Shira Meir Heumann

	Mr. Israel **Shnitzer** First Secretary Mrs. Etty Shnitzer
	Mr. Tomer **Morad** First Secretary
499-5488	Mr. Yaacov **Timsit** Attaché

Address:	Permanent Mission of Italy to the United Nations One Dag Hammarskjöld Plaza 885 Second Avenue, 49th Floor New York, N.Y. 10017
Telephone:	(212) 486-9191, (646) 840-5300
Telefax:	(212) 486-1036
e-mail:	info.italyun@esteri.it; archives.italyun@esteri.it
website:	www.italyun.esteri.it
Correspondence:	English
National holiday:	2 June Anniversary of the Republic

---

(646) 840-5307 H.E. Mr. Sebastiano **Cardi**
Ambassador Extraordinary and Plenipotentiary
Permanent Representative (DPC: 20 September 2013)

---

(646) 840-5302 H.E. Mr. Inigo **Lambertini**
Ambassador
Deputy Permanent Representative
Mrs. Maria Grazia Gragnano Lambertini

(646) 840-5373 Mrs. Emilia **Gatto**
Minister

(646) 840-5311 Mr. Paolo **Campanini**
First Counsellor

(646) 840-5323 Mr. Giovanni **Davoli**
First Counsellor

(646) 840-5309 Mrs. Cecilia **Piccioni**
First Counsellor

(646) 840-5313 Mrs. Valeria **Biagiotti**
First Counsellor
Mr. Andrea Tappi

(646) 840-5326 Mr. Pier Luigi **Zamporlini**
First Counsellor
Mrs. Marianna Santoro

(646) 840-5304 Mr. Andrea **Biagini**
First Counsellor
Mrs. Ramune Jacikeviciute

(646) 840-5320 Ms. Cristiana Maria **Mele**
Counsellor

(646) 840-5308	Mr. Cesare **Morbelli** Counsellor Mrs. Maria Saveria Veltri
(646) 840-5317	Mr. Andrea **Romussi** Counsellor Mrs. Valentina Anselmi
(646) 840-5316	Ms. Emanuela **Curnis** Counsellor
(646) 840-5359	Mr. Carlo Gino **Sanfilippo** First Secretary Mrs. Tania Cagiotti
(646) 840-5375	Mr. Paolo **Mari** First Secretary
(646) 840-5347	Mr. Daniele Giuseppe **Sfregola** First Secretary
(646) 840-5330	Ms. Alessandra Fabrizia **Rossi** Attaché (Head, Administrative Affairs)
(646) 840-5379	Mr. Mauro **Marcello** Attaché (Administrative Affairs)
(646) 840-5324	Ms. Antonella **D'Angelosante** Attaché (Economic and Development Affairs)
(646) 840-5335	Mr. Alfredo Alessandro **Lo Faro** Attaché (Administrative Affairs) Mrs. Iulia Andreea Panait
(646) 840-5336	Mr. Luigi **Marini** Attaché (Legal Affairs)
(646) 840-5305	Mr. Salvatore **Zappalá** Attaché (Legal Affairs) Mrs. Elena Irene Geraci
(646) 840-5356	Lieutenant General Paolo **Serra** Minister Counsellor Military and Police Adviser Mrs. Antonella Filippi
(646) 840-5355	Captain (N) Daniele **Romano** Counsellor Deputy Military Adviser Mrs. Michela Ragazzi
(646) 840-5376	Colonel Gabriele **Failla** Attaché Mrs. Emanuela Bona

Address:	Permanent Mission of Jamaica to the United Nations 767 Third Avenue, 9th Floor New York, N.Y. 10017
Telephone:	(212) 935-7509
Telefax:	(212) 935-7607
e-mail:	jamaica@un.int
website:	www.un.int/jamaica
Correspondence:	English
National holiday:	6 August Independence Day

Ext. 120 — H.E. Mr. E. Courtenay **Rattray**
Ambassador Extraordinary and Plenipotenriary
Permanent Representative (DPC: 25 June 2013)
Mrs. Tanya Rattray

Ext. 122 — Miss Shorna-Kay Marie **Richards**
Minister
Deputy Permanent Representative

Ext. 104 — Miss Farrah Lamour Demoya **Brown**
Counsellor

Ext. 116 — Mr. Kurt Oliver **Davis**
Counsellor
Mrs. Suzanne Sherine Robinson Davis

Ext. 103 — Miss Melissa Jodeanna **Johnson**
First Secretary

Ext. 121 — Miss Christine Millicent **Fenton**
Attaché

Ext. 123 — Miss Michelle Anita **Coy**
Attaché

Ext. 108 — Mrs. Natasha Marie **Irving-Patterson**
Attaché (Finance)
Mr. Ewart Carl Patterson

Address:	Permanent Mission of Japan to the United Nations 866 United Nations Plaza, Suite 230, 2nd Floor New York, N.Y. 10017
Telephone:	(212) 223-4300
Telefax:	(212) 751-1966
	(212) 308-1580 (Protocol Section) (212) 521-0671 (General Section) (212) 308-1451 (Political Section) (212) 308-1468 (Economic Section) (212) 521-0672 (Social Section) (212) 521-0675 (Administrative and Budgetary Section)
e-mail:	p-m-j@dn.mofa.go.jp
Correspondence:	English
National holiday:	23 December Birthday of the Emperor

521-1505	H.E. Mr. Motohide **Yoshikawa** Ambassador Extraordinary and Plenipotentiary Permanent Representative (DPC: 13 September 2013) Mrs. Corinne Yoshikawa
521-1506	H.E. Mr. Yoshifumi **Okamura** Ambassador Extraordinary and Plenipotentiary Deputy Permanent Representative Mrs. Kaoriko Okamura
521-1511	H.E. Mr. Hiroshi **Minami** Ambassador Deputy Permanent Representative
521-1546	Mr. Toshihiro **Aiki** Minister (Administrative and Budgetary Affairs) Mrs. Hiroko Aiki
521-1510	Mr. Shinsuke **Shimizu** Minister (General Affairs) Mrs. Mariko Shimizu
521-1507	Mr. Hiroshi **Ishikawa** Minister (Political Section)
521-1569	Mr. Kazuhiro **Kuno** Minister (Social Affairs) Mrs. Sawako Kuno
521-1556	Mr. Noboru **Sekiguchi** Minister (Economic Affairs) Mrs. Hiromi Sekiguchi

521-1563	Mr. Masato **Usui** Counsellor (Economic Affairs) Mrs. Tomoko Usui
521-1560	Mr. Naoki **Takahashi** Counsellor (Political Affairs) Mrs. Naoko Takahashi
521-1520	Mr. Sho **Ono** Counsellor (Administrative and Budgetary Affairs) Mrs. Yuki Ono
521-1525	Ms. Michiko **Miyano** Counsellor (Economic Affairs) Mr. Atsushi Tanase
521-1594	Mr. Shigetoshi **Nagao** Counsellor (Administrative and Budgetary Affairs) Mrs. Yuka Nagao
521-1516	Mr. Ryo **Fukahori** Counsellor (Political Section)
521-1566	Mr. Manabu **Sumi** Counsellor (Economic Affairs) Mrs. Kayako Sumi
521-0644	Mr. Kaitaro **Nonomura** Counsellor (Political Affairs) Mrs. Kaori Nonomura
521-1524	Mr. Hisao **Nishimaki** Counsellor (General Affairs)
521-1508	Mr. Taro **Tsutsumi** Counsellor (Social Affairs) Mrs. Ikuko Tsutsumi
521-1530	Mr. Yoshio **Kawano** First Secretary (General Affairs) Mrs. Mirian Kawano
521-1540	Mr. Kazuhiro **Takeda** First Secretary (General Affairs) Mrs. Yumi Takeda
521-1595	Mr. Takashi **Shimoda** First Secretary (General Affairs) Mrs. Junko Shimoda
521-1575	Ms. Eriko Yajima **Koyama** First Secretary (Administrative, Budgetary and UN Recruitment) Mr. Satoshi Koyama
521-1588	Mr. Masahiko **Kobayashi** First Secretary (Political Affairs)

521-1521	Mr. Yoshibumi **Ogura** First Secretary (Political Affairs) Defense Attaché Mrs. Kanako Ogura
521-0658	Mr. Yoshiyuki **Mikami** First Secretary (Economic Affairs) Mrs. Rina Mikami
521-1536	Mr. Chihiro **Tsurusaki** First Secretary (General Affairs)
521-1522	Mr. Yasuaki **Momita** First Secretary (Economic Affairs) Mrs. Eriko Momita
521-1513	Mr. Yoshimitsu **Morihiro** First Secretary (Political Affairs) Mrs. Megumi Morihiro
521-1558	Mr. Hiroshi **Onuma** First Secretary (Administrative and Budgetary Affairs) Mrs. Yasue Onuma
521-1590	Ms. Naomi **Kuroda** First Secretary (Social Affairs) Mr. Tatsuaki Kuroda
521-1581	Mr. Akihiko **Watanabe** First Secretary (General Affairs) Mrs. Narumi Watanabe
521-1557	Ms. Tomoko **Onishi** First Secretary (Economic Affairs)
521-1572	Mr. Yoshitaka **Kinoshita** First Secretary (Political Affairs)
521-1514	Ms. Chiho **Horiuchi** First Secretary (Political Affairs) Mr. Hamid Radjai
521-1552	Mr. Junichi **Sumi** First Secretary (Social Affairs) Mrs. Yukiko Sumi
521-1526	Ms. Yoko **Takushima** First Secretary (Economic Affairs)
521-1517	Mr. Yusuke **Shimizu** First Secretary (Political Affairs)
521-1591	Mr. Kenta **Kamamura** Second Secretary (Social Affairs) Mrs. Kayo Kamamura
521-1542	Mr. Norio **Matsuda** Second Secretary (General Affairs) Mrs. Kanako Matsuda

521-1592	Mr. Shohei **Tadome** Second Secretary (General Affairs)
521-1573	Ms. Eri **Hiroshima** Second Secretary (General Affairs)
521-1523	Mr. Yukiya **Tsuno** Second Secretary (Political Affairs) Mrs. Megumi Tsuno
521-1518	Mr. Satoru **Okano** Second Secretary (General Affairs) Mrs. Yurika Okano
521-1564	Mr. Nobuyuki **Sano** Attaché (General Affairs) Mrs. Hiromi Sano
521-1553	Ms. Mitsuyo **Takahashi** Third Secretary (General Affairs) Mr. Muneo Takahashi
521-1589	Mr. Daisuke **Shiragaki** Third Secretary (Protocol)
521-1533	Mr. Kenichi **Kawashima** Attaché (General Affairs) Mrs. Ayaka Kawashima
521-1544	Ms. Yukako **Honka** Attaché (General Affairs)

Jordan

Address:	Permanent Mission of the Hashemite Kingdom of Jordan to the United Nations 866 Second Avenue, 4th Floor New York, N.Y. 10017
Telephone:	(212) 832-9553
Telefax:	(212) 832-5346
e-mail:	missionun@jordanmissionun.com
Correspondence:	English
National holiday:	25 May Independence Day

Ext. 225	H.E Mrs. Dina **Kawar** Ambassador Extraordinary and Plenipotentiary Permanent Representative (DPC: 19 August 2014)

867-0291 Ext.201	H.E. Mr. Mahmoud Daifallah Mahmoud **Hmoud** Ambassador Senior Deputy Permanent Representative Mrs. Kirsty Ann Reid Hmoud
Ext. 226	Mr. Eihab **Omaish** Minister Plenipotentiary (Political Coordinator) Deputy Permanent Representative
867-0291 Ext. 208	Mr. Samer Anton Ayed **Naber** Minister Plenipotentiary
Ext. 222	Mr. Amjad Mohammad Saleh **Al-Moumani** Counsellor Mrs. Dina Nabil A. Maraqa
867-0291 Ext.204	Mr. Adi Ghassan Moh'd **Khair** Counsellor
867-0291 Ext. 202	Ms. Sonia Ishaq Ahmad **Sughayar** First Secretary
Ext. 239	Mr. Muaz Mohamad A-K **Al-Otoom** First Secretary
867-0291 Ext. 205	Mr. Omar Mohammad Theeb **Ababneh** Second Secretary Ms. Faten Jamal Abdelrahman Alwaked
Ext. 230	Mr. Moh'd Kais Mufleh **Albatayneh** Second Secretary
867-0291 Ext.206	Mr. Faris Musa Mohamd **Al-Adwan** Second Secretary

Ext. 232	Mr. Laith Ibrahim A. **Obeidat** Third Secretary Ms. Nour Mamdouh Kaseb **Aljazi** Third Secretary
Ext. 237	Brig. Gen. Mohammad Subhi Mohammad **Almhairat** Counsellor Military Adviser Mrs. Ghada Sabah Abdelhafez Elamaireh
Ext. 228	Brig. Gen. Ibrahim Salim Ibrahim **Marji** Counsellor Police Adviser Lt. Col. Ahmad Saleh Khalaf **Al Ghwiriin** Second Secretary Police Adviser Mrs. Rasha Tayseer Karim Alzyoud
Ext. 227	Mr. Issa Adib Kalaf **Shahatit** Attaché (Finance) Mrs. Abla Tawfiq Suleiman Ammari

Address:	Permanent Mission of the Republic of Kazakhstan to the United Nations 3 Dag Hammarskjöld Plaza 305 East 47th Street, 3rd Floor New York, N.Y. 10017
Telephone:	(212) 230-1900
Telefax:	(212) 230-1172 (212) 446-6782
e-mail:	kazakhstan@un.int
website:	www.kazakhstanun.org
Correspondence:	English
National holiday:	16 December Independence Day

Ext. 301 H.E. Mr. Kairat **Abdrakhmanov**
Ambassador Extraordinary and Plenipotentiary
Permanent Representative (DPC: 9 January 2014)
Mrs. Maira Abdrakhmanova

Ext. 320 Mr. Akan **Rakhmetullin**
Minister Counsellor
Deputy Permanent Representative
Mrs. Intizara Rakhmetullina

Ext. 322 Mr. Israil U. **Tilegen**
Minister Counsellor
Mrs. Elmira M. Tlegenova

Ext. 332 Mr. Kanat **Tumysh**
Minister Counsellor
Mrs. Leila Tumysh

Ext. 315 Mr. Tleuzhan S. **Seksenbay**
Counsellor
Mrs. Gulnar Seksenbayeva

Ext. 331 Ms. Akmaral **Kinzhebayeva**
Counsellor

Ext. 305 Colonel Alexandr **Kabentayev**
Counsellor
Military Adviser
Mrs. Bagdat Kabentayeva

Ext. 303 Mr. Ruslan **Bultrikov**
Counsellor
Mrs. Aliya Bultrikova

Ext. 329 Ms. Almagul **Konurbayeva**
Counsellor

Ext. 324	Mrs. Gulmira **Satybaldy** First Secretary
Ext. 314	Mr. Sergey **Viktorov** First Secretary Mrs. Maria Kravchenko
Ext. 313	Mr. Assan **Abdirov** First Secretary Mrs. Gulya Abdirova
Ext. 302	Mr. Talgat **Iliyas** First Secretary Mrs. Aigerim Ilyassova
Ext. 304	Mr. Azat **Shakirov** Second Secretary Mrs. Assel Shakirova
Ext. 325	Mr. Bekzat **Aitzhanov** Attaché Mrs. Zhazira Aitzhanova
Ext. 306	Ms. Damira **Zhanatova** Attaché Mr. Askar Zhumabayev

Address:	Permanent Mission of the Republic of Kenya to the United Nations 866 United Nations Plaza, Room 304 New York, N.Y. 10017
Telephone:	(212) 421-4740-4744
Telefax:	(212) 486-1985
e-mail:	info@kenyaun.org
Correspondence:	English
National holiday:	12 December Independence Day

H.E. Mr. Macharia **Kamau**
Ambassador Extraordinary and Plenipotentiary
Permanent Representative (DPC: 16 December 2010)

H.E. Ms. Koki Muli **Grignon**
Ambassador
Deputy Permanent Representative
Mr. Francois Michel Francis Grignon

Mr. Arthur Amaya **Andambi**
Minister Counsellor
Ms. Jacqueline Jonas Chirwa

Mr. Robert Ngei **Mule**
First Counsellor
Mrs. Dorothy Nthenya Kimeu

Mr. George **Kwanya**
First Counsellor
Mrs. Lizzie Mghoi Kwanya

Ms. Susan Wangeci **Mwangi**
First Counsellor

Mr. James Ndiragu **Waweru**
Second Counsellor
Mrs. Susan Wangechi Mwangi Ndirangu

Mr. Evans Simiyu **Maturu**
Second Counsellor

Mr. Tom Mboya **Adala**
Second Secretary
Ms. Habiba Yahya Seby

Mr. Sospeter Karani **Ikiara**
Second Secretary
Mrs. Jacinta Marigu Njue

Mr. Tobias Otieno **Ogweno**
Second Secretary
Ms. Ruth Achola Magak

Mr. John Maina **Kimani**
Attaché (Finance)
Mrs. Faith Wambui Kiarii

Ms. Marie Kinigonda **Odero**
Attaché (Administration)

Mrs. Grace Njeri **Mbabu**
Attaché (Administration)
Mr. Humphrey Mbabu Rithaa

Mr. Zachaeus Tirop **Psenjen**
Attaché (Finance)

Colonel Aphaxard Muthuri **Kiugu**
Attaché (Defence)
Mrs. Lucy Joy Kagwiria Muthuri

Colonel James Tajeu **Kenana**
Attaché (Defence)
Mrs. Dorcas Njeri

Kiribati

Address:	Permanent Mission of the Republic of Kiribati to the United Nations 800 Second Avenue, Suite 400A New York, N.Y. 10017
Telephone:	(212) 867-3310
Telefax:	(212) 867-3320
e-mail:	Kimission.newyork@mfa.gov.ki
website:	
Correspondence:	English
National holiday:	12 July

H.E. Mrs. Makurita **Baaro**
Ambassador Extraordinary and Plenipotentiary
Permanent Representative (DPC: 19 August 2013)
Mr. Baraniko Baaro

Mr. Baraniko **Baaro**
First Secretary
Deputy Permanent Representative
H.E. Mrs. Makurita Baaro

Address: Permanent Mission of the State of Kuwait to the United Nations
321 East 44th Street
New York, N.Y. 10017

Telephone: (212) 973-4300

Telefax: (212) 370-1733

e-mail: contact@kuwaitmission.org

website: www.kuwaitmission.com

Correspondence: English

National holiday: 25 February

H.E. Mr. Mansour Ayyad SH A **Alotaibi**
Ambassador Extraordinary and Plenipotentiary
Permanent Representative (DPC: 4 March 2010)
Mrs. Soad Alotaibi

Mr. Abdulaziz S M A **AlJarallah**
First Secretary
Deputy Permanent Representative
Mrs. Lulwah Albuaijan

Mr. Abdulaziz A M A **AlAjmi**
Second Secretary
Mrs. Danah M A Z H AlHuwailah

Mr. Hasan SH J Y A **Abulhasan**
Third Secretary
Mrs. Fatemah AlAryan

Mr. Abdullah A KH A KH **Alsharrah**
Third Secretary

Mr. Bashar Abdulah E R S **AlMowaizri**
Third Secretary

Mr. Abdulrazzaq E A M **AlAmiri**
Attaché

Mrs. Alia Abdullah A Y **AlMuzaini**
Attaché
Mr. Khaled Mohammad A T AlMulaifi

Mr. Waddah S. S. S. **AlFahad**
Attaché (Administrative Affairs)
Mrs. Manar AlMane

Miss Lolwa Saoud A **AlRasheed**
Attaché

Ms. Farah T A S H **AlGharabally**
Attaché

Ms. Haifa Ali E.N. **AlNaser**
Attaché

Address:	Permanent Mission of the Kyrgyz Republic to the United Nations 866 United Nations Plaza, Suite 477 New York, N.Y. 10017
Telephone:	(212) 486-4214, -4654
Telefax:	(212) 486-5259
e-mail:	kyrgyzstan@un.int
website:	www.un.int/kyrgyzstan
Correspondence:	English
National holiday:	31 August Independence Day

H.E. Mr. Talaibek **Kydyrov**
Ambassador Extraordinary and Plenipotentiary
Permanent Representative (DPC: 19 November 2010)
Mrs. Juparkul Abakirova

Mr. Nuran **Niyazaliev**
Counsellor
Deputy Permanent Representative
Mrs. Janara Niaspekova

Mrs. Madina **Karabaeva**
First Secretary

Mrs. Nuraiym **Tynybekova**
First Secretary

Mr. Ermek **Isakov**
Third Secretary
Mrs. Seidana Djusaeva

Lao People's Democratic Republic

Member State since 14 December 1955

Address: Permanent Mission of the Lao People's Democratic Republic to the United Nations
317 East 51st Street
New York, N.Y. 10022

Telephone: (212) 832-2734, -0095

Telefax: (212) 750-0039

e-mail: lao.pr.ny@gmail.com

website: www.un.int/lao

Correspondence: English and French

National holiday: 2 December

H.E. Mr. Khiane **Phansourivong**
Ambassador Extraordinary and Plenipotentiary
Permanent Representative (DPC: 16 April 2014)
Mrs. Phaichit Phansourivong

Mr. Maythong **Thammavongsa**
Minister Counsellor
Deputy Permanent Representative
Mrs. Kongkham Thammavongsa

Ms. Viengxay **Thammavong**
First Secretary

Mr. Thiphasone **Sengsourinha**
Second Secretary

Mr. Sengsoulivanh **Nhotlusay**
Second Secretary

Mr. Khamphinh **Philakone**
Second Secretary

Mr. Visasacksith **Snookphone**
Third Secretary

Mr. Phetthanousone **Phommalath**
Third Secretary

Mr. Keopaseuth **Chanthaphim**
Third Secretary

Mr. Vassana **Mounsaveng**
Third Secretary

Mr. Soulikone **Samounty**
Third Secretary

Mr. Sylaphet **Thinkeomeuangneua**
Third Secretary

Address: Permanent Mission of the Republic
of Latvia to the United Nations
333 East 50th Street
New York, N.Y. 10022

Telephone: (212) 838-8877

Telefax: (212) 838-8920

e-mail: mission.un-ny@mfa.gov.lv

Correspondence: English

National holiday: 18 November
Independence Day

H.E. Mr. Jānis **Mažeiks**
Ambassador Extraordinary and Plenipotentiary
Permanent Representative (DPC: 3 September 2013)
Mrs. Dace Mažeika

Ms. Inese **Freimane-Deksne**
Counsellor
Deputy Permanent Representative

Ms. Agnese **Vilde**
First Secretary

Ms. Viktorija **Karamane**
Second Secretary

Ms. Dace **Zalāne**
Third Secretary

Ms. Dace **Patmalniece**
Third Secretary

Address: Permanent Mission of Lebanon to the United Nations
866 United Nations Plaza, Room 531-533
New York, N.Y. 10017

Telephone: (212) 355-5460

Telefax: (212) 838-2819, -6756

e-mail: contact@lebanonun.org

website: lebanonun.com

Correspondence: English/French

National holiday: 22 November
Independence Day

Ext. 201

H.E. Mr. Nawaf **Salam**
Ambassador Extraordinary and Plenipotentiary
Permanent Representative (DPC: 13 July 2007)
Mrs. Sahar Baassiri Salam

Ext. 211

Ms. Caroline **Ziade**
Counsellor
Deputy Permanent Representative

Ms. Maya **Dagher**
Counsellor

Mr. Hassan **Abbas**
Counsellor

Address: Permanent Mission of the Kingdom of Lesotho to the United Nations
815 Second Avenue, 8th Floor
New York, N.Y. 10017

Telephone: (212) 661-1690

Telefax: (212) 682-4388

e-mail: lesothonewyork@gmail.com

Correspondence: English

National holiday: 4 October

H.E. Mr. Kelebone **Maope**
Ambassador Extraordinary and Plenipotentiary
Permanent Representative (DPC: 25 June 2013)
Mrs. Nkhetheleng Regina Maope

Mr. Mafiroane Edmond **Motanyane**
Counsellor (Political Affairs)
Mrs. Mamaime Eunice Motanyane

Mr. Malefetsane Seth **Moseme**
Counsellor (Legal Affairs)

Ms. Khopotso **Lehohla**
First Secretary

Mr. Kamohelo Thabo **Phenithi**
Third Secretary
Mrs. Joalane Maphenithi Anacletta Phenithi

Liberia

Member State since 2 November 1945

Address: Permanent Mission of the Republic of Liberia to the United Nations
866 United Nations Plaza, Suite 480
New York, N.Y. 10017

Telephone: (212) 687-1033, -1034

Telefax: (212) 687-1846, 1035

e-mail: Liberia@un.int

Correspondence: English

National holiday: 26 July
Independence Day

H.E. Ms. Marjon V. **Kamara**
Ambassador Extraordinary and Plenipotentiary
Permanent Representative (DPC: 8 October 2009)

Mr. Remongar T. **Dennis**
Minister
Deputy Permanent Representative

Mr. George S. W. **Patten**, Sr.
Minister Counsellor
Mrs. Virginia Nudeh Torbor Patten

Mr. Abu M. **Kamara**
Minister Counsellor (Press and Information)
Mrs. Aisha Kamara

Ms. Gail **Farngalo**
Counsellor

Mr. Erastus Saye **Wieh**
First Secretary (Financial Affairs)
Mrs. Esther Wieh

Mrs. Maggie Henrietta **Gibson-Glay**
Third Secretary (Executive Assistant)

Mr. Sam Zobon **Horace**
Attaché (Documents Officer)

Mr. Kawyienee Karl **Andrews**
Attaché

Libya

Member State since 14 December 1955

Address: Permanent Mission of Libya
to the United Nations
309-315 East 48th Street
New York, N.Y. 10017

Telephone: (212) 752-5775

Telefax: (212) 593-4787

e-mail: info@libyanmission-un.org

website: www.Libyanmission-un.org

Correspondence: English

National holiday: 24 December
Independence Day

H.E. Mr. Ibrahim O. A. **Dabbashi**
Ambassador Extraordinary and Plenipotentiary
Permanent Representative (DPC: 23 July 2013)
Mrs. Fatima M. A. Dabbashi

H.E. Mr. Elmahdi S. **Elmajerbi**
Ambassador
Deputy Permanent Representative
Mrs. Badria I. M. Benhasan

H.E. Mr. Omar A. A. **Annakou**
Ambassador
Mrs. Fauzia A. A. Emseek

Ms. Samira A. **Abubakar**
Counsellor

Mr. Nagib I. S. **Kafou**
Counsellor
Mrs. Mrwa A. M. Hasaieri

Mr. Salah M. S. **Said**
Counsellor
Mrs. Mahbuba A. M. Lmfatrsh

Mr. Ibrahim K. M. **Almabruk**
Counsellor (Financial Affairs)
Mrs. Massauda R. M. Almabruk

Mr. Nasser S. Z. **Ashaftt**
Counsellor (Administration)
Mrs. Laila M. Z. Eshofti

Mr. Zakaria S. M. **Nattah**
Counsellor (Administration)
Mrs. Awatef A. M. Alezmerli

Mr. Abdulmonem A. H. **Eshanta**
First Secretary
Mrs. Khoulud A. A. Galaly

Mr. Essa A. E. **Essa**
First Secretary
Mrs. Haneen A. A. Emhmed

Mr. Imad I. A. **Taguri**
First Secretary
Mrs. Eyman B. L. Belgasem

Mrs. Malak M. M. **Salim**
First Secretary
Mr. Fouad K. M. Binameer

Mr. Adel S. M. **Hamasi**
First Secretary
Mrs. Ghalia E. A. Elghawi

Mr. Adam A. M. **Tarbah**
First Secretary
Mrs. Tetiana Pokhvalona

Mr. Mohamed H. S. **Elmodir**
First Secretary
Mrs. Turkeya A. A. Alkekli

Mr. Hamza A. B. **Alokly**
Second Secretary

Mr. Jasem K. S. **Harari**
Second Secretary
Mrs. Amani H. A. Furgha

Mr. Hamza B. S. **Almagrabi**
Attaché (Administrative)
Mrs. Ahlam I. A. Maghrbi

Mr. Mohamed A. E. **Grad**
Assistant Attaché (Financial)
Mrs. Nora B.S. Aboseta

Liechtenstein

Member State since 18 September 1990

Address: Permanent Mission of the Principality of Liechtenstein to the United Nations
633 Third Avenue, 27th Floor
New York, N.Y. 10017

Telephone: (212) 599-0220

Telefax: (212) 599-0064

e-mail: mission@nyc.llv.li

Social Media: Twitter: @LiechtensteinUN

Correspondence: English

National holiday: 15 August

Ext. 221 — H.E. Mr. Christian **Wenaweser**
Ambassador Extraordinary and Plenipotentiary
Permanent Representative (DPC: 1 October 2002)

Ext. 225 — Mr. Stefan **Barriga**
Minister (Legal Affairs)
Deputy Permanent Representative
Mrs. Shantha Rau Barriga

Ext. 228 — Ms. Kathrin **Nescher**
Second Secretary

Address: Permanent Mission of the Republic of Lithuania to the United Nations
708 Third Avenue, 10th Floor
New York, N.Y. 10017

Telephone: (212) 983-9474

Telefax: (212) 983-9473

e-mail: lithuania@un.int

website: mission-un-ny.mfa.lt/

Correspondence: English

National holiday: 16 February
Independence Day

H.E. Ms. Raimonda **Murmokaitė**
Ambassador Extraordinary and Plenipotentiary
Permanent Representative (DPC: 25 October 2012)

Colonel Darius **Petryla**
Envoy Extraordinary and Minister Plenipotentiary
Mrs. Reda Petrylienė

Mrs. Nida **Jakubonė**
Minister Counsellor
Deputy Permanent Representative
Mr. Mindaugas Jakubonis

Mr. Dainius **Baublys**
Minister Counsellor
Mrs. Jūratė Baublienė

Ms. Rosita **Šorytė**
Minister Counsellor

Mrs. Vaida **Hampe**
Counsellor

Mrs. Diana **Pranevičienė**
Counsellor
Mr. Julius Pranevičius

Mr. Aleksas **Dambrauskas**
First Secretary
Mrs. Daiva Dambrauskienė

Ms. Rasma **Ramoškaitė**
First Secretary

Ms. Agnė **Gleveckaitė**
First Secretary

Mrs. Neringa **Juodkaitė Putrimienė**
Second Secretary

Mr. Dovydas **Špokauskas**
Second Secretary

Mr. Aidas **Sunelaitis**
Second Secretary
Mrs. Evelina Steponaitytė

Ms. Viktorija **Budreckaitė**
Second Secretary

Ms. Agnė **Pipiraitė**
Second Secretary

Ms. Rūta **Jazukevičiūtė**
Third Secretary

Ms. Solveiga **Vailionytė**
Attaché

Address:	Permanent Mission of Luxembourg to the United Nations 17 Beekman Place New York, N.Y. 10022
Telephone:	(212) 935-3589
Telefax:	(212) 935-5896
e-mail:	newyork.rp@mae.etat.lu
website:	www.un.int/luxembourg
Correspondence:	French
National holiday:	23 June

H.E. Ms. Sylvie **Lucas**
Ambassador Extraordinary and Plenipotentiary
Permanent Representative (DPC: 25 August 2008)

715-3910	Mr. Olivier **Maes** First Counsellor Deputy Permanent Representative Mrs. Ioulia Maes
715-3916	Mr. Jacques **Flies** Counsellor
715-3914	Mr. Thomas **Reisen** First Secretary
715-3903	Mr. José **Quintus** First Secretary Mrs. Jin Hana
715-3919	Ms. Maïté **van der Vekene** Second Secretary
715-3935	Mr. Sina **Khabirpour** Second Secretary
715-3938	Ms. Anne **Dostert** Second Secretary
715-3912	Ms. Anne **Schintgen** Second Secretary
	Ms. Françoise **Droulans** Second Secretary

Madagascar

Address: Permanent Mission of the Republic
of Madagascar to the United Nations
820 Second Avenue, Suite 800
New York, N.Y. 10017

Telephone: (212) 986-9491, -9492, -2827

Telefax: (212) 986-6271

e-mail: repermad@verizon.net

Correspondence: French

National holiday: 26 June
Independence Day

H.E. Mr. Zina **Andrianarivelo-Razafy**
Ambassador Extraordinary and Plenipotentiary
Permanent Representative (DPC: 9 September 2002)
Mrs. Elise Bako Andrianarivelo-Razafy

Mrs. Héléna Bernadette **Rajaonarivelo**
Minister Plenipotentiary
Deputy Permanent Representative

Mrs. Lydia **Randrianarivony**
Counsellor

Mrs. Hantasoa Fida Cyrille **Klein**
Counsellor
Mr. Steve Alain Marc Klein

Ms. Lila Nadia **Andrianantoandro**
Counsellor

Mr. Tony Emmanuel **Randriamarolahy**
Attaché
Mrs. Zafinirina Philomène Hova

Address:	Permanent Mission of the Republic of Malawi to the United Nations 866 United Nations Plaza, Suite 486 New York, N.Y. 10017
Telephone:	(212) 317-8738, -8718
Telefax:	(212) 317-8729
e-mail:	MalawiNewyork@aol.com; MalawiU@aol.com
Correspondence:	English
National holiday:	6 July Republic Day

Ext. 308	H.E. Mr. Brian **Bowler** Ambassador Extraordinary and Plenipotentiary Permanent Representative (DPC: 17 December 2014) Mrs. Kelly Ann Ernst
Ext. 303	Mr. Charles Cliff **Mkandawire** Counsellor Mrs. Mabel Maseda Mkandawire
Ext. 306	Mrs. Chrissie **Mahuka** First Secretary (Economic Affairs) Mr. Mike Peter Mahuka
Ext. 319	Mrs. Janet Zeenat **Karim** First Secretary (Social Affairs)
Ext. 320	Mr. John Daniel **Kachenjera** First Secretary (Political Affairs) Mrs. Lonely Kachenjera
Ext. 305	Mr. Timothy Richard **Sandram** First Secretary (Economic Affairs) Mrs. Ruth Sandram
Ext. 315	Mr. Living **Kalimanjira** First Secretary (Social Development) Mrs. Fiskani Regina Kalimanjira
Ext. 307	Mr. Aburey **Saiwala** First Secretary (Administration) Mrs. Christarbell Saiwala
Ext. 304	Colonel George Alexander **Jaffu**, Jr. Counsellor Military Adviser Mrs. Rachel Faida Kishabaga Jaffu

Address:	Permanent Mission of Malaysia to the United Nations 313 East 43rd Street New York, N.Y. 10017
Telephone:	(212) 986-6310
Telefax:	(212) 490-8576
e-mail:	mwnewyorkun@kln.gov.my
website:	www.un.int/malaysia , www.kln.gov.my/web/usa_un_new_york/home
Correspondence:	English
National holiday:	31 August

H.E. Mr. Ramlan Bin **Ibrahim**
Ambassador Extraordinary and Plenipotentiary
Permanent Representative (DPC: 22 April 2015)

Ext. 219	Mrs. Siti Hajjar **Adnin** Minister Deputy Permanent Representative Mr. Abdul Rahim Othman
Ext. 215	Mr. Raja Reza bin **Raja Zaib Shah** Minister Deputy Permanent Representative Mrs. Roslina Ismail
Ext. 272	Mr. Shaharuddin **Onn** Minister Counsellor Mrs. Zuraini Khalil
Ext. 203	Mr. Kennedy **Mayong Onon** Minister Counsellor Mrs. Rose Irene Tonggiling
Ext. 208	Mr. Sazali Mustafa **Kamal** Minister Counsellor
Ext. 236	Colonel Nazari **Abd Hadi** Counsellor Defence Adviser Mrs. Rasilah Shaari
Ext. 209	Mr. Mohammad Azri **Mohtar** Counsellor Mrs. Farah Adlina Adnan
Ext. 228	Mr. Tengku Mohd Dzaraif **Kadir** Counsellor Mrs. Noor Lily Mohamed Zaidel

Ext. 276	Mr. **Hew** Tse Hou Counsellor
Ext. 274	Mr. Johan Ariff **Abdul Razak** Counsellor Mrs. Syarifah Nurhafizah binti Syed Omar
Ext. 273	Mrs. Murni **Abdul Hamid** Counsellor Mr. Amin Abdul Majid
Ext. 275	Mr. Ahmad Dzaffir **Mohd Yussof** Counsellor
Ext. 216	Mr. Riaz **Abdul Razak** Second Secretary Mrs. Iranie Abdul Wahab
Ext. 225	Ms. Rosfazidah **Razi** Varathau Rajoo Second Secretary
Ext. 213	Ms. Shazana **Mokhtar** Second Secretary
Ext. 223	Mr. Mustapha Kamal **Rosdi** Second Secretary Mrs. Noor Sabrina Mohammed
Ext. 222	Mr. Mohd Ridzwan **Shahabudin** Second Secretary Mrs. Elisa Tjuddin
Ext. 230	Mr. Dzulfefly **Mustapha** Second Secretary (Administration) Mrs. Siti Marzilah Lasa
Ext. 231	Mr. Sahharon **Omar** Second Secretary (Administration) Mrs. Hasnah Mohamad Akhir

Address: Permanent Mission of the Republic of Maldives to the United Nations
800 Second Avenue, Suite 400E
New York, N.Y. 10017

Telephone: (212) 599-6194, -6195

Telefax: (212) 661-6405

e-mail: info@maldivesmission.com

website: www.MaldivesMission.com

Correspondence: English

National holiday: 26 July
Independence Day

H.E. Mr. Ahmed **Sareer**
Ambassador Extraordinary and Plenipotentiary
Permanent Representative (DPC: 20 December 2012)
Mrs. Fathimah Athifa

Mr. Jeffrey Salim **Waheed**
Minister
Deputy Permanent Representative

Mr. Hassan Hussain **Shihab**
First Secretary

Ms. Fathimath **Liusa**
Third Secretary

Mr. Hussain Abdul **Latheef**
Third Secretary

Mali

Address: Permanent Mission of the Republic of Mali to the United Nations
111 East 69th Street
New York, N.Y. 10021

Telephone: (212) 737-4150, 794-1311

Telefax: (212) 472-3778

e-mail: malionu@aol.com

website: www.un.int/mali

Correspondence: French

National holiday: 22 September
Independence Day

H.E. Mr. Sékou **Kassé**
Ambassador Extraordinary and Plenipotentiary
Permanent Representative (DPC: 23 July 2013)
Mrs. Kadidia Boly Kassé

Mr. Dianguina dit Yaya **Doucouré**
Minister Counsellor
Mrs. Nathalia Panthelievna Doucouré

Mr. Sidiky **Koita**
Second Counsellor
Mrs. Minata Wereme Koita

Mr. Matiné **Coulibaly**
Third Counsellor
Mrs. Hawa Coulibaly

Mr. Noël **Diarra**
Fourth Counsellor
Mrs. Marie Sienwa Coulibaly Diarra

Mr. Bagname **Simpara**
Fifth Counsellor

Mr. Gaoussou Bougadary dit Tiémoko **Dioni**
First Secretary
Mrs. Assitan Foune Wane Dioni

Address:	Permanent Mission of Malta to the United Nations 249 East 35th Street New York, N.Y. 10016
Telephone:	(212) 725-2345
Telefax:	(212) 779-7097
e-mail:	malta-un.newyork@gov.mt ;malta@un.int
Correspondence:	English
National holiday:	21 September Independence Day

H.E. Mr. Christopher **Grima**
Ambassador Extraordinary and Plenipotentiary
Permanent Representative (DPC: 10 February 2012)
Mrs. Mateja Prosek Grima

Ext.105	Mrs. Natasha Meli **Daudey** Counsellor Deputy Permanent Representative Mr. Xavier Rémi Daudey
Ext. 109	Mr. David Ian **Mansfield** First Secretary
Ext. 109	Mr. Bernard Charles **Mifsud** First Secretary
	Mr. Alan **Cordina** First Secretary Mrs. Mariella Cassar Cordina

Marshall Islands

Member State since 17 September 1991

Address:	Permanent Mission of the Republic of the Marshall Islands to the United Nations 800 Second Avenue, 18th Floor New York, N.Y. 10017
Telephone:	(212) 983-3040
Telefax:	(212) 983-3202
e-mail:	marshallislands@un.int
website:	marshallislands.un.int
Correspondence:	English
National holiday:	1 May Constitution Day

H.E. ...
Ambassador Extraordinary and Plenipotentiary
Permanent Representative (DPC: ...)

Ms. Deborah **Barker-Manase**
Minister Counsellor
Deputy Permanent Representative

Address: Permanent Mission of the Islamic Republic of Mauritania to the United Nations
116 East 38th Street
New York, N.Y. 10016

Telephone: (212) 252-0113, -0141

Telefax: (212) 252-0175

e-mail: mauritaniamission@gmail.com

Correspondence: French

National holiday: 28 November
Independence Day

H.E. Mr. Sidi Mohamed Ould **Boubacar**
Ambassador Extraordinary and Plenipotentiary
Permanent Representative (DPC: 10 June 2014)
Mrs. Oumoulkiram Sid'Ahmed

Mr. Lebbatt **Mayouf**
First Counsellor (Military Adviser)

Mr. Jiddou **Jiddou**
First Counsellor

Mr. El Hacen **Eleyatt**
First Counsellor
Mrs. Ramla Jeddou

Mrs. Khouna **Keva**
First Counsellor

Mr. Nagi **Mohamed**
First Counsellor
Military Adviser

Mr. El Khalil **El Hacen**
Second Counsellor

Mr. Mohamed Lemine **Mohamed Saleh**
Second Counsellor

Mr. Taleb Jiddou **Tolba**
Second Counsellor

Mr. M'Hamed **Guelaye**
Second Counsellor

Mr. Yassa **Diawara**
Second Counsellor

Mr. Mohamed El Bechir Mohamed **Lemine**
Second Counsellor

Mr. Ralph A. **Kader**
Attaché
Mrs. Sally Kader

Mauritius

Member State since 24 April 1968

Address:	Permanent Mission of the Republic of Mauritius to the United Nations 211 East 43rd St., 22nd Floor New York, N.Y. 10017
Telephone:	(212) 949-0190, -0191
Telefax:	(212) 697-3829
e-mail:	mauritius@un.int
Correspondence:	English
National holiday:	12 March National Day

H.E. ...
Ambassador Extraordinary and Plenipotentiary
Permanent Representative (DPC: ...)

Ms. Nundini **Pertaub**
First Secretary

Mr. Kemrajsingh **Angateeah**
Second Secretary

Mexico

Address: Permanent Mission of Mexico to the United Nations
Two United Nations Plaza, 28th Floor
New York, N.Y. 10017

Telephone: (212) 752-0220

Telefax: (212) 752-0634 (General Number)
(212) 688-8533 (Permanent Representative's Office)

e-mail: onuusr1@sre.gob.mx

website: www.sre.gob.mx/onu

Correspondence: Spanish

National holiday: 16 September
Independence Day

H.E. Mr. Jorge **Montaño**
Ambassador Extraordinary and Plenipotentiary
Permanent Representative (DPC: 23 July 2013)
Mrs. Luz Maria Valdes de Montaño

H.E. Mr. Juan **Sandoval Mendiolea**
Ambassador
Deputy Permanent Representative

Ext. 8024 — Mrs. Gabriela **Colín Ortega**
Minister
Mr. Paul Simón Hernández Gómez

Ext. 8031 — Mr. Ricardo **Alday González**
Minister

Ext. 8025 — Mr. Salvador **De Lara Rangel**
Counsellor

Ext. 8029 — Mr. Alejandro **Sousa Bravo**
First Secretary

Ext. 8044 — Mrs. Claudia Yuriria **García Guiza**
Second Secretary
Mr. Juan Carlos Romero Ramírez

Ext. 8032 — Mrs. Lorena **Alvarado Quezada**
Second Secretary
Mr. Francisco Javier Esguevillas Ruíz

Ext. 8026 — Mr. Bruno **Ríos Sánchez**
Second Secrteary
Mrs. Armida Valdes Campos

Ext. 8028 — Mr. Felipe **García Landa**
Second Secretary

Ext. 8030 — Ms. Sara Luna **Camacho**
Third Secretary

Ext. 8027	Ms. Elisa **Diaz Gras** Third Secretary Mr. Julien Andre Gastelo Raglianti
Ext. 8063	Mr. Juan Manuel **Hernández** Attaché Mrs. Lilia Juárez de Hernández
Ext. 8036	Ms. Jessy **Otero Valle** Attaché
Ext. 8034	Ms. Adriana Asia **Aguiar Aguilar** Attaché

Ext. 8060	Mr. Gerardo **Wolburg Redondo** Military Counsellor Mrs. Sandra Ortega de La Vega
Ext. 8061	Mr. José Ricardo **Gómez Meillon** Counsellor (Navy) Mrs. Gabriela Aurora Rodríguez Zapata
Ext. 8059	Captain (Navy) Rafael Eduardo **García Urbina** Attaché Deputy Military Adviser Mrs. Maria Elizabeth Lacaud Landero
Ext. 8058	Mr. Román **Rosales Limón** Attaché Military Adviser Mrs. Sonia Santiago Zepahua

Micronesia (Federated States of)

Member State since 17 September 1991

Address:	Permanent Mission of the Federated States of Micronesia to the United Nations 300 East 42nd Street, Suite 1600 New York, N.Y. 10017
Telephone:	(212) 697-8370
Telefax:	(212) 697-8295
e-mail:	fsmun@fsmgov.org
website:	www.fsmgov.org/fsmun/
Correspondence:	English
National holiday:	3 November Independence Day

H.E. Mrs. Jane J. **Chigiyal**
Ambassador Extraordinary and Plenipotentiary
Permanent Representative (DPC: 2 December 2011)

Mr. Jeem **Lippwe**
Minister
Deputy Permanent Representative
Mrs. Lerina Lippwe

Mr. Martin **Zvachula**
Second Secretary

Monaco

Address:	Permanent Mission of the Principality of Monaco to the United Nations 866 United Nations Plaza, Suite 520 New York, N.Y. 10017
Telephone:	(212) 832-0721
Telefax:	(212) 832-5358
e-mail:	Monaco.un@gmail.com
Correspondence:	French
National holiday:	19 November

Ext. 3	H.E. Ms. Isabelle F. **Picco** Ambassador Extraordinary and Plenipotentiary Permanent Representative (DPC: 11 September 2009)
Ext. 5	Mrs. Valérie S. **Bruell-Melchior** First Counsellor Deputy Permanent Representative Mr. Claude Bruell
Ext. 6	Ms. Clotilde A. **Ferry** First Secretary
Ext. 2	Mr. Benjamin **Valli** Third Secretary
Ext. 23	Mr. Florian **Botto** Third Secretary

Address: Permanent Mission of Mongolia
to the United Nations
6 East 77th Street
New York, N.Y. 10075

Telephone: (212) 861-9460, 737-3874

Telefax: (212) 861-9464

e-mail: mongolianmission@twcmetrobiz.com

website: www.un.int/mongolia

Correspondence: English

National holiday: 11 July

H.E. Mr. Od **Och**
Ambassador Extraordinary and Plenipotentiary
Permanent Representative (DPC: 8 August 2012)
Mrs. Tsolmon Jadamba

Ms. Gankhuurai **Battungalag**
Minister Counsellor
Deputy Permanent Representative

Ext. 13 — Ms. Ulziibayar **Vangansuren**
Counsellor
Mr. Orgil Sharkhuu

Ext. 16 — Mr. Chinuukhei **Bat-Erdene**
Counsellor
Mrs. Amarjargal Tumursukh

Ext. 17 — Mr. Batbold **Isheekhuu**
Counsellor
Military Adviser
Mrs. Otgonjargal Dambii

Ext. 25 — Mr. Enkhbat **Altangerel**
Counsellor
Mrs. Tuya Gochoo

Montenegro

Address: Permanent Mission of Montenegro
to the United Nations
801 Second Avenue, 7th Floor
New York, N.Y. 10017

Telephone: (212) 661-3700

Telefax: (212) 661-3755

e-mail: UN.NewYork@mfa.gov.me

Correspondence: English

National holiday: 13 July

H.E. Mr. Želijko **Perović**
Ambassador Extraordinary and Plenipotentiary
Permanent Representative (DPC: 11 May 2015)

H.E. Ms. Ivana **Pajević**
Ambassador
Deputy Permanent Representative
Mr. Dušan Proročić

Mr. Nikola **Ivezaj**
Second Secretary

Morocco

Member State since 12 November 1956

Address:	Permanent Mission of the Kingdom of Morocco to the United Nations 866 Second Avenue, 6th and 7th Floors New York, N.Y. 10017
Telephone:	(212) 421-1580
Telefax:	(212) 980-1512, 421-7826
e-mail:	morocco.un@maec.gov.ma
Correspondence:	French
National holiday:	30 July National Day

H.E. Mr. Omar **Hilale**
Ambassador Extraordinary and Plenipotentiary
Permanent Representative (DPC: 23 April 2014)
Mrs. Leila Fatmi

H.E. Mr. Abdeslam **Jaidi**
Ambassador
Mrs. Maria Luisa Estrella Jaidi

Mr. Abderrazzak **Laassel**
Minister Plenipotentiary
Deputy Permanent Representative
Mrs. Loubna Laassel

Mr. Bouchaib **El Oumni**
Minister Plenipotentiary
Mrs. Rachida Lofti

Mr. Tarik **Iziraren**
Minister Plenipotentiary
Mrs. Khadija Zegmount

Mrs. Rabea **Jaidi**
Minister Plenipotentiary

Mr. Mohammed **Atlassi**
Minister Plenipotentiary
Mrs. Manar Tamsouri

Mr. Hicham **Oussihamou**
Minister Plenipotentiary
Mrs. Malika Naibat

Mr. Aziz **El Haouari**
Counsellor
Mrs. Karima Rhoulami

Mr. Omar **El Khadir**
Counsellor
Mrs. Lotiza Lamchaouri

Mr. Omar **Kadiri**
Counsellor
Mrs. Zineb Lahbabi

Mrs. Jamila **Alaoui**
Counsellor (Foreign Affairs)
Mr. David Garrett Kirksey

Mr. Mourad **Raoui**
Counsellor
Mrs. Saloua Haidar

Mr. Yasser **Halfaoui**
Counsellor

Mr. Ahmed Nouri **Salimi**
Counsellor (Foreign Affairs)
Mrs. Fatima Ouammou

Ms. Majda **Moutchou**
Counsellor

Mr. Omar **Rabi**
Counsellor

Mr. Abdellah **Larhmaid**
Counsellor
Mrs. Hanane El Idrissi

Mr. Taha **Kadri**
First Secretary
Mrs. Majda Touzani

Mr. Mustapha **El Achraoui**
First Secretary
Mrs. Hind El Oufir

Mr. Abdelaziz **Ben Boubker**
Third Secretary

Mrs. Najwa **Sarkis Stone**
Attaché (Protocol)

Mozambique

Member State since 16 September 1975

Address: Permanent Mission of the Republic of Mozambique to the United Nations
420 East 50th Street
New York, N.Y. 10022

Telephone: (212) 644-6800, -5965

Telefax: (212) 644-5972, -0528

e-mail: mozambique@un.int

Correspondence: English

National holiday: 25 June
Independence Day

H.E. Mr. António **Gumende**
Ambassador Extraordinary and Plenipotentiary
Permanent Representative (DPC: 20 October 2011)
Mrs. Simangaliso Gatsi Gumende

Mr. Carlos Manuel **Da Costa**
Minister Counsellor
Mrs. Michelle Kanji Noormahomed

Major Gen. Custodio Luiz **Pinto**
Counsellor
Military Adviser
Mrs. Amelia Timoteo Mucavele

Mr. Bernardo **Serage**
Counsellor
Ms. Madalena Pessa Antonio Serage

Mr. Albino José **Parruge**
Attaché (Administration and Finance)

Mrs. Joana Alberto **Chipande**
Attaché (Administration and Finances)

Myanmar

Address: Permanent Mission of the Republic of the Union of Myanmar to the United Nations
10 East 77th Street
New York, N.Y. 10075

Telephone: (212) 744-1271, -1275, -1279

Telefax: (212) 744-1290

e-mail: myanmarmission@verizon.net

Correspondence: English

National holiday: 4 January
Independence Day

H.E. Mr. Kyaw **Tin**
Ambassador Extraordinary and Plenipotentiary
Permanent Representative (DPC: 19 September 2012)
Mrs. Lwin Lwin Hman

H.E. Mr. Myint **Lwin**
Ambassador
Deputy Permanent Representative

Mr. Ye Gyaw **Mra**
Minister Counsellor
Mrs. Aye Aye Than

Ms. Yin Po **Myat**
Counsellor

Ms. Nang Phy Sin Than **Myint**
First Secretary

Mr. Han Thein **Kyaw**
First Secretary

Ms. Ei Mon **Swai**
First Secretary

Ms. Tin Marlar **Myint**
First Secretary

Ms. Sann Thit **Yee**
Second Secretary

Mr. Naing **Myint**
Third Secretary (Chief of Chancery)
Mrs. Sandar Win

Mr. Myo Zaw **Lin**
Attaché (Chief of Chancery I)

Ms. Ni Ni **Maung**
Attaché (Chief of Chancery II)

Mrs. Ni Ni **Khaing**
Attaché
Mr. Aung Zaw Min

Address:	Permanent Mission of the Republic of Namibia to the United Nations 135 East 36th Street New York, N.Y. 10016
Telephone:	(646) 627-8670, (212) 685-2003
Telefax:	(646) 627-8678, (212) 685-1561
e-mail:	namibia@un.int
Correspondence:	English
National holiday:	21 March Independence Day

Ext. 8660	H.E. Mr. Wilfried I. **Emvula** Ambassador Extraordinary and Plenipotentiary Permanent Representative (DPC: 31 August 2010) Mrs. Ester Emvula
Ext. 8661	Mr. Pendapala Andreas **Naanda** Minister Counsellor Deputy Permanent Representative Mrs. Abigail Naanda
Ext. 8663	Mr. Vasco Mushe **Samupofu** Counsellor Mrs. Judith Mbuli Samupofu
Ext. 8665	Ms. Sevelina E.N. **Ashipala** First Secretary
Ext. 8664	Mr. Immanuel **Hamunyela** First Secretary
Ext. 8666	Mr. Stephanus **Hendrickse** Second Secretary Mrs. Deardary Adellle Hendrickse
Ext. 8667	Mrs. Amabel Leticia **Strauss** Third Secretary

Address:	Permanent Mission of the Republic of Nauru to the United Nations 801 Second Avenue, Third Floor New York, N.Y. 10017
Telephone:	(212) 937-0074
Telefax:	(212) 937-0079
e-mail:	nauru@un.int nauru@onecommonwealth.org
website:	www.un.int/nauru
Correspondence:	English
National holiday:	31 January Independence Day

H.E. Ms. Marlene **Moses**
Ambassador Extraordinary and Plenipotentiary
Permanent Representative (DPC: 30 March 2005)

Mrs. Margo Reminisse **Deiye**
Third Secretary
Mr. Pyon Emage Deiye

Mr. Rennier **Gadabu**
Attaché
Mrs. Angelene Gadabu

Address:	Permanent Mission of the Federal Democratic Republic of Nepal to the United Nations 820 Second Avenue, Suite 17B (17th Floor) New York, N.Y. 10017
Telephone:	(212) 370-3988, -3989
Telefax:	(212) 953-2038
e-mail:	nepal@un.int; nepalmissionusa@gmail.com
Correspondence:	English
National holiday:	28 May

Ext. 118 H.E. Mr. Durga Prasad **Bhattarai**
Ambassador Extraordinary and Plenipotentiary
Permanent Representative (DPC: 19 August 2013)
Mrs. Muna Bhattarai

Ext. 115 Mrs. Sewa Lamsal **Adhikari**
Minister Plenipotentiary
Deputy Permanent Representative
Mr. Pradip Adhikari

Ext. 113 Mr. Ghana Shyam **Lamsal**
Counsellor
Mrs. Sita Lamsal

Mr. Shatrudhwan Prasad Sharma **Pokharel**
Second Secretary

Ms. Illa **Mainali**
Second Secretary

Ext. 155 Mr. Dilli Prasad **Acharya**
Third Secretary
Mrs. Chandrakala Acharya

Mr. Tikaram **Upadhyaya**
Attaché
Ms. Sobha Sigdel

Ext. 116 Colonel Yog Raj **Sharma**
Counsellor
Military Adviser
Mrs. Sabina Sharma

Netherlands

Member State since 10 December 1945

Address:	Permanent Mission of the Kingdom of the Netherlands to the United Nations 666 Third Avenue, 19th Floor New York, N.Y. 10017
Telephone:	(212) 519-9500
Telefax:	(212) 370-1954
e-mail:	nyv@minbuza.nl
website:	www.netherlandsmission.org
Social Media:	Twitter: @NLatUN, @KvanOosterom
Correspondence:	English
National holiday:	27 April King's Day

519-9612	H.E. Mr. Karel Jan Gustaaf **van Oosterom** Ambassador Extraordinary and Plenipotentiary Permanent Representative (DPC: 5 August 2013) Mrs. Anna van Oosterom
519-9518	Mr. Peter **van der Vliet** Minister Plenipotentiary Deputy Permanent Representative Mrs. Joan Mitchell-van der Vliet
519-9619	Colonel Robert **de Rave** Counsellor Military Adviser Mrs. Marianne J. H. van Vliet
519-9624	Ms. Hedda **Samson** Counsellor
519-9572	Mr. Gerben **Planting** First Secretary Mrs. Maud Hereman
519-9522	Mr. Marcellinus **van den Bogaard** First Secretary Mrs. Flor van den Bogaard
519-9530	Mr. Adriaan **Beenen** First Secretary Ms. Linda Kovačević
519-9624	Ms. Charlotte **van Baak** First Secretary Mr. Graham Alexander McCulloch
519-9534	Mr. Nicolaas Jacob **de Regt** First Secretary Mr. Casper Martijn van Hooren

519-9744 Mr. Ilan **Cohen**
First Secretary
Mrs. Iris Qureshi

519-9553 Ms. Peggy Henrica Johanna Maria **Vissers**
First Secretary
Mr. Andres Ignacio Calvi

519-9571 Ms. Ingrid **Kersjes**
First Secretary

519-9515 Ms. Eleonora **van Munster**
First Secretary

Mr. Frits Frans Marie **Kemperman**
First Secretary
Mrs. Catharina Elisabeth Kemperman

Ms. Eugenia **Boutylkova**
First Secretary
Mr. Anne Poorta

519-9751 Mr. Anne **Poorta**
Second Secretary
Ms. Eugenia Boutylkova

519-9617 Lt. Colonel Alexander **Jansen**
Deputy Defense Attaché
Mrs. Xandra Jansen

New Zealand

Member State since 24 October 1945

Address:	Permanent Mission of New Zealand to the United Nations 600 Third Avenue, 14th Floor New York, N.Y. 10016
Telephone:	(212) 826-1960
Telefax:	(212) 758-0827
e-mail:	nzpmun@gmail.com
Correspondence:	English
National holiday:	6 February Waitangi Day

317-3080	H.E. Mr. Gerard Jacobus **van Bohemen** Ambassador Extraordinary and Plenipotentiary Permanent Representative (DPC: 11 May 2015) Mrs. Barbara Joy Hunt
317-3077	H.E. Mr. Phillip **Taula** Ambassador Deputy Permanent Representative Mrs. Lidwina Jean Maria Taula
317-3077	H.E. Mrs. Carolyn **Schwalger** Ambassador Deputy Permanent Representative Mr. Robert Kenneth Schwalger
317-3063	Ms. Nicola **Hill** Minister Counsellor
317-3084	Colonel David James **Russell** Counsellor Military Adviser Ms. Colleen Mary Joyce Grindlay
317-3075	Ms. Angela **Hassan-Sharp** Counsellor Mr. Benjamin Ray Sharp
317-3085	Mr. Scott **Sheeran** Counsellor Ms. Haidi Willmot
317-3066	Mr. Bradley **Sawden** Counsellor Mrs. Johanna Claire Sawden
317-3084	Lieutenant Colonel Peter **Hall** First Secretary Deputy Military Adviser Mrs. Mihiwara Suan Hall

317-3067	Mr. Nicholas **Walbridge** First Secretary
317-3082	Ms. Felicity **Roxburgh** First Secretary Mr. Vincent Roxburgh
317-3068	Mr. Peter **Martin** First Secretary
317-3095	Ms. Alexandra **Lennox-Marwick** Second Secretary Mr. Daniel Mcclelland
317-3088	Ms. Laura-Lee **Sage** Second Secretary Mr. Matthew Sage
317-3087	Mr. Benjamin **Steele** Second Secretary Ms. Mette Mikkelsen
317-3064	Mr. Thomas **Kennedy** Second Secretary
317-3094	Mr. Paul **Ballantyne** Second Secretary (Elections, UN Management)
317-3097	Mr. Peter James **Wright** Attaché (Political Affairs)

Address: Permanent Mission of Nicaragua
to the United Nations
820 Second Avenue, 8th Floor
New York, N.Y. 10017

Telephone: (212) 490-7997

Telefax: (212) 286-0815

e-mail: nicaragua@un.int

Correspondence: Spanish

National holiday: 15 September
Independence Day

H.E. Mrs. María **Rubiales de Chamorro**
Ambassador Extraordinary and Plenipotentiary
Permanent Representative (DPC: 13 July 2007)

H.E. Mr. Jaime **Hermida Castillo**
Ambassador Extraordinary and Plenipotentiary
Deputy Permanent Representative

Ms. Alina Julia **Argüello González**
Minister Counsellor

Mr. Jasser **Jiménez**
Counsellor
Mrs. Yelba Moncada de Jiménez

Mrs. María Clarisa **Goldrick**
First Secretary
Mr. Gerald Malachy Goldrick

Ms. Juana **Sandoval**
Third Secretary
Mr. Lucas Henderson

Ms. Patricia **Bajaña**
Attaché
Mr. Javier Bajaña

Mr. Yimel **Aguilar Sandino**
Attaché

Mr. Manuel **Vallejos**
Attaché

Ms. Maria Deyanira **Tellez**
Attaché

Address: Permanent Mission of the Republic of Niger
to the United Nations
417 East 50th Street
New York, N.Y. 10022

Telephone: (212) 421-3260, -3261, -3286

Telefax: (212) 753-6931

Correspondence: French

e-mail: nigermission@ymail.com

National holiday: 18 December
Proclamation of the Republic

H.E. Mr. Boubacar **Boureima**
Ambassador Extraordinary and Plenipotentiary
Permanent Representative (DPC: 4 January 2012)
Mrs. Aissata Boureima

Mr. Laouali **Labo**
First Counsellor
Mrs. Oumma Aboubacar Labo Laou Ali

Mrs. Halimatou Djibo **Saddy**
First Counsellor
Mr. Namaran Saddy

Mr. Ibrahim **Seyni**
First Secretary
Mrs. Amina Seyni Ibrahim

Mr. Maman **Idi**
First Secretary
Mrs. Habiba Mali Nah Allah Maman

Colonel Hassane **Mossi**
Attaché
Mrs. Zeinab Mossi Hassane

Address: Permanent Mission of Nigeria to the United Nations
828 Second Avenue
New York, N.Y. 10017

Telephone: (212) 953-9130

Telefax: (212) 697-1970

Correspondence: English

e-mail: permny@nigeriaunmission.org

website: nigeriaunmission.org/

National holiday: 1 October
Independence Day

297-9316 H.E. Mrs. U. Joy **Ogwu**
Ambassador Extraordinary and Plenipotentiary
Permanent Representative (DPC: 7 May 2008)

H.E. Mr. Usman **Sarki**
Ambassador
Deputy Permanent Representative
Mrs. Maryam Usman Sarki

Mr. Kayode **Laro**
Minister
Mrs. Idowu Laro

Mr. Anthony **Bosah**
Minister

Mr. Onesimus Yanya **Atanze**
Minister
Mrs. Sarah Atanze

Mr. Emmanuel K. **Ojo**
Minister
Mrs. Sidikat Ayodele Ojo

Mr. Lawal Mohammed **Hamidou**
Minister
Mrs. Sakina Lawal Hamidou

297-9353 Mr. Abiodun Richards **Adejola**
Minister
Mrs. Arinola Olufunke Adejola

(917) 267-4429 Mr. Martin Senkom **Adamu**
Minister Counsellor
Mrs. Angela Egbi Adamu

297-9325 Mrs. Amina **Smaila**
Minister

Mr. Cyprian Terseer **Heen**
Minister Counsellor

Mr. Ezenwa C. **Nwaobiala**
Senior Counsellor
Mrs. Chidinma Nwaobiala

297-9313 Mr. Tiwatope Adeleye **Elias-Fatile**
Senior Counsellor
Mrs. Martha Oluwashola Elias-Fatile

Mr. Yakubu Audu **Dadu**
Senior Counsellor
Mrs. Alice Noro Yakubu Dadu

Mr. Emmanuel Oluwadare **Oguntuyi**
Senior Counsellor
Mrs. Oluwayemisi Ajike Oguntuyi

Mr. Mohammed I. **Haidara**
Senior Counsellor
Mrs. Rayyanatu M. Haidara

Mr. Magaji **Umar**
Senior Counsellor
Mrs. Umar Fatima Magaji

Mr. Mohammed Bello **Aliyu**
Counsellor
Mrs. Turai Halima Mohammed

Ms. Naret Joyce **Hirse**
Counsellor

Mr. Michael O. **Okwudili**
Counsellor
Mrs. Christiana A. Okwudili

Mr. Edem Sunday **Eyo**
First Secretary
Mrs. Sonia Ndunese Edem

Mr. Kingsley **Weinoh**
First Secretary
Mrs. Oboromeni Weinoh

Ms. Clement Mercy **Osebhon**
Second Secretary
Mr. Finian Clement

Mr. Aliyu **Omar**
Attaché (Maritime)
Mrs. Rukaiyat Aliyu

Mr. Sule Ndana **Imam**
Attaché (Financial Affairs)
Mrs. Kaka Hauwa Imam

Mr. Thaddeus Chkuwuka **Ogbonna**
Attaché (Financial Affairs)

---

(646) 227-0728

Major General Lincoln Jack **Ogunewe**
Minister
Defence Adviser

Mr. Mohammed **Nasiru**
Senior Counsellor
Assistant Commissioner of Police
Mrs. Zaiyanatu Mohammed

Commander (Navy) Saburi Abayomi **Lawal**
Counsellor
Deputy Defence Adviser
Mrs. Moriliat Temitayo Lawal

Lt. Colonel Saidu Tanko **Audu**
Counsellor
Deputy Defence Adviser
Mrs. Hindatu Audu Saidu

Ms. Josephine Mwuese **Adeh**
Third Secretary
Assistant Superintendent of Police

Norway

Member State since 27 November 1945

Address:	Permanent Mission of Norway to the United Nations 825 Third Avenue, 38th Floor New York, N.Y. 10022
Telephone:	(646) 430-7510
Telefax:	(646) 430-7591
e-mail:	delun@mfa.no un.newyork@mfa.no
Correspondence:	English
National holiday:	17 May Constitution Day

---

(646) 430-7571	H.E. Mr. Geir O. **Pedersen** Ambassador Extraordinary and Plenipotentiary Permanent Representative (5 September 2012) Mrs. Mona Christophersen
(646) 430-7512	H.E. Ms. May-Elin **Stener** Ambassador Deputy Permanent Representative
(646) 430-7514	Mrs. Susan **Eckey** Minister Counsellor Mr. Sivert Martin Falkeid
(646) 430-7513	Mr. Halvor **Sætre** Minister Counsellor Ms. Vibeke Borchgrevink
(646) 430-7525	Ms. Hilde **Klemetsdal** Minister Counsellor Mr. Erik Henningsen
(646) 430-7518	Mr. Trond Egil **With** Minister Counsellor Police Adviser Mrs. Dalia With
(646) 430-7517	Ms. Marte Lerberg **Kopstad** Counsellor (Press)
(646) 430-7516	Mr. Alf Håvard **Vestrheim** Counsellor Mrs. Eugenia Vidal Gil
(646) 430-7519	Ms. Anne Heidi **Kvalsøren** Counsellor
(646) 430-7521	Ms. Meena **Syed** Counsellor Mr. Erik Niklas Fjaellstaal Nordquist

(646) 430-7523	Ms. Iselin Hebbert **Larsen** First Secretary
(646) 430-7524	Mr. Bjoern Klouman **Bekken** First Secretary
(646) 439-7515	Mr. Andreas Motzfeldt **Kravik** First Secretary Mrs. Lindis Bjørnerem
	Ms. Eleonora **Van Munster** First Secretary

---

(646) 430-7522	Colonel Per Erik **Rønning** Counsellor Military Adviser Ms. Zubaida Rasul- Rønning
(646) 430-7520	Mr. Paal Zandstra **Krokeide** Counsellor Deputy Military Adviser Mrs. Silje Zandstra Krokeide

Oman

Address:	Permanent Mission of the Sultanate of Oman to the United Nations 3 Dag Hammarskjöld Plaza 305 East 47th Street, 12th Floor New York, N.Y. 10017
Telephone:	(212) 355-3505
Telefax:	(212) 644-0070
e-mail:	oman@un.int
Correspondence:	English
National holiday:	18 November

Ext. 211	H.E. Mrs. Lyutha S. **Al-Mughairy** Ambassador Extraordinary and Plenipotentiary Permanent Representative (DPC: 8 April 2011) Mr. M. S. Stoby
Ext. 228	Mr. Mohamed Ahmed Salim **Al-Shanfari** Minister Plenipotentiary Deputy Permanent Representative Mrs. Al-Shanfari
Ext. 209	Mr. Khalid Saeed Mohamed **Al Shuaibi** Minister Plenipotentiary Mrs. Sumaiya Al-Rajhi
Ext. 208	Mr. Mohammed Ahmed **Ba-Omar** Counsellor Mrs. Ba-Omar
Ext. 206	Mr. Majid Yahya Khalifa **Al Murghairi** First Secretary Mrs. Al Murghairi
Ext. 225	Mr. Adallah Juma Ali **Al Araimi** First Secretary Mrs. Maryam Abdullah Al Arimi
Ext. 227	Ms. Azza Hamood Ali **Al-Busaidi** First Secretary
Ext. 217	Mr. Sulaiman Salim Mohamed **Al-Abdali** Third Secretary
Ext. 207	Mr. Yasir Abdullah Rashid **Al Wahaibi** Third Secretary Mrs. Al Wahaibi

Pakistan

Member State since 30 September 1947

Address:	Permanent Mission of Pakistan to the United Nations Pakistan House 8 East 65th Street New York, N.Y. 10065
Telephone:	(212) 879-8600, -8603, 8025, 8028, 8031, 8033
Telefax:	(212) 744-7348
e-mail:	pakistan@un.int
website:	www.pakun.org
Correspondence:	English
National holiday:	23 March Pakistan Day

Ext. 125	H.E. Ms. Maleeha **Lodhi** Ambassador Extraordinary and Plenipotentiary Permanent Representative (DPC: 10 March 2015)
Ext. 199	H.E. Mr. Sahebzada Ahmed **Khan** Ambassador Deputy Permanent Representative Mrs. Sara Khan
Ext. 198	Mr. Nabeel **Munir** Minister Mrs. Saema Nabeel
Ext. 155	Mr. Khalil Ur Rahman **Hashmi** Minister Mrs. Marium Mahmoud
Ext. 116	Mr. Diyar **Khan** Counsellor Mrs. Tasleem Diyar
	Mr. Bilal **Ahmad** Counsellor Mrs. Naila Bilal Ahmad
Ext. 152	Mr. Farrukh Iqbal **Khan** Counsellor Mrs. Erum Farrukh Khan
	Mr. Nauman Bashir **Bhatti** First Secretary Mrs. Ajla Nauman
	Mr. Yasar Ammar Third Secretary Mrs. Salma Mukhtar

Ext. 142	Mr. Shahzad **Naseer** Counsellor Military Adviser
	Mr. Masood **Anwar** Minister (Press)
Ext. 143	Mr. Aqeel Nawaz **Siddiqui** Attaché (Finance and Accounts) Mrs. Aqeela Azhar

Address:	Permanent Mission of the Republic of Palau to the United Nations 866 United Nations Plaza, Suite 575 New York, N.Y. 10017
Telephone:	(212) 813-0310
Telefax:	(212) 813-0317
e-mail:	mission@palauun.org
website:	www.palauun.org
Correspondence:	English
National holiday:	1 October Independence Day

H.E. Dr. Caleb **Otto**
Ambassador Extraordinary and Plenipotentiary
Permanent Representative (DPC: 3 September 2013)
Mrs. Judy Buster Otto

H.E. Mr. Stuart **Beck**
Ambassador
Mrs. Ebiltulik M. L. Beck

Address:	Permanent Mission of Panama to the United Nations 866 United Nations Plaza, Suite 4030 New York, N.Y. 10017
Telephone:	(212) 421-5420, -5421
Telefax:	(212) 421-2694
e-mail:	emb@panama-un.org
website:	www.panama-un.org
Correspondence:	Spanish
National holiday:	3 November Independence Day

H.E. Ms. Laura Elena **Flores Herrera**
Ambassador Extraordinary and Plenipotentiary
Permanent Representative (DPC: 4 September 2014)

H.E. Ms. Paulina María **Franceschi Navarro**
Ambassador
Deputy Permanent Representative

H.E. Mr. Hernán **Tejeira**
Ambassador

Ms. Elena **Ng**
Counsellor

Ms. Carmen **Ávila**
Second Secretary

Mrs. María de los Angeles **Peña de Sgro**
Attaché
Mr. John J. Sgro

Mr. Jaime Antonio **Ruiz Jayes**
Attaché
Police Adviser

Ms. Desirée del Carmen **Cedeño Rengifo**
Attaché

Mr. Cedric Oscar **Miró Weeden**
Attaché

Papua New Guinea

Member State since 10 October 1975

Address:	Permanent Mission of the Independent State of Papua New Guinea to the United Nations 201 East 42nd Street, Suite 2411 New York, N.Y. 10017
Telephone:	(212) 557-5001
Telefax:	(212) 557-5009
e-mail:	pngun@pngmission.org
Correspondence:	English
National holiday:	16 September Independence Day

Ext. 17 — H.E. Mr. Robert Guba **Aisi**
Ambassador Extraordinary and Plenipotentiary
Permanent Representative (DPC: 25 June 2002)
Mrs. Susan Iamonama Aisi

Mr. Fred **Sarufa**
Counsellor

Mr. Peter **Bonny**
First Secretary

Ms. Nelly Luavagi **Peni**
Third Secretary

Colonel Michael Augustine **Daniels**
Defence Attaché

Paraguay

Address: Permanent Mission of Paraguay to the United Nations
801 Second Avenue, Suite 702
New York, N.Y. 10017

Telephone: (212) 687-3490, -3491

Telefax: (212) 818-1282

e-mail: paraguay@un.int

Correspondence: Spanish

National holiday: 15 May
Independence Day

H.E. Mr. Federico Alberto **González Franco**
Ambassador Extraordinary and Plenipotentiary
Permanent Representative (DPC: 20 January 2015)
Mrs. Silvia Maria Riquelme de González

Mr. Marcelo Eliseo **Scappini Ricciardi**
Minister
Deputy Permanent Representative
Mrs. Fabiola María Torres Figueredo

Ms. Julia Anselmina **Maciel González**
Counsellor

Mr. Luis **Benítez Rodríguez**
First Secretary
Mrs. Diva Riquelme de Benítez

Mrs. Maria Gloria Beatriz **Sanabria de Montiel**
First Secretary
Mr. Marcos Antonio Montiel Sosa

Mr. Jose Osvaldo **Sanabria Rivarola**
First Secretary

Mrs. Ana Edelmira **Rolon Candia**
Second Secretary

Mr. Enrique José María **Carrillo Gómez**
Second Secretary

Mrs. Ana Soledad **Sandoval Espínola**
Second Secretary

Ms. Ethel **Peña**
Attaché

Ms. Rita **Arce**
Attaché

Ms. Marta Angélica **Cristaldo**
Attaché

Mr. Rubén **Esquivel**
Attaché

Colonel DEM Sebastian **Acevedo Mujica**
Attaché
Military Adviser
Mrs. Luz Marina Alvarenga de Acevedo

Colonel DEM Edgar **Noceda Figueredo**
Attaché
Military Adviser
Mrs. Maria Elena Castillo Martinez

Address:	Permanent Mission of Peru to the United Nations 820 Second Avenue, Suite 1600 New York, N.Y. 10017
Telephone:	(212) 687-3336 (212) 937-0567 (Press Matters)
Telefax:	(212) 972-6975 (212) 883-0591 (Permanent Representative's Office)
e-mail:	onuper@unperu.org
website:	www.un.int/peru
Correspondence:	Spanish
National holiday:	28 July Independence Day

937-0569	H.E. Mr. Gustavo **Meza-Cuadra** Ambassador Extraordinary and Plenipotentiary Permanent Representative (DPC: 24 October 2013) Mrs. Sonia Balcazar de Meza-Cuadra
687-3336	Mr. Augusto **Thornberry** Minister Deputy Permanent Representative Mrs. Maritza Mendoza de Thornberry
937-0564	Ms. Ana **Peña** Minister Counsellor
937-0563	Mr. Víctor **Muñoz** Counsellor Mrs. Eliana Tapia de Muñoz
937-0570	Mr. Glauco **Seoane** Counsellor
	Mr. Walter **Habich Morales** First Secretary
937-0559	Mr. Jorge **Medina** First Secretary Mrs. Gabriela Higa
937-0574	Mr. Eduardo **López** First Secretary Mrs. Eugenia Yzique
	Ms. Veronika **Bustamante Gomez** First Secretary
	Mr. Angel **Horna** Second Secretary

937-0561	Mrs. Lucía **Amiri-Talesh** Second Secretary Mr. Kjiel Vargas Legovic
937-0572	Gen. Luis **Howell** Counsellor (Peacekeeping Affairs) Mrs. Sonia Violeta Helfer

Address:	Permanent Mission of the Republic of the Philippines to the United Nations 556 Fifth Avenue, 5th Floor New York, N.Y. 10036
Telephone:	(212) 764-1300
Telefax:	(212) 840-8602
e-mail:	newyorkpm@gmail.com
website:	www.un.int/philippines
Correspondence:	English
National holiday:	12 June Independence Day

Ext. 126	H.E. Ms. Lourdes Ortiz **Yparraguirre** Ambassador Extraordinary and Plenipotentiary Permanent Representative (DPC: 22 April 2015)

Ext. 112	Mrs. Irene Susan Barreiro **Natividad** Minister Deputy Permanent Representative
Ext. 125	Mr. Julio Camara **Dery** Minister Mrs. Ruena de Guzman Espino-Dery
Ext. 137	Mr. Igor Garlit **Bailen** Minister
Ext. 120	Ms. Maria Angela **Ponce** Minister
Ext. 123	Mrs. Noemi Tan **Diaz** First Secretary Mr. Jon Mannion
Ext. 133	Ms. Shirley Liwanag **Flores** Second Secretary
Ext. 124	Ms. Anita **Parado-Brillo** Attaché
Ext. 132	Mr. Moises Hidalgo **Ocampo** Attaché Mrs. Lynda Jewel Pobre-Ocampo
Ext. 139	Mrs. Cecilia Sanchez **Tomas** Attaché Mr. Renie Pascual Tomas

Ext. 130	Mr. Lazaro Melendez **Garcia**, Jr. Attaché Mrs. Arlette Garcia
Ext. 128	Mrs. Maria Teresa Endozo **Narbuada** Attaché Mr. Samuel Lelis Narbuada
Ext. 141	Mr. German C. **Punzalan** Attaché Mrs. Susana G. Punzalan
Ext. 116	Mr. Edwin R. **de Pacina** Attaché Mrs. Carolyn C. de Pacina
Ext. 131	Mrs. Rachel Anne **Nicerio-Moran** Attaché
Ext. 126	Mrs. Maria Carmen Lucena **Romanillos** Attaché Mr. Bernabe Bangot Romanillos, Jr.
Ext. 111	Ms. Maria Flordeliza Aspera **Tuiza** Attaché
Ext. 134	Mr. Joseph Arnel S. **Santos** Attaché Mrs. Angelita Panton Alvarado-Santos
Ext. 115	Mr. Alfredo Minanga **Labrador V** Attaché Ms. Sheryl Abuan Labrador
Ext. 138	Ms. Elea Vergara **Perez** Attaché
Ext. 142	Col. Jaime Fernando Rillorta **Hidalgo** Military Attaché Mrs. Joy Corazon Lorenzo Hidalgo

Address:	Permanent Mission of the Republic of Poland to the United Nations 750 Third Avenue, 30th Floor New York, N.Y. 10017
Telephone:	(212) 744-2506
Telefax:	(212) 517-6771; (212) 744-2510
e-mail:	poland.un@msz.gov.pl
Website:	www.nowyjorkonz.msz.gov.pl
Correspondence:	English
National holiday:	3 May Constitution Day

---

(646) 559-7552	H.E. Mr. Bogusław **Winid** Ambassador Extraordinary and Plenipotentiary Permanent Representative (DPC: 4 September 2014) Mrs. Beata Winid
(646) 559-7553	Mr. Paweł **Radomski** Minister Counsellor Deputy Permanent Representative
(646) 559-7577	Mr. Marek Jerzy **Michalewski** Minister Counsellor
(646) 559-7570	Colonel Jacek Andrzej **Stochel** Counsellor Mrs. Milena Anna Wronska-Stochel
(646) 559-7573	Ms. Ewa **Małys** Counsellor
(646) 559-7562	Ms. Monika Agnieszka **Ekler** Counsellor
(646) 559-7583	Mr. Tomasz Grzegorz **Stefanik** First Secretary
(646) 559-7559	Mr. Mateusz **Sakowicz** First Secretary Mrs. Bogna Bernaciak Sakowicz
(646) 559-7578	Mrs. Agata Ewelina **Duda-Plonka** First Secretary
(646) 559-7556	Mr. Adam **Krzywosądzki** First Secretary Mrs. Hanna Grażyna Krzywosądzka
(646) 559-7576	Ms. Joanna Aurelia **Fiodorow** Second Secretary

(646) 559-7582	Mrs. Karina Helena **Węgrzynowska** Second Secretary Mr. Marcin Paweł Nędzi
(646) 559-7560	Mrs. Aleksandra **Stępowska** Second Secretary Mr. Konrad Stępowski
(646) 559-7581	Mrs. Joanna Elzbieta **Honkisz** Second Secretary Mr. Piotr Adam Kleśta
(646) 559-7555	Mr. Jacek **Jakubowski** Second Secretary
(646) 559-7587	Mr. Aleksander Jerzy **Romanowski** Second Secretary Mrs. Olga Aleksandra Romanowska
(646) 559-7571	Mr. Tomasz **Tokarski** Third Secretary
(646) 559-7584	Mrs. Sylwia **Wojtaszek** Attaché Mr. Rafał Paweł Wojtaszek
(646) 559-7585	Mr. Krzysztof **Konieczny** Attaché
(646) 559-7552	Mrs. Agnieszka **Wietecha-Michalak** Attaché Mr. Janusz Michalak

Portugal

Member State since 14 December 1955

Address:	Permanent Mission of Portugal to the United Nations 866 Second Avenue, 9th Floor New York, N.Y. 10017
Telephone:	(212) 759-9444, -9445, -9446, -9447
Telefax:	(212) 355-1124
e-mail:	portugal@un.int
website:	www.un.int/portugal
Correspondence:	English
National holiday:	10 June

Ext. 2902/2903	H.E. Mr. Álvaro **Mendonça e Moura** Ambassador Extraordinary and Plenipotentiary Permanent Representative (DPC: 16 April 2013) Mrs. Maria Cristina Mendonça e Moura
Ext. 2912	Mrs. Cristina Maria Cerqueira **Pucarinho** Minister Counsellor Deputy Permanent Representative Mr. Pedro Manuel Soares de Oliveira
Ext. 2238	Mr. Manuel Frederico **Pinheiro da Silva** Counsellor
Ext. 2911	Ms. Maria João Franco **Coutinho** First Secretary
Ext. 2807	Ms. Maria Inês de Almeida **Coroa** First Secretary
Ext. 2805	Ms. Maria Raquel **de Oliveira Martins** First Secretary
Ext. 2802	Mr. André **Abreu Costa Monteiro** First Secretary
Ext. 2808	Mr. João Miguel **Madureira** Minister Counsellor (Legal Affairs)
Ext. 2803	Lieutenant Colonel Jorge Manuel dos Reis Gamito **Torres** Counsellor Military Adviser
Ext. 2815	Mr. José António Martins **Cortes Palma** Counsellor Mrs. Elisabete Proença Rodrigues e Cortes Palma
Ext. 2801	Ms. Vanessa **Gomes** Attaché

Qatar

Member State since 21 September 1971

Address: Permanent Mission of the State of Qatar to the United Nations
809 United Nations Plaza, 4th Floor
New York, N.Y. 10017

Telephone: (212) 486-9335, -9336

Telefax: (212) 758-4952

e-mail: pmun@mofa.gov.qa

Correspondence: English

National holiday: 18 December
National Day

H.E. Ms. Alya Ahmed Saif **Al-Thani**
Ambassador Extraordinary and Plenipotentiary
Permanent Representative (DPC: 24 October 2013)

Mr. Yousef Sultan **Laram**
First Secretary
Deputy Permanent Representative
Mrs. Maryam Yousuf Al-Hammadi

Mr. Abdulrahman Yaaqob Y.A. **Al-Hamadi**
Second Secretary

Mr. Ghanim Al-Hudaifi **Al-Kuwari**
Third Secretary

Ms. AlDaana Mohammed A.H. **Al-Mulla**
Third Secretary

Sheikh Ahmad Mohamed **Al-Thani**
Third Secretary

Ms. Alanoud Qassim M. A. **Al-Temimi**
Third Secretary

Republic of Korea

Address: Permanent Mission of the Republic of Korea to the United Nations
335 East 45th Street
New York, N.Y. 10017

Telephone: (212) 439-4000

Telefax: (212) 986-1083

e-mail: korea.un@mofa.go.kr

website: un.mofat.go.kr

Correspondence: English

National holiday: 3 October

439-4011 H.E. Mr. **Oh** Joon
Ambassador Extraordinary and Plenipotentiary
Permanent Representative (DPC: 20 September 2013)
Mrs. Kim Miri

439-4089 H.E. Ms. **Paik** Ji-ah
Ambassador
Deputy Permanent Representative
Mr. Choi Joonsoo

439-4002 H.E. Mr. **Hahn** Choonghee
Ambassador
Deputy Permanent Representative
Mrs. Kim Kyunghee

439-4004 Mr. **Koo** Jin Joo
Minister
Mrs. Lee Jihee

439-4028 Mr. **Lim** Hoon-Min
Minister Counsellor
Mrs. Kwon Jin Kyung

439-4028 Mr. **Yoo** Dae Jong
Minister Counsellor
Mrs. Song Soo Kyung

439-4024 Mr. **Park** Taeil
Counsellor
Mrs. Choi Wanseob

439-4088 Mr. **Suh** Sangpyo
Counsellor
Mrs. Lee Min Sun

439-4008 Mr. **Chung** Byung-ha
Counsellor

439-4023 Mr. **Lim** Sang Beom
Counsellor
Ms. Noh Hae Sook

439-4064 Mr. **Jeong** Seon Yong
Counsellor
Mrs. Kang Ihn Kyoung

439-4091 Mr. **Won** Hoshin
Counsellor
Ms. Choi Min Yong

439-4062 Mr. **Shin** Seoung Ho
Counsellor

439-4042 Mr. **Kang** Sangwook
Counsellor

439-4090 Mr. **Rhee** Zha-hyoung
Counsellor

439-4030 Mr. **Lee** Moon Hee
Counsellor
Mrs. Seo Seung Hee

439-4017 Mr. **Choi** Chun
Counsellor
Ms. Oum Heasun

439-4027 Mr. **Lee** Hwangroh
Counsellor

439-4008 Mr. **Lee** Tong-a
Counsellor
Mrs. Yoo Haerim

439-4052 Ms. **Cho** Eun Hee
First Secretary

439-4057 Mr. **Ko** Jae Sin
First Secretary
Mrs. Kim Eun Jung

439-4087 Mr. **Kim** Ileung
First Secretary
Mrs. Jang Sukyong

439-4038 Mr. **Park** Jang Ho
First Secretary
Mrs. Cho Hyeseung

439-4029 Mr. **Choi** Won Seok
First Secretary
Mrs. Choi Wan Jung

439-4025 Mr. **Yoo** Jongyul
First Secretary
Mrs. Kwon Youngim

439-4010	Ms. **Han** Li Sa First Secretary Mr. Lee Jonghun
439-4020	Ms. **Kim** Hye-Jin First Secretary
439-4060	Ms. **Hong** Yujin First Secretary
439-4051	Mr. **Kim** Il-hoon First Secretary Mrs. Kim Minyoung
439-4009	Ms. **Lee** Eun Joo Second Secretary
439-4056	Mr. **Kim** Namki Second Secretary Mrs. Park Su Seong
439-4051	Mr. **Lee** Sang Yun Second Secretary Mrs. Kim Kyeongmin
439-4067	Mr. **Kim** Sangil Second Secretary Ms. Lee Youngeun
439-4040	Ms. **Park** Jee Won Second Secretary
439-4019	Mr. **Kim** Kyoung Un Third Secretary Mrs. Shin Bo Ra
439-4078	Mr. **Kim** Hyun Keun Attaché Mrs. Yoo Hyein

439-4021	Lt. Colonel **Kim** Taedong Attaché Military Adviser Mrs. Choi Eunkyoung

Republic of Moldova

Member State since 2 March 1992

Address:	Permanent Mission of the Republic of Moldova to the United Nations 35 East 29th Street New York, N.Y. 10016
Telephone:	(212) 447-1867
Telefax:	(212) 447-4067
e-mail:	unmoldova@aol.com
website:	www.onu.mfa.md
Correspondence:	English
National holiday:	27 August

Ext. 201	H.E. Mr. Vlad **Lupan** Ambassador Extraordinary and Plenipotentiary Permanent Representative (DPC: 18 January 2012) Mrs. Rodica Lupan
Ext. 202	Mrs. Larisa **Miculeț** Counsellor Deputy Permanent Representative
Ext. 203	Ms. Carolina **Podoroghin** Second Secretary

Romania

Member State since 14 December 1955

Address:	Permanent Mission of Romania to the United Nations 573-577 Third Avenue (& 38th Street) New York, N.Y. 10016
Telephone:	(212) 682-3273, -3274, 818-1491, -1496 (212) 972-3230 (Ambassador's Office)
Telefax:	(212) 682-9746
e-mail:	misiune@romaniaun.org
website:	www.mpnewyork.mae.ro
Correspondence:	English/French
National holiday:	1 December

---

(212) 972-3230	H.E. Mrs. Simona Mirela **Miculescu** Ambassador Extraordinary and Plenipotentiary Permanent Representative (DPC: 5 June 2008)
Ext. 202	Mrs. Elena Anca **Jurcan** Minister Counsellor Deputy Permanent Representative Mr. Petru Jurcan
Ext. 214	Ms. Narcisa Daciana **Vlădulescu** Counsellor
Ext. 221	Mrs. Elisabeta-Maria **David** First Secretary Mr. Gabriel David
Ext. 213	Ms. Corina-Monica **Badea** Second Secretary
Ext. 210	Mr. Dan Alexandru **Oanţă** Second Secretary Mrs. Katalin Oanţă
Ext. 212	Ms. Oana Maria **Rebedea** Second Secretary
Ext. 211	Mrs. Katalin **Oanţă** Second Secretary Mr. Dan Alexandru Oanţă
Ext. 288	Mr. Viorel **Stan** Attaché Mrs. Silvia Stan
	Mr. Ştefan **Mircea** Attaché (Communication) Mrs. Tania Gabriela Mircea

Ext. 230	Mr. Lucian Constantin **Andrei** Minister Counsellor Military Adviser Mrs. Lucia-Elena Andrei

Address: Permanent Mission of the Russian Federation
to the United Nations
136 East 67th Street
New York, N.Y. 10065

Telephone: (212) 861-4900, -4901

Telefax: (212) 628-0252, 517-7427

e-mail: press@russiaun.ru

website: www.russiaun.ru

Correspondence: English

National holiday: 12 June
Day of Russia

H.E. Mr. Vitaly I. **Churkin**
Ambassador Extraordinary and Plenipotentiary
Permanent Representative (DPC: 1 May 2006)
Mrs. Irina Y. Churkina

Mr. Dmitry I. **Maksimychev**
Envoy Extraordinary and Minister Plenipotentiary
Deputy Permanent Representative
Mrs. Elena V. Maksimycheva

Mr. Petr V. **Iliichev**
Envoy Extraordinary and Minister Plenipotentiary
First Deputy Permanent Representative
Mrs. Olga V. Iliicheva

Mr. Evgeny T. **Zagaynov**
Envoy Extraordinary and Minister Plenipotentiary
Deputy Permanent Representative
Mrs. Ksenia Y. Novikova

Mr. Vladimir K. **Safronkov**
Envoy Extraordinary and Minister Plenipotentiary
Deputy Permanent Representative
Mrs. Elena D. Safronkova-Alekseeva

Mr. Igor O. **Gribok**
Senior Counsellor
Mrs. Irina G. Gribok

Ms. Irina A. **Medvedeva**
Senior Counsellor

Mr. Evgeny V. **Senkin**
Senior Counsellor
Mrs. Lilia N. Senkina

Mr. Evgeny I. **Kolesnikov**
Senior Counsellor
Mrs. Marina V. Kolesnikova

Mr. Sergey V. **Khalizov**
Senior Counsellor
Mrs. Ekaterina V. Chumicheva

Mrs. Dilyara S. **Ravilova-Borovik**
Senior Counsellor

Mr. Maxim V. **Musikhin**
Senior Counsellor
Mrs. Marina A. Ustinova

Mr. Mikael V. **Agasandyan**
Counsellor
Mrs. Victoria V. Agasandyan

Mr. Andrey A. **Listov**
Counsellor
Mrs. Tatiana V. Listova

Mr. Stepan A. **Govorunenko**
Counsellor
Mrs. Elena Y. Govorunenko

Mr. Anton Y. **Morozov**
Counsellor
Mrs. Yulia A. Sobachevskaya

Mr. Vasily S. **Makarov**
Counsellor
Mrs. Natalia I. Makarova

Mr. Alexander V. **Letoshnev**
Counsellor
Mrs. Elena K. Letoshneva

Ms. Galina S. **Khvan**
Counsellor

Mr. Sergey V. **Tsygankov**
Counsellor
Mrs. Irina N. Tsygankova

Mrs. Olga V. **Mozolina**
Counsellor
Mr. Petr Y. Osipkin

Mr. Vyacheslav V. **Dunaev**
Counsellor
Mrs. Larisa M. Lopushinskaya

Mr. Alexander A. **Volgarev**
Counsellor
Mrs. Tatiana A. Volgareva

Mr. Dmitry V. **Bogachev**
Counsellor
Mrs. Natalia S. Bogacheva

Ms. Anna M. **Evstigneeva**
Counsellor

Mr. Alexey A. **Zaytsev**
Counsellor
Mrs. Anastasia Y. Zaytseva

Mr. Evgeny A. **Ustinov**
First Secretary
Mrs. Nadezda A. Ustinova

Mr. Sergey V. **Antropov**
First Secretary
Mrs. Irina A. Antropova

Mr. Dmitry O. **Maksimov**
First Secretary
Mrs. Natalia S. Maksimova

Mr. Evgeny Y. **Varganov**
First Secretary
Mrs. Lidia N. Varganova

Mr. Georgy N. **Tushkanov**
First Secretary
Mrs. Alexandra A. Tushkanova

Mr. Vadim Y. **Sergeev**
First Secretary
Mrs. Daria D. Sergeeva

Mr. Vladislav I. **Dolgiy**
First Secretary
Mrs. Tamara V. Dolgaya

Ms. Elena S. **Mukhametzyanova**
First Secretary

Mr. Kirill E. **Shershnev**
First Secretary
Mrs. Olga N. Shershneva

Mr. Ivan A. **Korovyakovskiy**
First Secretary
Mrs. Svetlana K. Umrikhina

Mr. Roman O. **Katarskiy**
First Secretary

Mr. Evgeny V. **Kalugin**
First Secretary
Mrs. Yana V. Kalugina

Mr. Konstantin P. **Degtyarev**
First Secretary
Mrs. Zarina A. Shil

Mr. Alexandr V. **Repkin**
First Secretary
Mrs. Olga V. Repkina

Mr. Alexander E. **Sviridov**
First Secretary

Mr. Alexey N. **Terekhov**
First Secretary
Mrs. Inna P. Terekhova

Mr. Dmitry Y. **Dalmatov**
Second Secretary
Mrs. Marina L. Dalmatova

Mr. Alexander S. **Lankevich**
Second Secretary
Mrs. Ekaterina V. Lankevich

Mr. Sergey P. **Yakushev**
Second Secretary
Mrs. Natalia V. Yakusheva

Mr. Ivan I. **Nechaev**
Second Secretary

Mr. Ilya Y. **Gerasin**
Second Secretary
Mrs. Marina G. Gerasina

Mr. Anton S. **Shamarin**
Second Secretary
Mrs. Angelina V. Shamarina

Mr. Nikita V. **Piontkovskiy**
Second Secretary
Mrs. Natalia G. Piontkovskaya

Mr. Alexander I. **Khomenko**
Second Secretary
Mrs. Elena N. Zykova

Mr. Alexander A. **Smirnov**
Second Secretary
Mrs. Iraida D. Smirnova

Mr. Sergey Y. **Dutov**
Second Secretary
Mrs. Irina S. Dutova

Mr. Dmitry I. **Nekrasov**
Second Secretary
Mrs. Svetlana S. Nekrasova

Mr. Vadim V. **Sergeev**
Second Secretary
Mrs. Alla G. Sergeeva

Mr. Vladimir A. **Ponomarev**
Second Secretary
Mrs. Natalia V. Ponomareva

Mr. Sergey N. **Donets**
Second Secretary
Mrs. Ekaterina Y. Donets

Mr. Anton D. **Orlov**
Third Secretary
Mrs. Oxana I. Orlova

Mrs. Yulia A. **Plokhova**
Third Secretary

Mr. Oleg O. **Filimonov**
Third Secretary
Mrs. Anna A. Filimonova

Mr. Sergey A. **Leonidchenko**
Third Secretary

Mr. Ivan A. **Kulikov**
Third Secretary
Mrs. Kristina G. Kulikova

Ms. Elena A. **Melikbekyan**
Third Secretary

Mr. Dmitry V. **Perfilov**
Third Secretary
Mrs. Natalia Y. Perfilova

Mr. Pavel A. **Fondukov**
Third Secretary

Mr. Dmitry V. **Podlesnykh**
Third Secretary
Mrs. Ekaterina A. Podlesnykh

Mr. Alexey D. **Militskiy**
Third Secretary
Mrs. Yulia S. Militskaya

Mr. Dmitry V. **Shchichko**
Third Secretary
Mrs. Veronika E. Klimanova

Mr. Roman G. **Bryulgart**
Third Secretary

Mr. Alexey V. **Eremin**
Attaché
Mrs. Margarita A. Eremina

Mr. Anatoly A. **Titov**
Attaché
Mrs. Natalia S. Titova

Mr. Daniil I. **Poddubnyy**
Attaché
Mrs. Elena A. Poddubnaya

Mr. Sergey V. **Saveliev**
Attaché
Mrs. Olga V. Savelieva

Mr. Roman O. **Annenkov**
Attaché
Mrs. Valentina V. Annenkova

Mr. Alexey V. **Ermolenko**
Attaché
Mrs. Tatiana S. Ermolenko

Mr. Sergey A. **Kuryatnikov**
Attaché

Mr. Sergey V. **Leus**
Attaché
Mrs. Alesya A. Leus

Mr. Evgeny N. **Mitrofanov**
Attaché
Mrs. Tatiana I. Mitrofanova

Mr. Roman P. **Bondarenko**
Attaché
Mrs. Ekaterina Y. Kaplina

Mr. Andrey A. **Lyubchikov**
Attaché
Mrs. Tatiana P. Lyubchikova

Mr. Ilya L. **Kozhokaru**
Attaché
Mrs. Irina A. Malinina

Mr. Dmitry A. **Soloviev**
Attaché
Mrs. Yulia V. Solovieva

Mr. Igor I. **Bykov**
Attaché
Mrs. Anzhela A. Mikhina

Mr. Konstantin V. **Fomin**
Attaché
Mrs. Irina I. Aparneva

Mr. Valery I. **Kuzmenkov**
Attaché
Mrs. Valeria S. Kuzmenkova

Mr. Dmitry A. **Lopaev**
Attaché
Mrs. Olga R. Lopaeva

Mrs. Yulia N. **Kudasova**
Attaché

Mr. Andrey O. **Zinoviev**
Attaché
Mrs. Natalia V. Zinovieva

Mr. Valery F. **Dybunov**
Attaché
Mrs. Liudmila A. Dybunova

Mr. Egor S. **Shulgin**
Attaché

Mr. Roman A. **Teslenko**
Attaché
Mrs. Anna Y. Teslenko

Address: Permanent Mission of the Republic
of Rwanda to the United Nations
370 Lexington Avenue, Suite 401
New York, N.Y. 10017

Telephone: (212) 679-9010

Telefax: (212) 679-9133

e-mail: ambanewyork@minaffet.gov.rw

ambanewyork@gmail.com

Correspondence: French/English

National holiday: 1 July
Independence Day

H.E. Mr. Eugène-Richard **Gasana**
Ambassador Extraordinary and Plenipotentiary
Permanent Representative (DPC: 17 July 2009)
Mrs. Agnès Gasana

Mr. Olivier **Nduhungirehe**
Minister Counsellor
Deputy Permanent Representative
Mrs. Virginie Ingabire

Mrs. Jeanne d'Arc **Byaje**
Minister Counsellor
Deputy Permanent Representative

Mr. Lawrence **Manzi**
First Counsellor

Mr. Robert **Kayinamura**
First Counsellor

Mr. Emmanuel **Nibishaka**
First Counsellor
Ms. Seraphine Uwamahoro

Mr. Maboneza **Sana**
First Counsellor

Mr. Isaïe **Bagabo**
Second Counsellor

Mr. Etienne **Nkerabigwi**
Second Counsellor

Mr. Mustapha **Sibomana**
Second Counsellor

Mr. Emmanuel **Biraro**
Second Counsellor

Ms. Aline **Mukashyaka**
Second Counsellor

Colonel Vincent **Nyakarundi**
Military Attaché
Mrs. Immaculée Uwimana

Mrs. Virginie **Ingabire**
Attaché

Saint Kitts and Nevis

Member State since 23 September 1983

Address: Permanent Mission of Saint Kitts and Nevis
to the United Nations
414 East 75th Street, 5th Floor
New York, N.Y. 10021

Telephone: (212) 535-1234

Telefax: (212) 535-6854

e-mail: sknmission@aol.com

Correspondence: English

National holiday: 19 September
Independence Day

H.E. Mr. Delano Frank **Bart**
Ambassador Extraordinary and Plenipotentiary
Permanent Representative (DPC: 30 November 2006)

Mr. Samuel Alharjai **Berridge**
Counsellor

Ms. Ghislaine **Williams**
First Secretary
Mr. Sylvester Clarke

Ms. Nyian **Farrell**
Second Secretary

Ms. Thouvia **France**
Third Secretary

Saint Lucia

Address: Permanent Mission of Saint Lucia
to the United Nations
800 Second Avenue, 5th Floor
New York, N.Y. 10017

Telephone: (212) 697-9360, -9361

Telefax: (212) 697-4993

e-mail: info@stluciamission.org

Correspondence: English

National holiday: 22 February
Independence Day

H.E. Ms. Menissa **Rambally**
Ambassador Extraordinary and Plenipotentiary
Permanent Representative (DPC: 6 June 2012)

H.E. Mr. Aziz **Debbagh**
Ambassador (Economic Development and Foreign Relations)

Ms. Kimberly K. **Louis**
First Secretary

Ms. Maria **Jean Baptiste**
Second Secretary

Saint Vincent and the Grenadines

Member State since 16 September 1980

Address: Permanent Mission of Saint Vincent and the Grenadines to the United Nations
800 Second Avenue, Suite 400F
New York, N.Y. 10017

Telephone: (212) 599-0950, -0955

Telefax: (212) 599-1020

e-mail: mission@svg-un.org; svgmission@gmail.com

Correspondence: English

National holiday: 27 October
Independence Day

H.E. Ms. Inga Rhonda **King**
Ambassador Extraordinary and Plenipotentiary
Permanent Representative (DPC: 13 September 2013)

Ms. Nedra P. **Miguel**
Counsellor
Deputy Permanent Representative

Ms. Isma Nicole **Richards**
Counsellor

Address: Permanent Mission of the Independent State of Samoa to the United Nations
800 Second Avenue, Suite 400J
New York, N.Y. 10017

Telephone: (212) 599-6196

Telefax: (212) 599-0797

e-mail: samoa@un.int

website: www.samoa.un.int

Correspondence: English

National holiday: 1 June
Independence Celebration Day

H.E. Mr. Ali'ioaiga Feturi **Elisaia***
Ambassador Extraordinary and Plenipotentiary
Permanent Representative (DPC: 18 September 2003)
Mrs. Maria Lei Sam-Elisaia

Mrs. Maureen Francella **Strickland-Simonet**
Counsellor
Deputy Permanent Representative
Mr. Benoît Simonet

Ms. Ida Tifitifi **Fuimaono**
First Secretary

* Ambassador Extraordinary and Plenipotentiary to the United States of America.

San Marino

Member State since 2 March 1992

Address: Permanent Mission of the Republic of San Marino to the United Nations
327 East 50th Street
New York, N.Y. 10022

Telephone: (212) 751-1234

Telefax: (212) 751-1436

e-mail: sanmarinoun@gmail.com

Correspondence: English

National holiday: 3 September

H.E. Mr. Daniele D. **Bodini**
Ambassador Extraordinary and Plenipotentiary
Permanent Representative (DPC: 9 August 2005)

Mr. Damiano **Beleffi**
Counsellor
Deputy Permanent Representative
Mrs. Hiromi Matsuzaki

Mr. Roberto **Balsimelli**
First Secretary
Mrs. Carol Balsimelli

Ms. Natascia **Bartolini**
First Secretary

Sao Tome and Principe

Member State since 16 September 1975

Address: Permanent Mission of Sao Tome and Principe
to the United Nations
675 Third Avenue, Suite 1807
New York, NY 10017

Telephone: (212) 651-8116

Telefax/phone: (212) 651-8117

e-mail: rdstppmun@gmail.com

Correspondence: French

National holiday: 12 July
Independence Day

H.E. Mr. Carlos Filomeno **Agostinho das Neves**
Ambassador Extraordinary and Plenipotentiary
Permanent Representative (DPC: 19 September 2012)
Mrs. Faustina Silva de Oliveira Cassandra das Neves

H.E. Mr. Angelo Antonio **Toriello**
Ambassador
Special Adviser

Saudi Arabia

Address: Permanent Mission of Saudi Arabia
to the United Nations
809 United Nations Plaza, 10th/11th Floors
New York, N.Y. 10017

Telephone: (212) 557-1525

Telefax: (212) 983-4895

e-mail: saudi-mission@un.int

Correspondence: English

National holiday: 23 September

H.E. Mr. Abdallah Y. **Al-Mouallimi**
Ambassador Extraordinary and Plenipotentiary
Permanent Representative (DPC: 23 June 2011)
Mrs. Sahar Haider O. Hajjar

Mr. Abdulmohsen F. A. **Alyas**
Counsellor
Deputy Permanent Representative
Mrs. Rouaa M. A. Atyah

Mr. Mohamed Bahjat Saad Kh. A **Hijazi**
Counsellor
Mrs. Manal Abdullah A. Khoja

Mr. Abdulaziz Saleh M. **AlRodiman**
Counsellor

Ms. Maisah Mohamed A. **Sobaihi**
Counsellor

Mr. Saad Abdullah N. **Al Saad**
Counsellor
Mrs. Shaima Shahwan H. Al Rizqi

Mr. Abdulaziz S. S. **Al Salloom**
First Secretary
Mrs. Haila S. S. Al Gadi

Mr. Mohammed Abdulhamid M. **Khan**
First Secretary
Mrs. Heba Mohammed Ali A. Bangash

Ms. Manal Hassan **Radwan**
First Secretary

Mr. Abdullah Khalid O. **Tawlah**
First Secretary
Mrs. Marwah Mohammed A. Bederi

Mr. Nasser M. **Al Faridi**
First Secretary
Mrs. Muna Hassan Abed

Mr. Khalid Hulayyiil M. **Alotaibi**
First Secretary
Mrs. Awatf Ghazai M. AlOsaimi

Mr. Saad Dakheel Saad **Al Sehli**
First Secretary
Mrs. Fozeyah Turki M. Al Aufi

Mr. Hassan Saeed H. **AlJomae**
First Secretary
Mrs. Ghalia Mohammad H. Jadallah

Mr. Raid Abdullah M. **AlHnaki**
Second Secretary
Mrs. Arwa Mohsen H. AlAwajy

Mr. Abdulrahman A. A. **AlAbdulwahab**
Second Secretary

Ms. Rania Talal A. **Abdulbaqi**
Second Secretary

Mr. Dahham Saad SH. **Al Muttairi**
Third Secretary
Mrs. Jamila Yahya A. Al Salim

Mr. Abdullah Mohammed A. **AlGhunim**
Third Secretary
Mrs. Deemah Abdulrahman A. AlMarshoud

Mr. Abdulrahman M. R. **Jamalhariri**
Third Secretary
Mrs. Sarah Abdullah D. Al Hajri

Mr. Hekmat Mohammed N. **AlSaeed**
Third Secrteary
Mrs. Zubaida Hamed M. Abo Suliman

Mr. Majid M. Y. **Alharbi**
Attaché
Mrs. Raniah Abdullah M. Zahran

H.H. Princess Lubna **Al Saud**
Attaché

Mr. Abdulaziz A. **Al Mughamis**
Attaché
Mrs. Ibtisam Saud A. Alsayari

Mr. Walid Saad Abdulrahman **Al Bawardi**
Attaché

Mr. Ahmed Abdulaziz A. **AlTuwaijri**
Attaché

H.H. Princess Nour Bint Bandar Bin Mohammed Bin Abdulrahman **Al Saud**
Attaché

Ms. Farah Abdulaziz I. **AlSweel**
Attaché

Mr. Faisal A.M. **Jedea**
Attaché

Mr. Mohammed Awad S. **Mosalim**
Attaché
Mrs. Sahar Suwailem I. Nasser

Mr. Yousef Mohammed A. **AlHamdan**
Attaché
Mrs. Amal Abdullah A. AlHoshan

Mr. Suliman Abdullah Saleh **AlNafea**
Attaché
Mrs. Hessah Homoud Mohammed AlNassar

Address: Permanent Mission of the Republic of Senegal to the United Nations
747 Third Avenue 21st Floor (b. 46th & 47th Street)
New York, N.Y. 10017

Telephone: (212) 517-9030, -9031, -9032

Telefax: (212) 517-3032

e-mail: senegal.mission@yahoo.fr

Correspondence: French

National holiday: 4 April
Independence Day

H.E. Mr. Fodé **Seck**
Ambassador Extraordinary and Plenipotentiary
Permanent Representative (DPC: 19 September 2014)
Mrs. Marieme Cisse

H.E. Mr. Gorgui **Ciss**
Ambassador
Deputy Permanent Representative

Mr. Barthelemy **Diouf**
Minister Counsellor
Military Adviser

Mrs. Fatou Gaye **Diagne**
First Counsellor

Mr. Mamadou **Mbodj**
First Counsellor
Mrs. Matilde Diatta Mbodj

Mr. Mame Oumar **Thiaw**
First Counsellor
Mrs. Mhayang Dieng Thiaw

Mr. Isidor Marcel **Sene**
First Counsellor

Mr. Pierre **Faye**
First Counsellor

Mr. Cheikh Tidiane **Deme**
First Counsellor

Mrs. Khady Mbacké **Diop**
Second Counsellor
Mr. Khalilou Diop

Mr. Papa Gallo **Ndiaye**
Second Counsellor

Mr. Papa Baba **Guisse**
Second Counsellor

Mr. Alioune **Lo**
First Secretary

Mr. Paul Etienne **Ndiaye**
First Secretary

Ms. Ndeye Oumy **Gueye**
First Secretary

Mr. Babacar **Diouf**
Second Secretary
Mrs. Khadidiatou Seck Diouf

Mrs. Aissatou Sankharé **Dembele**
Second Secretary

Mrs. Djimith Faye **Diarra**
Second Secretary
Mr. Babacar Diarra

Mrs. Khoudia Ndiaye Bousso **Cisse**
Second Secretary

Mr. Paul **Mendy**
Attaché
Mrs. Christiane Mendy

Address:	Permanent Mission of the Republic of Serbia to the United Nations 854 Fifth Avenue New York, N.Y. 10065
Telephone:	(212) 879-8700, (646)490-7067
Telefax:	(212) 879-8705
e-mail:	info@serbiamissionun.org
website:	www.un.int/serbia
Correspondence:	English
National holiday:	15 February Day of Statehood

Ext. 230	H.E. Mr. Milan **Milanović** Ambassador Extraordinary and Plenipotentiary Permanent Representative (DPC: 19 August 2013) Mrs. Maja Milanović

Ext. 231	H.E. Mrs. Katarina **Lalic Smajevic** Ambassador Deputy Permanent Representative Mr. Aleksandar Smajevic
Ext. 250	Mr. Boris **Holovka** Minister Counsellor Mrs. Slađana Holovka
Ext. 237	Mr. Radiša **Grujić** Minister Counsellor
Ext. 239	Ms. Ana **Ilić** First Counsellor
Ext. 229	Ms. Lidija **Bubanja** Counsellor
Ext. 233	Ms. Marija **Perišić** First Secretary
	Ms. Marina **Nikodijevic** Third Secretary
	Mr. Zoran **Zdravkovic** Attaché Mrs. Milena Zdravkovic
	Mr. Dragan **Bosković** Attaché
Ext. 254	Mr. Dejan **Bucalo** Attaché Mrs. Violeta Bucalo

Ext. 254	Mr. Djordje **Bogdanović** Attaché
Ext. 235	Colonel Milan **Ranković** Minister Counsellor Military Adviser Mrs. Danijela Ranković

Address: Permanent Mission of the Republic
of Seychelles to the United Nations
800 Second Avenue, Suite 400G
New York, N.Y. 10017

Telephone: (212) 972-1785

Telefax: (212) 972-1786

e-mail: seychelles@un.int , seychellesmissionun@gmail.com

Correspondence: English

National holiday: 18 June
Constitution Day

H.E. Ms. Marie-Louise **Potter**
Ambassador Extraordinary and Plenipotentiary
Permanent Representative (DPC: 5 September 2012)
Mr. Clement Alfred Herman Potter

H.E. Mr. Ronald Jean **Jumeau**
Ambassador (Climate Change and SIDS Issues)

Mr. Thomas Selby **Pillay**
Minister Counsellor

Ms. Wendy Guilian **Isnard**
Second Secretary

Ms. Deborah Jane **Cholmondeley**
Attaché

Address:	Permanent Mission of the Republic of Sierra Leone to the United Nations 245 East 49th Street New York, N.Y. 10017
Telephone:	(212) 688-1656, -6748
Telefax:	(212) 688-4924
e-mail:	sierraleone@un.int
Correspondence:	English
National holiday:	27 April Independence Day

688-4097 H.E. Mr. Vandi Chidi **Minah**
Ambassador Extraordinary and Plenipotentiary
Permanent Representative (DPC: 18 September 2013)
Mrs. Rosemarie Minah

H.E. Mr. Amadu **Koroma**
Ambassador
Deputy Permanent Representative
Mrs. Seray Koroma

Mr. Leroy **Kanu**
Minister Plenipotentiary

Mr. Alhusine Mohammed **Sesay**
Minister Counsellor
Mrs. Margaret Y. Sesay

Mr. Saidu **Nallo**
Counsellor
Mrs. Augusta Yeawa Nallo

Mr. Franklyn Brima **Fawundu**
Counsellor
Mrs. Elfreda Kadie Brima-Fawundu

Mr. Vahfomba Foday **Bawoh**
Counsellor (Finance)
Mrs. Mariama Bawoh

Mr. Sheku **Mesali**
Counsellor
Mrs. Bithadon Alice Mesali

Colonel Muana Brima **Massaquoi**
Counsellor
Military Adviser
Mrs. Betty Massaquoi

Mr. Mohamed Lamin **Khan**
First Secretary
Mrs. Emmencia A.C. Khan

Mr. Saifu **George**
Third Secretary
Mrs. Musu Eleen George

Address: Permanent Mission of the Republic of Singapore to the United Nations
318 East 48th Street
New York, N.Y. 10017

Telephone: (212) 826-0840

Telefax: (212) 826-2964

e-mail: singapore@un.int

website: www.mfa.gov.sg/newyork

Correspondence: English

National holiday: 9 August

Ext. 604	H.E. Ms. Karen **Tan** Ambassador Extraordinary and Plenipotentiary Permanent Representative (DPC: 19 August 2013)
Ext. 506	Mr. Joseph **Teo** Choon Heng Minister Counsellor Deputy Permanent Representative Mrs. Jessica Jayeswari Letchamanan
Ext. 405	Colonel **Foo** Khee Loon Counsellor Military Advisor Mrs. Lee Hoa Clara NG
Ext. 512	Mr. Ken **Siah** Counsellor
Ext. 511	Ms. Natalie Y. **Morris-Sharma** Counsellor (Legal) Mr. Neeraj Dylan Sharma
Ext. 119	Ms. Winnie Ting Ting **Tan** Counsellor (Administration)
Ext. 513	Ms. Adele **Li** Wei First Secretary
Ext. 514	Ms. Seema Gail **Parkash** First Secretary
Ext. 120	Ms. Felicia **Low** Attaché (Administration)

Address: Permanent Mission of the Slovak Republic
to the United Nations
801 Second Avenue, 12th Floor
New York, N.Y. 10017

Telephone: (212) 286-8880; -8401; -8418; -8452 (General Numbers)
(212) 286-8476 (Permanent Representative's Office)
(212) 286-8451 (Military Adviser's Office)

Telefax: (212) 286-8419 (Permanent Representative's Office)
(212) 286-8451 (Military Adviser's Office)

e-mail: un.newyork@mzv.sk

website www.mzv.sk/unnewyork

Correspondence: English

National holiday: 1 September
Constitution Day

Ext. 101 H.E. Mr. František **Ružička**
Ambassador Extraordinary and Plenipotentiary
Permanent Representative (DPC: 5 September 2012)
Mrs. Ingrid Ružičková

Ext. 128 Mr. Peter **Agha**
First Secretary

Ext. 105 Mr. Michal **Komada**
First Secretary

Ext. 134 Mr. Peter **Selepec**
First Secretary

Ext. 136 Mrs. Valéria **Zolcerová**
Second Secretary
Mr. Mikulaš Zolcer

Ext. 104 Mr. Slavomir **Kantor**
Third Secretary
Mrs. Lucia Kantorová

Ext. 106 Mr. Miroslav **Halinkovic**
Attaché
Mrs. Karin Halinkovičová

Ext. 109 Mr. František **Boško**
Attaché

Address:	Permanent Mission of the Republic of Slovenia to the United Nations 630 Third Avenue, 20th Floor New York, N.Y. 10017
Telephone:	(212) 370-3007
Telefax:	(212) 370-1824
e-mail:	slovenia@un.int
website:	www.un.int/slovenia/
Correspondence:	English
National holiday:	25 June

Ext. 11	H.E. Mr. Andrej **Logar** Ambassador Extraordinary and Plenipotentiary Permanent Representative (DPC: 3 September 2013) Mrs. Cvetka Logar
Ext. 18	Mrs. Martina **Skok** Minister Counsellor
Ext. 13	Ms. Barbara **Kremžar** Minister Counsellor
Ext. 12	Mr. Matej **Marn** Counsellor Deputy Permanent Representative Mrs. Ajda Marn
Ext. 19	Mrs. Saša **Jurecko** First Secretary Mr. Andraž Naglič
Ext. 34	Mrs. Urša **Ponikvar** Third Secretary Mr. Klemen Ponikvar
Ext. 30	Major General Dobran **Božič** First Counsellor Military Advise

Solomon Islands

Member State since 19 September 1978

Address:	Permanent Mission of Solomon Islands to the United Nations 800 Second Avenue, Suite 400L New York, N.Y. 10017-4709
Telephone:	(212) 599-6192, -6193
Telefax:	(212) 661-8925
e-mail:	simun@solomons.com
Correspondence:	English
National holiday:	7 July

H.E. Mr. Collin D. **Beck**
Ambassador Extraordinary and Plenipotentiary
Permanent Representative (DPC: 26 November 2003)
Mrs. Helen Beck

Mrs. Helen **Beck**
Counsellor
H.E. Mr. Collin D. Beck

Mrs. Vanessa M. **Kenilorea**
Third Secretary
Mr. Peter Kenilorea

Address:	Permanent Mission of the Federal Republic of Somalia to the United Nations 425 East 61st Street, Suite 702 New York, N.Y. 10065
Telephone:	(212) 688-9410, -5046
Telefax:	(212) 759-0651
e-mail:	somalia@un.int
Correspondence:	English
National holiday:	1 July

H.E. Mr. Elmi Ahmed **Duale**
Ambassador Extraordinary and Plenipotentiary
Permanent Representative (DPC: 18 October 2005)
Mrs. Ashura Hilal Duale

Address:	Permanent Mission of the Republic of South Africa to the United Nations 333 East 38th Street, 9th Floor New York, N.Y. 10016
Telephone:	(212) 213-5583
Telefax:	(212) 692-2498
e-mail:	pmun.newyork@dirco.gov.za
Correspondence:	English
National holiday:	27 April Freedom Day

692-2465 H.E. Mr. Jeremiah Nyamane Kingsley **Mamabolo**
Ambassador Extraordinary and Plenipotentiary
Permanent Representative (DPC: 13 March 2013)
Mrs. Alenore Cecilia Mamabolo

692-2466 Mr. Ephraim Leshala **Mminele**
Minister Plenipotentiary
Deputy Permanent Representative
Mrs. Julia Ngokoana Mminele

692-2484 Mr. Petrus Sipho **Seakamela**
Minister Counsellor (Political Affairs)

692-2496 Mr. Thembela Osmond **Ngculu**
Counsellor (Sustainable Development & Climate Change)
Mrs. Bomikazi Wendy Ngculu

692-2471 Mr. Mlungisi Cedrick **Mbalati**
Counsellor (Political Affairs)
Mrs. Hershney Mbalati

692-2450 Ms. Bahiyyih Angelia Mpho **Masetlha**
Counsellor (Political Affairs)

692-2420 Mr. Albertus Johannes **Laubscher**
Counsellor (Corporate Services)
Mrs. Irina Evgenyevna Laubscher

692-2402 Ms. Karen **Lingenfelder**
Counsellor (Political Affairs)

692-2414 Mr. David Robin **Wensley**
Counsellor (Political Affairs)
Mrs. Ronel Wensley

692-2460 Mr. Raymond Thulane **Nyembe**
Counsellor (Political Affairs)

692-2473 Mr. Thembile Elphus **Joyini**
Counsellor (Legal Affairs)

692-2459	Mr. Wouter Hofmeyr **Zaayman** Counsellor (Political Affairs) Mrs. Izabela Zaayman
692-2458	Mr. Lyle Patrick **Davidson** Counsellor (Political Affairs)
692-2424	Mr. Tshamano Combrick **Milubi** First Secretary (Political Affairs) Mrs. Vhonani Tryphinah Milubi
692-2425	Ms. Nichola Nokulunga **Sabelo** First Secretary (Political Affairs)
692-2452	Ms. Karen Lizelle **Burger** First Secretary (Political Affairs) Ms. Mercia Nelmarie Schoeman
692-2464	Mr. Lawrence Xolani **Malawane** First Secretary (Political Affairs)
692-2497	Ms. Mmalebone Catherine **Mmekoe** First Secretary (Administration)
692-2495	Mr. Oyama **Mgobozi** First Secretary (Political Affairs)
692-2474	Mr. Simon Poni **Marobe** First Secretary (Political Affairs) Mrs. Linda Jabulisiwe Marobe
692-2457	Mr. Lesetla Andreas **Teffo** First Secretary (Political Affairs) Mrs. Morongoa Francina Teffo
692-2446	Mr. Mbulungeni Sydney **Muenda** First Secretary (Political Affairs) Mrs. Mpho Cathrine Muenda
692-2466	Ms. Faith Thandi **Zondo** Third Secretary (Administration)
692-2491	Ms. Neo Theressa **Moroeng** Third Secretary
692-2465	Miss Nozipho **Ncobeni** Third Secretary
692-2454	Colonel Mongezi Michael **Kweta** Attaché (Defence) Military Adviser Mrs. Nosipho Claudia Kweta

Address:	Permanent Mission of the Republic of South Sudan to the United Nations 336 East 45th Street, 5th Floor New York, N.Y. 10017
Telephone:	(212) 937-7977
Telefax:	(212) 867-9242
e-mail:	info@rssun-nyc.org
Correspondence:	English
National holiday:	9 July

Ext. 2008	H.E. Mr. Francis Mading **Deng** Ambassador Extraordinary and Plenipotentiary Permanent Representative (DPC: 19 September 2012) Mrs. Dorothy Deng
Ext. 2003	Mr. Amanuel Yoanes **Ajawin** Counsellor
	Mr. Emmanuel Pothwei **Benjamin** First Secretary
Ext. 2012	Mr. Agok Anyar **Madut** Second Secretary
	Mr. Oryem Jacob **Opoka** Second Secretary Mrs. Paska Disan Ojwee Olweny
Ext. 2011	Ms. Savia Akujo Henry **Minga** Third Secretary
Ext. 2009	Ms. Aliyah Akur Ago **Wek** Third Secretary
	Mr.Bak Barnaba Chol **Bak** Third Secretary
	Mr. Marious Ben **Angu** Attaché (Financial Affairs) Mrs. Rose Juan Andrew Poggo
	Ms. Hellen Rita **Merekaje** Attaché (Administrative Affairs) Mr. John Okwera Lawery Pai

Spain

Address:	Permanent Mission of Spain to the United Nations One Dag Hammarskjöld Plaza 245 East 47th Street, 36th Floor New York, N.Y. 10017
Telephone:	(212) 661-1050
Telefax:	(212) 949-7247; 697-8690
e-mail:	Rep.nuevayorkonu@maec.es
website:	www.spainun.org
Correspondence:	Spanish
National holiday:	12 October

294-2569	H.E. Mr. Román **Oyarzun Marchesi** Ambassador Extraordinary and Plenipotentiary Permanent Representative (DPC: 9 January 2014) Mrs. Begoña Allendesalazar Ruiz de Arana
Ext. 309	H.E. Mr. Juan Manuel **González de Linares Palou** Ambassador Deputy Permanent Representative Mrs. Claire Cêtre
Ext. 342	Mr. Fernando **Fernández-Arias Minuesa** Minister Counsellor Mr. Neil John Mann
	Mr. Ignacio **Díaz de la Guardia Beuno** Minister Counsellor Mrs. María Palacios Palacios
Ext. 324	Mr. Francisco Javier **Gasso Matoses** Minister Counsellor Mrs. María Teresa Soler Rodenas
Ext. 322	Colonel Luis **Viñas Casado** Counsellor Military Adviser Mrs. Eva María Talens Alfonso
Ext. 317	Mr. Florentino **Sotomayor Basabe** Counsellor Mrs. Maria Teresa Suarez Martínez
Ext. 356	Mr. José Antonio **Latorre Remón** Counsellor Deputy Military Adviser Mrs. María Esther Laudo Tesan
	Mr. Félix **Manjón Martín** Counsellor

Ext. 320	Mr. José Javier **Gutiérrez Blanco Navarrete** Counsellor Ms. Rebekah Kosinski
	Mrs. María **Palacios Palacios** Counsellor Mr. Ignacio Díaz de la Guardia Beuno
Ext. 321	Mr. Alberto Pablo **de la Calle García** Counsellor
Ext. 305	Mr. Luis Francisco **Martínez Montes** Counsellor Mrs. Masae Muraoka
Ext. 357	Mr. Francisco Javier **García-Larrache** Counsellor
Ext. 334	Ms. Alejandra **del Río Novo** Counsellor
	Mr. Agustín **Rebollo Fuente** Counsellor Mrs. María Victoria Arnal Martínez
	Mrs. Marta **Navarro Cuellas** Counsellor Mr. Miguel Angel Palacios Fernández
Ext. 323	Ms. Ana Esmeralda **Martínez Saez** Counsellor
Ext. 350	Mr. Juan Antonio **Rios Reviejo** Counsellor
Ext. 319	Mr. Manuel **Pablos López** Counsellor Mrs. Ana María Villen Otero
Ext. 327	Mr. Antonio **Sánchez Gil** Counsellor (Military) Mrs. Maria Estela García Berzas
Ext. 333	Ms. Carmen **Castiella Ruiz de Velasco** Counsellor
Ext. 340	Mr. Nicolás **Cimarra Etchenique** First Secretary
Ext. 335	Ms. Victoria **Ortega Gutiérrez** First Secretary Mr. Eduardo Martínez Moriano
	Ms. Maria Luisa **Marteles Gutiérrez del Alamo** First Secretary
	Mr. Carlos **López Ortíz** First Secretary

Address: Permanent Mission of the Democratic Socialist Republic of Sri Lanka to the United Nations
820 Second Avenue, 2nd Floor
New York, N.Y. 10017

Telephone: (212) 986-7040

Telefax: (212) 986-1838

e-mail: mail@slmission.com

website: www.slmission.com

Correspondence: English

National holiday: 4 February
Independence Day

H.E. Mr. Amrith Rohan **Perera**
Ambassador Extraordinary and Plenipotentiary
Permanent Representative (DPC: 22 April 2015)

Mr. Niluka Prabhath **Kadurugamuwa**
Counsellor
Mrs. Kamani Priyanga Gunawardana

Ms. Lanka Varuni **Muthukumarana**
First Secretary

Mr. Madhuka Sanjaya **Wickramarachchige**
First Secretary
Mrs. Dhaneera Manjaree Wijesinghe Ekanayaka

Mr. Bothalage Bede Herman **Fernando**
Attaché (Administration)
Mrs. Shanuka Kumudu Ratnayake

Mrs. Yanthrawaduge Mihiri Hemarani **Fernando**
Attaché (Accounts)

Address: Permanent Mission of the Republic
of the Sudan to the United Nations
305 East 47th Street
3 Dag Hammarskjöld Plaza, 4th Floor
New York, N.Y. 10017

Telephone: (212) 573-6033

Telefax: (212) 573-6160

e-mail: sudan@sudanmission.org

Correspondence: English

National holiday: 1 January
Independence Day

H.E. ...
Ambassador Extraordinary and Plenipotentiary
Permanent Representative (DPC: ...)

H.E. Mr. Hassan Hamid **Hassan**
Ambassador
Deputy Permanent Representative
Mrs. Nagla Mohamed

Mr. Elhafiz Eisa Abdalla **Adam**
Minister Plenipotentiary

Mr. Idrees Mohammed Ali Mohammed **Saeed**
Counsellor
Mrs. Hanan Siliman Ahmed Mohamed

Mr. Khalid **M. Osman Sid Ahmed Mohammed Ali**
Counsellor
Mrs. Aisha Ibrahim Ahmed Omer

Mr. Mohamed Ibrahim Mohamed **Elbahi**
Counsellor
Mrs. Mawahib Abdelrazig Mohamed Elbahi

Mr. Hassan Elsiddig Ahmed **Abdalhay**
Counsellor
Mrs. Selwa Abdalsadig Mohammed Abdallah

Mr. Mustafa Elhossein **Elshareef**
First Secretary
Ms. Rihab Mahmoud Elsayed Suliman

Ms. Rwayda Izzeldin Hamid **Elhassan**
First Secretary

Ms. Shafaq Abdaljaleel Jubartallah **Mokwar**
Third Secretary

Mr. Almustafa Mubarak Hussein **Rahamtalla**
Third Secretary
Mrs. Allara Ali Osman Mohamed

Mr. Sami Elzein Elamin **Mohammed**
Attaché (Administration)

Mr. Mohamed Abdalmoniem Mohamed **Hussaien**
Attaché (Administration)
Mrs. Hadeel Mohie Eldin Abuelabass

Mr. Mohammed Abdalla Ali **Mohammed**
Attaché (Finance)
Mrs. Nidal Alsaid Mohamedahmed Alsayadi

Address: Permanent Mission of the Republic of Suriname to the United Nations
866 United Nations Plaza, Suite 320
New York, N.Y. 10017-1822

Telephone: (212) 826-0660, -0661, -0662, -0663

Telefax: (212) 980-7029

e-mail: suriname@un.int

Correspondence: English

National holiday: 25 November
Independence Day

H.E. Mr. Henry Leonard **Mac-Donald**
Ambassador Extraordinary and Plenipotentiary
Permanent Representative (DPC: 16 August 2007)
Mrs. Hyacinth Mac-Donald

Mrs. Kitty **Sweeb**
Counsellor
Deputy Permanent Representative

Mr. Raymond Harold **Landveld**
Counsellor
Mrs. Rinalda Landveld

Ms. Miriam **MacIntosh**
First Secretary

Mr. Furgil Harry **Pinas**
Attaché

Address: Permanent Mission of the Kingdom
of Swaziland to the United Nations
408 East 50th Street
New York, N.Y. 10022

Telephone: (212) 371-8910, -8911, -8775; mobile: (917) 517-0589

Telefax: (212) 754-2755

e-mail: swaziland@un.int; swazinymission@yahoo.com

Correspondence: English

National holiday: 6 September
Independence Day

H.E. Mr. Zwelethu **Mnisi**
Ambassador Extraordinary and Plenipotentiary
Permanent Representative (DPC: 24 August 2010)
Mrs. Lucia Nonhlanhla Mnisi

Mrs. Antoinette Fanie **Henwood-Ronald**
First Secretary
Mr. Sibusiso Clive Ronald

Mr. Vulindlela Simphiwe **Kunene**
First Secretary
Mrs. Welile Thembelihle Mathonsi

Mr. Mduduzi Kieth Kenneth **Mbingo**
First Secretary
Mrs. Zanele Pinky Mbingo

Mr. Sonnyboy Sandziso **Hlatshwako**
Third Secretary
Mrs. Nompumelelo Goodness Hlatshwako

Mrs. Thabsile Yvonne **Tshabalala**
Attaché

Sweden

Address:	Permanent Mission of Sweden to the United Nations One Dag Hammarskjöld Plaza 885 Second Avenue, 46th Floor New York, N.Y. 10017-2201
Telephone:	(212) 583-2500
Telefax:	(212) 583-2549
e-mail:	sweden@un.int
website:	www.swedenabroad.com/un
Social Media:	Twitter: @SwedenUN
Correspondence:	English
National holiday:	6 June

583-2501 H.E. Mr. Olof **Skoog**
Ambassador Extraordinary and Plenipotentiary
Permanent Representative (DPC: 10 March 2015)

583-2503 H.E. Mr. Per **Thöresson**
Ambassador
Deputy Permanent Representative
Ms. Dorkas Thöresson

583-2509 Mr. Magnus **Lennartsson**
Minister (Economic and Social Affairs)
Ms. Izumi Nakamitsu

583-2511 Mr. Gunnar **Aldén**
Counsellor (Political Affairs)
Ms. Sara Aldén

583-2507 Mr. Andreas **Hilmersson**
Counsellor (Economic and Social Affairs)
Mr. Laurent Oster

583-2517 Mr. Carl **Orrenius Skau**
Counsellor (Electoral and Political Affairs)
Ms. Lisa Orrenius Skau

583-2519 Ms. Gunilla **Dahlin**
Councellor, Head of Chancery

583-2512 Mr. Nicolas **Weeks**
Counsellor (Political Affairs)
Ms. Le Zhang

583-2516 Mr. Frederik **Nivaeus**
Counsellor (Political Affairs)

583-2536	Mr. Daniel **Peterson** First Secretary (Economic and Social Affairs) Ms. Nadia Boussaid Peterson
583-2510	Ms. Karin **Nilsson Snellman** First Secretary (Economic and Social Affairs) Mr. Claes Nilsson
583-2506	Ms. Johanna **Nilsson** First Secretary (Human Rights and Social Affairs) Mr. David Karlsson
583-2535	Mr. Frederick **Lee-Olsson** First Secretary (Political Affairs)
583-2520	Ms. Angela **Kennedy** Second Secretary Mr. Carl Kennedy
583-2523	Ms. Berit **Lindberg** Second Secretary (Archives) Mr. Mattias Lindberg
583-2513	Ms. Hanna **Stenberg** Second Secretary (Economic and Social Affairs) Mr. Karl Jonas Poulsen

---

583-2534	Colonel Claes **Naréus** Counsellor Military Adviser Ms. Marie-Louise Naréus
583-2540	Mr. Dan **Peterson** Counsellor Police Adviser Ms. Helene Diyabanza Peterson

Switzerland

Address:	Permanent Mission of Switzerland to the United Nations 633 Third Avenue, 29th Floor New York, N.Y. 10017
Telephone:	(212) 286-1540
Telefax:	(212) 286-1555
e-mail:	nyc.vertretung-un@eda.admin.ch
website:	www.eda.admin.ch/missny
Correspondence:	French
National holiday:	1 August

Ext. 1117	H.E. Mr. Paul **Seger** Ambassador Extraordinary and Plenipotentiary Permanent Representative (DPC: 4 June 2010) Mrs. Colette Seger-Schneiter

---

Ext. 1126	Mr. Olivier Marc **Zehnder** Minister Deputy Permanent Representative Mrs. Frederique Zehnder-Merot
Ext. 1154	Mrs. Tatjana **von Steiger Weber** Minister Mr. Alexandre Weber
Ext. 1144	Mr. Adrian Michael **Sollberger** Counsellor
Ext. 1128	Mr. Frédéric Marc-André **Tissot-Daguette** Counsellor Military Adviser Mrs. Laura Anne Ruhnke Tissot Daguette
Ext. 1152	Mr. Cyril Gabriel Telva **Prissette** Counsellor
Ext. 1154	Mr. Nicolas Manuel **Randin** Counsellor Mrs. Cristina Martinez Randin
Ext. 1127	Ms. Nathalie Véronique **Chuard** First Secretary
Ext. 1137	Ms. Beate **Elsaesser** First Secretary
Ext. 1140	Mr. Christoph **Fuchs** First Secretary
Ext. 1143	Mrs. Christine Elisabeth **Loew** First Secretary

Ext. 1119	Ms. Maja **Messmer Mokhtar** First Secretary Mr. Jamil Mokhtar
Ext. 1114	Ms. Eliane **Kiener** First Secretary Christian Georg Maeder
Ext. 1151	Mrs. Damaris **Carnal** First Secretary Mr. Jonathan Mueller
Ext. 1153	Mr. Matthias **Dettling** First Secretary Mrs. Cari Dettling
Ext.1145	Mr. Matteo **Fachinotti** Second Secretary Mrs. Se Young Jang
Ext. 1125	Mrs. Cynthia **Kunz** Attaché Mr. Michel Kunz
Ext. 1117	Mrs. Elisabeth **Karppinen-Hauser** Attaché Mr. Juhani Karppinen
Ext. 1212	Mr. Gérald Alexis **Pachoud** Attaché Mrs. France Jaton Pachoud
Ext. 1101	Mr. Alfred **Boeni** Assistant Attaché Mrs. Monica Boeni

Syrian Arab Republic

Member State since 24 October 1945

Address: Permanent Mission of the Syrian Arab Republic to the United Nations
820 Second Avenue, 15th Floor
New York, N.Y. 10017

Telephone: (212) 661-1313

Telefax: (212) 983-4439

e-mail: exesec.syria@gmail.com

Correspondence: English

National holiday: 17 April
Independence Day

H.E. Mr. Bashar **Ja'afari**
Ambassador Extraordinary and Plenipotentiary
Permanent Representative (DPC: 31 July 2006)
Mrs. Shohreh Eskandari

Mr. Ali Ahmad **Haydar**
Counsellor
Mrs. Rasha Mouzahem

Mr. Koussay Abduljabbar **Aldahhak**
Counsellor
Mrs. Hala Medhat Badr

Mr. Asaad **Ibrahim**
First Secretary

Mr. Ihab **Hamed**
Second Secretary
Mrs. Amani Shonshou

Ms. Monia **Alsaleh**
Second Secretary

Mr. Ismail Bassel **Ayzouki**
Third Secretary
Mrs. Dima Al Kahwaje

Mr. Rabee **Jawhara**
Third Secretary

Mr. Muhanad **Haydar**
Attaché

Tajikistan

Member State since 2 March 1992

Address:	Permanent Mission of the Republic of Tajikistan to the United Nations 216 East 49th Street, 5th Floor New York, N.Y. 10017
Telephone:	(212) 207-3315
Telefax:	(212) 207-3855
e-mail:	tajikistan@un.int; tajikistanun@aol.com
Website:	www.tajikistan-un.org
Correspondence:	English
National holiday:	9 September Independence Day

H.E. Mr. Mahmadamin **Mahmadaminov**
Envoy Extraordinary and Minister Plenipotentiary
Permanent Representative (DPC: 25 February 2014)
Mrs. Shodigul Asaulova

Mr. Lukmon **Isomatov**
Counsellor

Mr. Bilol **Bobojon**
Attaché
Mrs. Khojarmoh Abdulloeva

Mr. Bakhtiyor **Muhamedjanov**
Attaché

Address:	Permanent Mission of Thailand to the United Nations 351 East 52nd Street New York, N.Y. 10022
Telephone:	(212) 754-2230
Telefax:	(212) 688-3029
e-mail:	thailand@un.int
Correspondence:	English
National holiday:	5 December Celebration of the birthday anniversary of His Majesty the King

---

Ext. 154 H.E. Mr. Virachai **Plasai**
Ambassador Extraordinary and Plenipotentiary
Permanent Representative (DPC: 10 March 2015)
Mrs. Elizabeth Plasai

Ext. 146 H.E. Mr. Chayapan **Bamrungphong**
Ambassador
Deputy Permanent Representative
Mrs. Ganniga Bamrungphong

Ext. 135 Colonel Orgrob **Amarachgul**
Minister
Military Adviser
Mrs. Thanwalai Amarachgul

Ext. 139 Mr. Paisan **Rupanichkij**
Minister Counsellor
Mrs. Puangporn Rupanichkij

Ext. 130 Ms. Jirusaya **Birananda**
Minister Counsellor
Head of Chancery

Ext. 153 Ms. Sirithon **Wairatpanij**
Counsellor

Ext. 152 Ms. Chonvipat **Changtrakul**
First Secretary
Mr. Chaiwut Gamonpilas

Ext. 138 Mrs. Pimpida Ravirat **Thanarat**
First Secretary

Ext. 148 Mr. Thaweechot **Tatiyapermpoon**
First Secretary

Ext. 140 Mr. Vachara **Pawutiyapong**
First Secretary

Ext. 141	Ms. Thanavon **Pamaranon** Second Secretary
Ext. 128	Mr. Nawin **Chirapant** Second Secretary
Ext. 151	Mrs. Leena **Bordeenithikasem** Attaché (Administrative/Technical) Mr. Chanchai Bordeenithikasem
Ext. 150	Mrs. Ploenpit **Phongphan** Attaché (Administrative/Technical)

The former Yugoslav Republic of Macedonia

Member State since 8 April 1993

Address: Permanent Mission of the former Yugoslav Republic of Macedonia to the United Nations
866 United Nations Plaza, Suite 517
New York, N.Y. 10017

Telephone: (212) 308-8504, -8723

Telefax: (212) 308-8724

e-mail: newyork@mfa.gov.mk

Website: www.missions.gov.mk/un-newyork

Correspondence: English

National holiday: 2 August

H.E. Mr. Vasile **Andonoski**
Ambassador Extraordinary and Plenipotentiary
Permanent Representative (DPC: 14 March 2014)

 Member State since 27 September 2002

Address: Permanent Mission of the Democratic
Republic of Timor-Leste to the United Nations
866 United Nations Plaza, Suite 441
New York, N.Y. 10017

Telephone: (212) 759-3675

Telefax: (212) 759-4196

e-mail: timor-leste@un.int

Correspondence: English

National holiday: 20 May

H.E. Mrs. Sofia **Mesquita Borges**
Ambassador Extraordinary and Plenipotentiary
Permanent Representative (DPC: 4 March 2010)
Mr. Hansjoerg Walter Strohmeyer

Mr. Almerio **do Carmo Vieira**
Second Secretary
Mrs. Genoveva Delita Pereira Nunes

Address: Permanent Mission of Togo to the United Nations
336 East 45th Street
New York, N.Y. 10017

Telephone: (212) 490-3455, -3456

Telefax: (212) 983-6684

Correspondence: French

e-mail: togo@un.int; togo.mission@yahoo.fr

National holiday: 27 April
National Day

H.E. Mr. Kodjo **Menan**
Ambassador Extraordinary and Plenipotentiary
Permanent Representative (DPC: 25 June 2009)
Mrs. Ayawavi Attoessi Menan

Mrs. Kouméalo **Anate Balli**
Minister Counsellor

Mr. Waké **Yagninim**
Second Counsellor
Mrs. Hodalo Mariki

Mr. Edem Komi **Amoudokpo**
First Secretary
Mrs. Edem Elodie Koffi-Agomu

Mr. Kodjovi **Dosseh**
First Secretary
Mrs. Damyal Bombona

Mr. Norbert Komlanvi **Guidiglo**
Attaché
Mrs. Mamouwézim Wiyao

Colonel Wiyaoh Blakimwe **Balli**
Attaché (Defense)

Mrs. Amebo Essi Dziedzom **Samtou Adjogli**
Attaché
Mr. Kokou Justin Adjogli

Address:	Permanent Mission of the Kingdom of Tonga to the United Nations 250 East 51st Street New York, N.Y. 10022
Telephone:	(917) 369-1025
Telefax:	(917) 369-1024
e-mail:	tongaunmission@gmail.com
Correspondence:	English
National holiday:	4 November

H.E. Mr. Mahe'uli'uli Sandhurst **Tupouniua**
Ambassador Extraordinary and Plenipotentiary
Permanent Representative (DPC: 19 August 2013)

Mr. Tevita Suka **Mangisi**
Counsellor
Deputy Permanent Representative
Mrs. Toshiko Mangisi

Ms. Odette **Tupouohomohema**
First Secretary

Trinidad and Tobago

Member State since 18 September 1962

Address: Permanent Mission of the Republic
of Trinidad and Tobago to the United Nations
633 Third Avenue, 12th Floor
New York, N.Y. 10017

Telephone: (212) 697-7620, -7621, -7622, -7623

Telefax: (212) 682-3580

e-mail: tto@un.int

Correspondence: English

National holiday: 31 August

646-589-8206	H.E. ... Ambassador Extraordinary and Plenipotentiary Permanent Representative (DPC: ...)
646-589-8207	H.E. Mr. Eden **Charles** Ambassador Extraordinary and Plenipotentiary Deputy Permanent Representative Mrs. Joanne Murray Charles
646-589-8202	Ms. Melissa Ann Marie **Boissiere** Second Secretary
646-589-8203	Ms. Rueanna **Haynes** Second Secretary
646-589-8204	Ms. Charlene **Roopnarine** Second Secretary
	Ms. Lizanne **Aching** Second Secretary
646-589-8205	Mrs. Tessa **Guiseppi-Legier** Attaché (Financial Affairs)
646-589-8206	Ms. Jacquline **Britto** Attaché (Administrative Affairs)

Tunisia

Member State since 12 November 1956

Address:	Permanent Mission of Tunisia to the United Nations 31 Beekman Place New York, N.Y. 10022
Telephone:	(212) 751-7503, -7534, -5069
Telefax:	(212) 751-0569; (212) 319-4752
e-mail:	tunisnyc@nyc.rr.com ; Tunisia@un.int
Correspondence:	French
National holiday:	20 March Independence Day

Ext. 42	H.E. Mr. Mohamed Khaled **Khiari** Ambassador Extraordinary and Plenipotentiary Permanent Representative (23 November 2012) Mrs. Miriem Oueslati Khiari
Ext. 32	Mr. Riadh **Ben Sliman** Minister Plenipotentiary Deputy Permanent Representative Mrs. Samia Ben Youssef Ben Sliman
Ext. 26	Mr. Anouar **Missaoui** Counsellor Mrs. Rahma Hamdi Missaoui
	Mrs. Karima **Bardaoui** Counsellor
	Mr. Ramzi **Louati** Counsellor Mrs. Imane Gharrass Louati
Ext. 27	Mrs. El Khansa **Arfaoui Harbaoui** First Secretary Mr. Anis Harbaoui
Ext. 31	Mrs. Nour **Zarrouk Boumiza** First Secretary Mr. Wissem Boumiza
Ext. 16	Mr. Mekki **Mansouri** Attaché Mrs. Aida Mansouri
Ext. 24	Mr. Ghazi **Karchoud** Attaché Mrs. Kaouther Boughanmi Karchoud
Ext. 22	Mr. Ourabi **Taggazi** Attaché

Address:	Permanent Mission of Turkey to the United Nations 1 Dag Hammarskjöld Plaza 885 2nd Avenue, 45th Floor New York, N.Y. 10017
Telephone:	(212) 949-0150
Telefax:	(212) 949-0086
e-mail:	tr-delegation.newyork@mfa.gov.tr
Website	www.turkuno.dt.mfa.gov.tr
Correspondence:	English
National holiday:	29 October Republic Day

450-9112 H.E. Mr. Y. Halit **Çevik**
Ambassador Extraordinary and Plenipotentiary
Permanent Representative (DPC: 25 October 2012)
Mrs. R. Nihal Çevik

450-9113 Mr. Levent **Eler**
Minister Plenipotentiary
Deputy Permanent Representative
Mrs. Ayten Eler

450-9108 Colonel Namık Kemal **Çil**
Counsellor
Military Adviser
Mrs. Hatice Çil

450-9135 Mrs. Makbule Başak **Yalçın**
Counsellor
Mr. Ertan Yalçın

450-9134 Mr. Efe **Ceylan**
Counsellor
Mrs. Ayşe Yilmaz Ceylan

450-9158 Ms. Gizem **Sucuoğlu**
Counsellor

450-9131 Mr. Murat **Uğurluoğlu**
Counsellor

450-9121 Ms. Elif **Çalışkan**
Counsellor

450-9109 Mrs. Ceren Hande **Özgür**
Counsellor
Mr. Reyhan Özgür

450-9102 Mrs. İpek Zeytinoğlu **Özkan**
Counsellor

867-9023	Mr. İslam **Doğru** Counsellor (Press)
450-9104	Mr. Muhammet Üzeyir **Karabıyık** Counsellor (Legal Affairs) Mrs. Nurgül Şenel Karabıyık
949-0150	Mr. Muharrem **Turgut** First Secretary Mrs. Tuba Tola Turgut
450-9184	Mr. Serdar **Özaydın** First Secretary
450-9175	Mr. Yavuz Selim **Çubukcu** First Secretary
450-9172	Mr. Bilal Emre **Biral** Second Secretary Mrs. Azime Biral
450-9103	Ms. Derle **Demirel** Second Secretary
450-9116	Mr. Yiğit **Canay** Second Secretary
450-9105	Ms. Merve Neva **Ünal** Second Secretary
450-9145	Ms. Tülay **Bağ** Second Secretary
450-9128	Mr. Tahsin Oğuz **Özçelik** Second Secretary Mrs. Remziye Emir Özçelik
450-9120	Mr. Hüseyin **İspir** Third Secretary Mrs. Emine İspir
450-9171	Mr. Ahmet Şükrü **Özdemir** Attaché
450-9155	Mr. Ferhat **Güneş** Attaché
450-9137	Mr. Özkan **Şahintürk** Attaché Mrs. Gamze Şahintürk
450-9137	Mr. Mustafa **Bilir** Attaché Mrs. Norasiah BTE Sulaimi

Address:	Permanent Mission of Turkmenistan to the United Nations 866 United Nations Plaza, Suite 540 New York, N.Y. 10017
Telephone:	(212) 486-8908
Telefax:	(212) 486-2521
e-mail:	turkmenistan@un.int
Website:	www.turkmenistanun.org
Correspondence:	English
National holiday:	27 October Independence Day

H.E. Mrs. Aksoltan **Ataeva**
Ambassador Extraordinary and Plenipotentiary
Permanent Representative (DPC: 23 February 1995)
Mr. Chary Pirmoukhamedov

Ext. 2	Mr. Ata **Eyeberdiyev** Counsellor Mrs. Mahri Eyeberdiyeva
Ext. 4	Mr. Rovshen **Annaberdiyev** First Secretary Mrs. Kumushgozel Annaberdiyeva
Ext. 9	Mr. Azat **Sahetmyradov** Attaché Mrs. Jenet Sahetmyradova

Address:	Permanent Mission of Tuvalu to the United Nations 800 Second Avenue, Suite 400D New York, N.Y. 10017
Telephone:	(212) 490-0534
Telefax:	(212) 808-4975
e-mail:	tuvalu.un@gmail.com
website:	www.un.int/wcm/content/site/tuvalu
Correspondence:	English
National holiday:	1 October Independence Day

H.E. Mr. Aunese Makoi **Simati**
Ambassador Extraordinary and Plenipotentiary
Permanent Representative (DPC: 20 December 2012)
Mrs. Sunema Pie Simati

Mrs. Sunema Pie **Simati**
First Secretary
H.E. Mr. Aunese Makoi Simati

Address: Permanent Mission of the Republic
of Uganda to the United Nations
336 East 45th Street
New York, N.Y. 10017

Telephone: (212) 949-0110, -0111, -0112, -0113

Telefax: (212) 687-4517

e-mail: ugandaunny@un.int

website: www.ugandamissionunny.net

Correspondence: English

National holiday: 9 October
Independence Day

H.E. Mr. Richard **Nduhuura**
Ambassador Extraordinary and Plenipotentiary
Permanent Representative (DPC: 15 May 2013)
Mrs. Clare Sanyu Nduhuura

H.E. Mr. Kintu **Nyago**
Ambassador
Deputy Permanent Representative

H.E. Mr. Arthur Sewankambo **Kafeero**
Ambassador
Mrs. Margaret Awino Kafeero

H.E. Mr. Duncan Laki **Muhumuza**
Ambassador
Mrs. Catherine Kanyesigye Muhumuza

Mr. Julius **Shariita**
Minister Counsellor
Mrs. Jane Shariita Busingye

Mr. John Leonard **Mugerwa**
Counsellor
Mrs. Maureen Mugerwa

Mr. Tom Tarcisius Onyai **Manano**
Counsellor

Mr. Rauben **Byereta**
First Secretary

Mrs. Maargaret Awino **Kafeero**
First Secretary

Mrs. Caroine **Nalwanga**
First Secretary
Mr. Tom Magambo

Mrs. Bernadette Mwesige **Ssempa**
Second Secretary
Mr. Deogratias Lwanga Ssempa

Ms. Zipporah **Mayanja**
Third Secretary

Mr. Beckham Robert **Mugimba**
Third Secretary
Mrs. Sarah Mugimba Abaho

Mr. Joseph **Barigye**
Third Secretary

Ms. Annet **Kabuye**
Attaché (Administration)

Maj. General Silver Moses **Kayemba**
Minister Counsellor
Military Adviser

Ukraine

Member State since 24 October 1945

Address: Permanent Mission of Ukraine to the United Nations
220 East 51st Street
New York, N.Y. 10022

Telephone: (212) 759-7003

Telefax: (212) 355-9455

e-mail: uno_us@mfa.gov.ua

website: www.mfa.gov.ua/uno

Correspondence: English

National holiday: 24 August
Independence Day

Ext. 100 H.E. Mr. Yuriy **Sergeyev**
Ambassador Extraordinary and Plenipotentiary
Permanent Representative (DPC: 15 May 2007)
Mrs. Nataliya Ivashyna

Ext. 117 Mr. Andriy **Tsymbaliuk**
Counsellor
Deputy Permanent Representative
Mrs. Tetiana Tsymbaliuk

Ext. 128 Mr. Mykhailo **Kyrylenko**
Counsellor
Military Adviser
Mrs. Liudmyla Kyrylenko

Ext. 107 Mr. Ihor **Yaremenko**
Counsellor

Mr. Eduard **Fesko**
Counsellor

Ext. 113 Mr. Taras **Kaiuk**
First Secretary
Mrs. Zoriana Kaiuk

Ext. 130 Mr. Yaroslav **Golitsyn**
First Secretary

Lieutenant Colonel Ihor **Dzera**
First Secretary
Deputy Military Adviser
Mrs. Lesia Dzera

Ext. 127 Mr. Volodymyr **Mialkovskyi**
First Secretary
Mrs. Iryna Mialkovska

Ext. 114 Mr. Yehor **Pyvovarov**
First Secretary

Ext. 112	Mr. Volodymyr **Leschenko** First Secretary Mrs. Mariya Leschenko
	Mr. Igor **Bondiuk** Second Secretary Mrs. Irina Bondiuk
Ext. 115	Mr. Oleksiy **Shapoval** Third Secretary Mrs. Zinaida Mansurova
Ext. 109	Mr. Ramiz **Ramazanov** Attaché

United Arab Emirates

Member State since 9 December 1971

Address: Permanent Mission of the United Arab Emirates
to the United Nations
3 Dag Hammarskjöld Plaza
305 East 47th Street, 7th Floor
New York, N.Y. 10017

Telephone: (212) 371-0480

Telefax: (212) 371-4923

e-mail: newyork@mofa.gov.ae

Correspondence: English

National holiday: 2 December

H.E. Mrs. Lana Zaki **Nusseibeh**
Ambassador Extraordinary and Plenipotentiary
Permanent Representative (DPC: 18 September 2013)
Mr. Omar Hameed Hadi

Ms. Hind Abdulaziz **Alowais**
Counsellor

Mr. Majid Hasan Mohammed Hasan **Alsuwaidi**
Counsellor

Mr. Jamal Jama Ahmed Abdulla **Al Musharakh**
Second Secretary
Deputy Permanent Representative

Mr. Saud Hamad Ghanem Hamad **Alshamsi**
Second Secretary
Mrs. Hana Abdalla S. AlMakhawi Alsuwaidi

Mr. Ahmed Abdelrahman Ahmed **Almahmoud**
Second Secretary

Mr. Suood Rashed Ali Alwali **Almazrouei**
Third Secretary
Mrs. Shamsa Obaid Rashid Alaqroubi Alsuwaidi

Mr. Ahmed Sultan Saqer Sultan **Alqassimi**
Third Secretary

Mrs. Ameirah Obaid Mohamed Obaid **Alhefeiti**
Third Secretary
Mr. Anwar Eid Saeed Saif Alazeezi

Mr. Anwar Eid Saeed Saif **Alazeezi**
Third Secretary
Mrs. Ameirah Obaid Mohamed Obaid Alhefeiti

Ms. Khaula Ali Khamis Obaid **Alshamsi**
Third Secretary

United Kingdom of Great Britain and Northern Ireland

Member State since 24 October 1945

Address:	Permanent Mission of the United Kingdom to the United Nations One Dag Hammarskjöld Plaza 885 Second Avenue New York, N.Y. 10017
Telephone:	(212) 745-9200
Telefax:	(212) 745-9316
e-mail:	uk@un.int
website:	ukun.fco.gov.uk/en
Correspondence:	English
National holiday:	13 June (2015) Celebration of the birthday of Her Majesty the Queen

---

745-9360	H.E. Mr. Matthew **Rycroft**, CBE Ambassador Extraordinary and Plenipotentiary Permanent Representative (DPC: 27 April 2015)
745-9337	H.E. Mr. Peter **Wilson** Ambassador Deputy Permanent Representative Mrs. Monica Roma Wilson
745-9356	H.E. Mr. Michael **Tatham** Ambassador Mrs. Belinda Cherrington
745-9318	H.E. Mr. Martin **Shearman** Ambassador Ms. Miriam Shearman
745-9247	Colonel Mark **Maddick** Counsellor Military Adviser Mrs. Gail Maddick
745-9200	Mr. Richard **Moon** Counsellor
745-9325	Ms. Corinne **Kitsell** Counsellor
	Mr. Steven **Hill** Counsellor Mrs. Geraldine Hill
745-9329	Mr. Thomas **Meek** Counsellor Ms. Anna Meek

745-9357	Ms. Alexandra **Davison** First Secretary (Political Affairs)
745-9395	Mr. Yasser **Baki** First Secretary
745-9225	Mr. Jesse **Clarke** First Secretary (Legal Affairs) Ms. Anthea Roberts
745-9235	Ms. Fiona Eileen **Ritchie** First Secretary
745-9258	Mr. Douglas **Benedict** First Secretary (Political Affairs)
745-9282	Ms. Lisa **Maguire** First Secretary
745-9214	Mr. Nicholas **Conway** First Secretary (Political Affairs) Mrs. Corey Stoughton
745-9370	Ms. Iona **Thomas** First Secretary
745-9311	Mr. Joseph **Beeley** First Secretary (Management Reform and Finance)
745-9275	Mr. Matthew **Jackson** First Secretary
	Mr. Dan **Pilkington** First Secretary Mrs. Jodie Beth Pilkington
	Mr. Simon **Horner** First Secretary Katherine Gallagher Horner
	Mr. Craig **Mills** First Secretary Mr. Matthew John Ireland
	Mr. Mark **Power** First Secretary
	Ms. Catherine **Carr** First Secretary
745-9350	Mr. Iain **Griffiths** Second Secretary
745-9253	Mr. Mungo **Woodifield** Second Secretary
745-9278	Ms. Eleanor Mary Beatrice **Dodd** Second Secretary

745-9215	Ms. Helen **Walker** Second Secretary
745-9211	Mr. Neil Ian **McKillop** Second Secretary
745-9244	Mr. Philip Edward **Reed** Second Secretary (Humanitarian Affairs) Mrs. Neysela Carla Da Silva-Reed
745-9321	Mr. Paul **Davies** Second Secretary (Technical Officer)
745-9398	Mr. Mohammed Tahir **Khan** Second Secretary Ms. Frances Roberts
745-9309	Mr. Christopher **Hunter** Second Secretary
745-9274	Mr. Alexander **Horne** Second Secretary Mrs. Elizabeth Horne
	Ms. Senay **Bulbul** Second Secretary Mr. Thomas Malcolm Brindle
	Ms. Raakhi **Sunak** Second Secretary
	Mr. Matthew **Thourne** Second Secretary
745-9345	Ms. Gemma **McDermott** Attaché
745-9360	Mrs. Kay **Sweet** Attaché (Private Secretary to the Permanent Representative) Mr. Jonathan Charles Sweet
	Ms. Sian **Brackett** Attaché
	Mr. James **Egan** Attaché

United Republic of Tanzania

Member State since 14 December 1961

Address: Permanent Mission of the United Republic of Tanzania to the United Nations
307 East 53rd Street, Suite 400
New York, N.Y. 10022

Telephone: (212) 697-3612

Telefax: (212) 697-3618

e-mail: tzrepny@aol.com

Correspondence: English

National holiday: 26 April
Union Day

H.E. Mr. Tuvako Nathaniel **Manongi**
Ambassador Extraordinary and Plenipotentiary
Permanent Representative (DPC: 19 September 2012)
Mrs. Upendo Tuvako Manongi

H.E. Mr. Ramadhan **Mwinyi**
Ambassador
Deputy Permanent Representative
Mrs. Fatma Khamis Mohamed

Mrs. Maura **Mwingira**
Minister Plenipotentiary

Mr. Songelael W. **Shilla**
Minister Plenipotentiary
Mrs. Atuhuvye Benedict Kayombo

Major Wilbert **Ibuge**
Minister Plenipotentiary
Ms. Mary Mdachi

Mr. Abdalla Othman **Khamis**
Minister Plenipotentiary
Mrs. Hidaya Said Mohamed

Mr. Justin **Kisoka**
Counsellor
Mrs. Regina James Moshy

Mr. Noel **Kaganda**
First Secretary
Mrs. Emmanuela Kaganda

Ms. Tully Malecela **Mwaipopo**
First Secretary

Ms. Ellen **Maduhu**
Second Secretary

Mrs. Roselinda Bernard **Mkapa**
Attaché (Administrative Affairs)

Mr. Yusuph **Tugutu**
Financial Attaché
Mrs. Ester Mboje

Address:	United States Mission to the United Nations 799 United Nations Plaza New York, N.Y. 10017
Telephone:	(212) 415-4000 (Information after hours, weekends and holidays)
Telefax:	(212) 415-4443 (General Number) (212) 415-4141 (Economic Section) (212) 415-4162 (Host Country Affairs) (212) 415-4209 (Legal Affairs) (212) 415-4415 (Political Section) (212) 415-4053 (Press and Public Affairs) (212) 415-4183 (Management and Reform) (212) 415-4154 (US Military Staff) (212) 415-4069 (US Mission Protocol Office)
e-mail:	USUNPolFax@state.gov
website:	usun.state.gov
Correspondence:	English
National holiday:	4 July Independence Day

415-4404	H.E. Ms. Samantha **Power** Ambassador Extraordinary and Plenipotentiary Permanent Representative (DPC: 5 August 2013) Mr. Cass Sunstein
415-4035	H.E. Ms. Isobel **Coleman** Ambassador Representative for Management and Reform
415-4232	H.E. Mr. David **Pressman** Ambassador Alternate Representative for Special Political Affairs
415-4261	H.E. Ms. Michele J. **Sison** Ambassador Deputy Permanent Representative
781-470-0644	Mr. James **Donovan** Minister Counsellor Mrs. Ratja Wiesbrock Donovan
415-4106	Mr. Thomas **Gallo** Minister Counsellor Mr. Joseph Merante
415-4058	Mr. Max **Gleischman** Minister Counsellor

415-4254	Mr. Christopher **Huttleston** Minister Counsellor Ms. Selma Huttleston
415-5175	Mr. Christopher **Klein** Minister Counsellor Ms. Anne Mah
415-4280	Mrs. Terri **Robl** Minister Counsellor Dr. Ahmed Esa
415-4220	Mr. Mark A. **Simonoff** Minister Counsellor Ms. Phyllis Hwang
415-4422	Mr. Michael **Vassalotti** Minister Counsellor Mrs. Tracey Vassalotti
415-4225	Mr. John **Arbogast** Counsellor Ms. Sonia Elliot
415-4277	Ms. Jill **Derderian** Counsellor
415-4316	Mr. Stephen **Gee** Counsellor
415-4330	Ms. Eileen P. **Merritt** Counsellor
415-4180	Mrs. Cherith A. **Norman Chalet** Counsellor Mr. Georges N. Chalet
415-4076	Mr. Jon **Piechowski** Counsellor Ms. Macarena Aristegui
415-4224	Mr. David **Pressman** Counsellor
415-4346	Mr. Curtis R. **Ried** Counsellor
415-4333	Mr. David A. **Traystman** Counsellor Mrs. Christine Traystman
415-4382	Mr. Michael **Abel** Adviser
415-4458	Mr. Eugene S. **Albrecht** Adviser
415-4097	Miss Tresa A. **Amaker** Adviser

415-4168	Ms. Mary A. **Ambrose** Adviser
415-4446	Mr. Raymond **Amey** Adviser Mrs. Arthelia Amey
415-4294	Ms. Elaine S. M. **Angeles** Adviser
	Ms. Mary-Kate **Barry** Adviser
415-4089	Ms. Sharon **Belluci** Adviser
415-4081	Mr. Joshua J. **Black** Adviser
415-4167	Mrs. Christine **Bousada** Adviser Mr. Hassan Bousada
415-4144	Ms. Lisa **Bowen** Adviser
415-4418	Ms. Kyla **Brooke** Adviser
415-4407	Mr. Thomas J. **Buda** Adviser
415-4491	Mr. Douglas **Carey** Adviser Ms. Yuko Carey
415-4349	Ms. Shane **Chase** Adviser
415-4233	Mr. Eugene B. **Chen** Adviser
415-4118	Mr. Donald J. **Conahan** Adviser Mrs. Toni Ann Conahan
415-4473	Ms. Kelly **Conley** Adviser
415-4301	Mr. Kurtis **Cooper** Adviser
415-4296	Mrs. Anne **Davis** Adviser
415-4153	Mr. Anthony **Deaton** Adviser Ms. Vanessa Pelizzon

415-4229	Mr. Neil **DiBiase** Adviser
415-4322	Ms. Anca S. **DiGiacomo** Adviser
415-4462	Mr. Hugh **Dugan** Adviser Mrs. Ute Dugan
415-4444	Mr. David **Dunn** Adviser Mrs. Maria-Ellena Dunn
415-4103	Mr. Ivan J. **Ferber** Adviser
(843) 217-1972	Mr. Carlos **Figueroa** Adviser Mrs. Lori Lynn Figueroa
415-5119	Major Larry **Fonder** (Army) Adviser
415-4265	Mr. Brendan **Fox** Adviser Ms. Katherine Fox
415-4368	Ms. Kate **Fox** Adviser
415-4035	Ms. Billie A. **Fulton** Adviser
415-4116	Ms. Martha **Fulton** Adviser
415-4306	Mrs. Emma **Garvin** Adviser Mr. Alfred T. Garvin
415-4137	Mrs. Leslie **Garvin-Ferguson** Adviser Mr. Raymond K. Ferguson
415-4152	Mr. Angelo M. **Guarnaccio** Adviser Mrs. Janise L. Gray Guarnaccio
646-338-9933	Mr. Paul Edward **Hanna** Adviser Mrs. Natalia Linos
703-462-3195	Ms. Adrienne **Harchik** Adviser
	Mrs. Kylie **Holmes** Adviser

415-4190	Ms. Gail **Horak** Adviser Mr. Matthew Horak
415-4100	Ms. Lorraine **Jacobs** Adviser
415-4182	Mr. Aalok **Kanani** Adviser
415-4054	Ms. Margaret A. **Kerry** Adviser Mr. George Kaler
415-4134	Ms. Colleen **King** Adviser
415-4292	Ms. Megan **Koilparampil** Adviser
415-4292	Ms. Lorraine C. **Konzet** Adviser
415-4453	Mr. Jason **Lang** Adviser
415-4372	Mr. David Y. **Lee** Adviser Ms. Soohyun Park
415-4117	Mr. Jesse S. **Levinson** Adviser
415-4295	Ms. Catherine **Lillie** Adviser
415-4214	Mr. Paul **Longo** Adviser Ms. Laura Hur
415-4193	Ms. Andrea **Lupi** Adviser
415-4078	Mr. Kevin **Lynch** Adviser
415-4147	Lt. Col. David **MacDonald** (Army) Adviser Ms. Amy MacDonald
415-4185	Ms. Jane C. **Malloy** Adviser Mr. Jermaine Emmanuel Kamau
415-4091	Ms. Genevieve **Maricle** Adviser
415-4356	Ms. Kimberly M. **McClure** Adviser

415-4122	Mr. Roy **Menendez** Adviser Mrs. Ana Menendez
415-4085	Ms. Millie **Meyers** Adviser
415-4029	Mr. Jeremy C. **Migden** Adviser
415-4346	Mr. Walter **Miller** Adviser
415-4098	Mr. Frederick N. **Morgan** Adviser Mrs. Sharon V. Morgan
415-4228	Mr. Tyler **Moselle** Adviser
415-4424	Mr. Frederick S. **Murriel** Adviser Mrs. Camille Grizzle Murriel
(928) 446-9559	Mr. Adam Lee **Musoff** Adviser Mrs. Jodi Lee Rind
415-4143	Ms. Denise **Nash** Adviser
415-4343	Mr. Nicholas P. **Newton** Adviser
415-4449	Mr. Jason **Ng** Adviser
(347) 234-6297	Mr. Youseline **Obas** Adviser
415-4486	Ms. Sevasti **Pandermarakis** Adviser
415-4204	Ms. Laurie Shestack **Phipps** Adviser Mr. Thomas J. Phipps
415-4250	Ms. Cynthia **Plath** Adviser
415-4215	Mr. Christopher **Pothoven** Adviser Mr. Timothy Fitzsimmons
415-4121	Ms. Rabia **Qureshi** Adviser
415-4012	Ms. Kelly L. **Razzouk** Adviser Mr. Michel Robert Diwan

415-4451	Mr. Brian **Reames** Adviser
415-4469	Mr. Davis **Richelsoph** Adviser
415-4146	Ms. Maria **Riofrio** Adviser
415-4480	Lt. Colonel Glenn J. **Sadowski**, (Marine Corps) Adviser Mrs. Claudia P. Sadowski
415-4361	Ms. Aisha **Sabar** Adviser Mr. Adnan Ahmad
415-4419	Ms. Hillary **Schrenell** Adviser
415-4471	Ms. Dawn **Schrepel** Adviser
415-4278	Ms. Natoschia **Scruggs** Adviser Mr. Walid Rawash
415-4429	Ms. Rebecca **Shivprasod** Adviser Mr. Chevalia Shivprasod
415-4176	Ms. Marc **Sims** Adviser
415-4012	Mr. Russel **Singer** Adviser Mrs. Eva Christina Delius
415-4203	Ms. Christina **Skewes-Cox** Adviser
415-4197	Ms. Esther Pan **Sloane** Adviser Mr. Robert Sloane
415-4264	SFC Caesar **Smith** (Army) Adviser Mrs. Illya Smith
415-4246	Mr. J. Patrick **Sowers** Adviser
415-4493	Mr. Nikolaus **Steinberg** Adviser
415-4093	Ms. Eleanor C. **Stone** Adviser Mr. Lorenzo Falciani

415-4327	Mr. Edward J. **Swoyer** Adviser Ms. Meghan Swoyer
415-4217	Ms. Sheila **Taharally** Adviser
415-4037	Ms. Paula **Thomas** Adviser
415-4101	Mr. Harry K. **Ting** Adviser
	Ms. Elizabeth C. **Tomaselli** Adviser
	Mr. Douglas Eugene **Towns** Adviser
415-4092	Mr. Amit **Upadhyay** Adviser Mrs. Smitaben Upadhyay
415-4102	Mr. Eugenio **Vargas** Adviser
858-232-8242	Mrs. Stephanie **Walker** Adviser Mr. Erik Walker
415-4358	Ms. Rae Lynn **Wargo** Adviser
(917) 454-8389	Mr. Carl **Watson** Adviser Mr. Evgeny Victorovich Relepey
415-4337	Mrs. Ann M. **Wharton** Adviser Mr. Royal Wharton
415-4067	Ms. Alexis **Wichowski** Adviser Mr. Jonathan Tepperman
415-4494	Mr. Richard F. **Williams** Adviser Mrs. Joleen Williams
415-4133	Mr. Eric E. **Wolf** Adviser
	Mrs. Kam Ting **Wong** Adviser Mr. Leslie James Bright
	Ms. Elisa **Yoshioka** Adviser

415-4376	Mr. Christopher T. **Zimmer** Adviser
(646) 282-2811	Mr. Thomas G. **Gallo** Regional Director Office of Foreign Missions Department of State Mr. Joseph Merante
(646) 282-2812	Mr. Murray J. **Smith** Deputy Regional Director Office of Foreign Missions Department of State

Uruguay

Member State since 18 December 1945

Address: Permanent Mission of Uruguay to the United Nations
866 United Nations Plaza, Suite 322
New York, N.Y. 10017

Telephone: (212) 752-8240

Telefax: (212) 593-0935

e-mail: uruguay@urudeleg.org

website: www.urudeleg.org

Correspondence: Spanish

National holiday: 25 August
Independence Day

H.E. Mr. Gonzalo **Koncke**
Ambassador Extraordinary and Plenipotentiary
Permanent Representative (DPC: 9 January 2014)

Mrs. Cristina **Carrión**
Minister
Deputy Permanent Representative
Mr. Gustavo Rodriguez

Mr. Álvaro **Ceriani**
Minister Counsellor
Mrs. Nadine Jasa de Ceriani

Mrs. Imelda **Smolcic**
Minister Counsellor
Mr. Andrés Tiribocchi

Mr. Jorge **Dotta**
Minister Counsellor

Mrs. Gabriela **Ortigosa**
Minister Counsellor
Mr. Rudy Lion

Mr. José Luis **Rivas**
Minister Counsellor

Mrs. Silvana **Della Gatta**
First Secretary
Mr. Damián Lechini

Ms. Silvana **García**
First Secretary

Ms. María Emilia **Eyheralde Geymonat**
Third Secretary

Colonel (Army) Alberto **Spada**
Attaché
Military Adviser

Colonel Ricardo **Fernandez**
Attaché
Military Adviser

Uzbekistan

Member State since 2 March 1992

Address:	Permanent Mission of the Republic of Uzbekistan to the United Nations 801 Second Avenue, 20th Floor New York, N.Y. 10017
Telephone:	(212) 486-4242
Telefax:	(212) 486-7998
e-mail:	uzbekistan.un@gmail.com
Correspondence:	English
National holiday:	1 September Independence Day

H.E. Mr. Muzaffarbek **Madrakhimov**
Ambassador Extraordinary and Plenipotentiary
Permanent Representative (DPC: 23 April 2014)

Mr. Ildar **Shigabutdinov**
Counsellor
Deputy Permanent Representative
Mrs. Negina Shigabutdinova

Mr. Gulyamjon **Pirimkulov**
Second Secretary
Mrs. Gulgun Pirimkulova

Address: Permanent Mission of the Republic
of Vanuatu to the United Nations
800 Second Avenue, Suite 400C
New York, N.Y. 10017

Telephone: (212) 661-4303

Telefax: (212) 661-5544

e-mail: vanunmis@aol.com

Correspondence: English

National holiday: 30 July
Independence Day

H.E. Mr. Odo **Tevi**
Ambassador Extraordinary and Plenipotentiary
Permanent Representative (DPC: 13 August 2014)
Mrs. Sharon Tevi

Mr. Eric Belleay **Kalotiti**
Minister Counsellor
Deputy Permanent Representative

Mrs. Evelyn **Adams**
Second Secretary
Mr. Timothy Adams

Venezuela (Bolivarian Republic of)

Member State since 15 November 1945

Address: Permanent Mission of the Bolivarian Republic of Venezuela to the United Nations
335 East 46th Street
New York, N.Y. 10017

Telephone: (212) 557-2055

Telefax: (212) 557-3528

e-mail: misionvenezuelaonu@gmail.com

Correspondence: Spanish

National holiday: 5 July
Independence Day

H.E. Mr. Rafael Darío **Ramírez Carreño**
Ambassador Extraordinary and Plenipotentiary
Permanent Representative (DPC: 16 January 2015)
Mrs. Beatrice Daniela Sansó de Ramírez

H.E. Ms. María Gabriela **Chávez Colmenares**
Ambassador
Deputy Permanent Representative

H.E. Mr. Henry Alfredo **Suárez Moreno**
Ambassador
Deputy Permanent Representative
Mrs. Argelia María Calzadilla Pérez

Mr. Wilmer Alfonzo **Méndez Graterol**
Minister Counsellor
Mrs. Yumaira Coromoto Rodríguez Silva

Mr. Zael Alexis **Fernández Rivera**
Minister Counsellor
Mrs. Yaritza María Paolini Hernández

Ms. Ana Carolina **Rodríguez de Febres-Cordero**
Minister Counsellor

Mrs. Glenna **Cabello de Daboin**
Counsellor
Mr. Nelson Daboin Rodríguez

Mr. Williams José **Suárez Moreno**
Counsellor

Ms. Cristiane **Engelbrecht Schadtler**
Counsellor

Mr. Alfredo Fernando **Toro-Carnevali**
First Secretary
Mrs. María Andreína Ruiz de Toro

Mr. Robert Alexander **Poveda Brito**
First Secretary

Ms. Marisela Eugenia **Gonzalez Tolosa**
First Secretary
Mr. Adolfo Rafael Martínez Noguera

Mr. Yaruma Ollantay **Rodríguez Silva**
First Secretary
Mrs. Mercedes Alexandra Acosta Sierra

Mr. Jonel Manuel **Ortiz Denis**
First Secretary

Mr. Roberto **Bayley Angeleri**
First Secretary
Mrs. Valeska Francoise Pina García

Ms. Liliana Josefina **Matos Juarez**
Second Secretary

Mrs. Yumaira Coromonto **Rodríguez Silva**
Second Secretary

Mr. Cesar Augusto **Chavarri Cabello**
Second Secretary

Ms. Sau Ming **Chan Shum**
Second Secretary

Mr. Joaquín Alberto **Pérez Ayestarán**
Second Secretary

Mr. Jhon Rafael **Guerra Sansonetti**
Second Secretary
Mrs. Yulisbhet Perez Nuñez

Brigadier General José Luis **Betancourt Marquez**
Attaché
Mrs. Flerida del Carmen Ramos Leon

Address: Permanent Mission of the Socialist Republic of Viet Nam to the United Nations
866 United Nations Plaza, Suite 435
New York, N.Y. 10017

Telephone: (212) 644-0594, -0831, -1564

Telefax: (212) 644-5732

e-mail: info@vietnam-un.org

website: www.un.int/vietnam

Correspondence: English

National holiday: 2 September
Independence Day

H.E. Mrs. **Nguyen** Phuong Nga
Ambassador Extraordinary and Plenipotentiary
Permanent Representative (DPC: 5 November 2014)
Mr. Phung Thang Tat

Ext. 42 Mr. **Nguyen** Trac Ba
Minister
Deputy Permanent Representative
Mrs. Vu Thi Kim Minh

Mr. **Pham** Quang Hieu
Minister Counsellor
Deputy Permanent Representative
Mrs. Thai Hong Thu

Mr. **Do** Hung Viet
Minister Counsellor
Deputy Permanent Representative
Mrs. Pham Mai Thi Huyen

Ext. 27 Mr. **Do** Van Minh
Counsellor
Mrs. Doan Minh Ha

Mr. **Vu** Van Mien
Counsellor
Mrs. Nguyen Ha Thi Bich

Mr. **Bui** Vu Hiep
Counsellor
Mrs. Nguyen Thanh Thi

Mr. **Do** Manh Son
Counsellor
Mrs. Nguyen Thi Lien

Ext. 35	Mr. **Luong** Phuc Hong First Secretary Mrs. Nguyen Lan Huong Thi
	Mr. **Pham** Viet Ha First Secretary
Ext. 37	Mr. **Vu** Chi Thanh First Secretary Mrs. Nguyen Thi Hoai Huong
	Mr. **Nguyen** Huu Hung First Secretary
	Mr. **Nguyen** Viet Lam Second Secretary (Head of Chancery) Mrs. Dang Thi Thanh Phuong
Ext. 32	Ms. **Nguyen** Cam Linh Second Secretary
	Ms. **Vu** Minh Thuy Second Secretary
	Mr. **Phan** Ho The Nam Second Secretary
	Mr. **Nguyen** Duc Cuong Second Secretary Mrs. Nguyen Thi Minh Tham
	Mr. **Nguyen** Van Dong Third Secretary Mrs. Vu Thi Kim Nguyen
	Mrs. **Khuat** Thi Minh Thao Third Secretary Mr. Khuat Duy Hai
	Mr. **Nguyen** Duy Thanh Third Secretary
	Mr. **Dinh** Viet Dung Third Secretary
	Mrs. **Nguyen** Ta Ha Mi Third Secretary
	Mr. **Ha** Thanh Chung Attaché Mrs. Pham Thi Huong Giang

Address:	Permanent Mission of the Republic of Yemen to the United Nations 413 East 51st Street New York, N.Y. 10022
Telephone:	(212) 355-1730, -1731
Telefax:	(212) 750-9613
e-mail:	YMISS-NEWYORK@MOFA.GOV.YE
Correspondence:	English
National holiday:	22 May

644-8627	H.E. Mr. Khaled Hussein Mohamed **Alyemany** Ambassador Extraordinary and Plenipotentiary Permanent Representative (DPC: 20 January 2015) Mrs. Haifa Abdullah Saeed Mater
	H.E. Mr. Mohamed Taha **Mustafa** Ambassador Adviser Mrs. Seena Omar Husein Ambool
Ext. 36	Mr. Ali Obadi **Mosaed** Counsellor Mrs. Amal Abdulmajid Alawi Al-Abbadi
Ext. 26	Mr. Talal Ali Rashed **Aljamali** First Secretary Mrs. Reem Abdulrahman Taha Alsharjabi
Ext. 35	Mr. Taha Hussein Daifallah **Al-Awadhi** Second Secretary Mrs. Eman Fadhl Moqbel Mansoor
Ext. 30	Mr. Belal Abdulgabar Ali **Abdo** Second Secretary Mrs. Eynas Abdullah Hamood Saeed
Ext. 28	Mr. Ahmed Abdullah Hames **Al-Ojari** Second Secretary Mrs. Bushra Hussain Faid Mojali
Ext. 29	Mr. Amjad Qaid Ahmed **Al-Kumaim** Second Secretary Mrs. Souha Taiser Zoudhi Ahmed
	Mrs. Intisar Nasser Mohammed **Abdullah** Third Secretary Mr. Mohammed Abdo Ali Dhaifallah

Ext. 58	Mr. Mohammed Kadri Saleh **Al Joumari** Counsellor Military Attaché Mrs. Khyria Molatf Ahmed Al Joumari

Zambia

Address: Permanent Mission of the Republic
of Zambia to the United Nations
237 East 52nd Street
New York, N.Y. 10022

Telephone: (212) 888-5770

Telefax: (212) 888-5213

e-mail: zambia@un.int

Correspondence: English

National holiday: 24 October

H.E. Dr. Mwaba Patricia **Kasese-Bota**
Ambassador Extraordinary and Plenipotentiary
Permanent Representative (DPC: 10 February 2012)
Mr. Simon Bota

Ms. Christine **Kalamwina**
Minister Counsellor
Deputy Permanent Representative

Mrs. Theresah Chipulu Luswili **Chanda**
Counsellor (Economic)

Ms. Beatrice Lungowe **Mutandi**
Counsellor (Political)
Mr. Paul Makuwa Kapanda

Brig. Gen. Erick **Mwewa**
Counsellor
Military Adviser
Mrs. Bridget Leya Ntembeni Mwewa

Mr. Silvester **Mwanza**
Counsellor (Political/Administration)
Mrs. Violet Bwalya Kasonde Mwanza

Mr. Chibaula David **Silwamba**
First Secretary (Press)
Mrs. Euphrasia Fara Mawere Silwamba

Mr. Kaswamu **Katota**
First Secretary (Legal)
Mrs. Yamishi Gloria Katota

Mr. Oliver **Munyonsi**
First Secretary (Accounts)
Mrs. Mary Bwanga Munyonsi

Mr. Langford **Banda**
Second Secretary
Mrs. Ellen Makwakwa Banda

Mrs. Martha Mposha **Munjile**
Second Secretary

Zimbabwe

Address:	Permanent Mission of the Republic of Zimbabwe to the United Nations 128 East 56th Street New York, N.Y. 10022
Telephone:	(212) 980-9511, -5084
Telefax:	(212) 308-6705
e-mail:	zimnewyork@gmail.com
Correspondence:	English
National holiday:	18 April

H.E. Mr. Frederick Musiiwa Makamure **Shava**
Ambassador Extraordinary and Plenipotentiary
Permanent Representative (DPC: 19 September 2014)
Mrs. Beatrice Foya-Shava

Mr. Vusumuzi **Ntonga**
Minister Counsellor
Mrs. Chipili L.M. Ntonga

Mrs. Kumbirayi **Taremba**
Minister Counsellor

Mr. Joel **Muzuwa**
Counsellor
Mrs. Ezeria Muzuwa

Mr. Tonderai Nyikayaparara **Mutarisi**
Counsellor
Mrs. Sharon Pepukai Mutarisi

Ms. Elizabeth **Kumire**
Counsellor

Air Commodore Simon **Nyowani**
Counsellor
Military Adviser
Mrs. Theresa Nyowani

Mrs. Bernadette Silungisile **Ntaba**
Counsellor
Mr. McLoddy Rutendo Kadyamusuma

Mr. Felix **Samakande**
Counsellor
Mrs. Ellen Samakande

Mr. Onismo **Chigejo**
Counsellor
Mrs. Espina Chigejo

Ms. Priscilla **Chikuturudzi**
Second Secretary

Mrs. Margaret **Chingono**
Third Secretary

II. Non-member States having received a standing invitation to participate as observers in the sessions and the work of the General Assembly and maintaining permanent observer missions at Headquarters

Holy See

Address: Permanent Observer Mission of the Holy See
to the United Nations
25 East 39th Street
New York, N.Y. 10016-0903

Telephone: (212) 370-7885

Telefax: (212) 370-9622

e-mail: office@holyseemission.org

website: www.holyseemission.org

National holiday: 13 March
Anniversary of the Pontificate of
His Holiness Pope Francis

H.E. Archbishop Bernardito Cleopas **Auza**
Apostolic Nuncio
Permanent Observer (since 19 September 2014)

Rev. Msgr. Joseph **Grech**
Second Secretary

Fr. Roger **Landry**
Attaché

Ms. Kallie **Aultman**
Attaché

Mr. Timothy **Herrmann**
Attaché

State of Palestine

Address: Permanent Observer Mission of the State of Palestine
to the United Nations
115 East 65th Street
New York, N.Y. 10065

Telephone: (212) 288-8500

Telefax: (212) 517-2377

e-mail: palestine@un.int

website: www.un.int/palestine

National holiday: 15 November

H.E. Mr. Riyad H. **Mansour***
Ambassador
Permanent Observer
Mrs. Caryl Mansour

H.E. Ms. Feda **Abdelhady-Nasser***
Ambassador
Deputy Permanent Observer
Mr. Tarik Nasser

Ms. Nadya Rifaat **Rasheed**
First Counsellor

Mr. Abdullah Abu **Shawesh**
Counsellor

Mrs. Sahar **Abushawesh**
First Secretary

Mr. Yussef F. **Kanaan**
Senior Adviser
Mrs. Abla Kanaan

Mrs. Somaia **Barghouti**
Senior Adviser

Ms. Reem Julia **Mansour**
Legal Adviser

Ms. Sahar **Salem**
Legal Adviser

Ms. Ghada **Hassan**
Assistant Attaché

* The title "Ambassador", if used with respect to the representative of an entity other than a Member State, should not be understood as indicating in itself an entitlement to diplomatic privileges and immunities.

III. Intergovernmental organizations having received a standing invitation to participate as observers in the sessions and the work of the General Assembly and maintaining permanent offices at Headquarters

The following intergovernmental organizations, which have received a standing invitation to participate in the sessions and the work of the General Assembly as observers, do not maintain permanent offices at Headquarters:

African, Caribbean and Pacific Group of States
African Development Bank
Agency for the Prohibition of Nuclear Weapons in Latin America and the Caribbean
Andean Community
Andean Development Corporation
Asian Development Bank
Association of Caribbean States
Association of Southeast Asian Nations
Black Sea Economic Cooperation Organization
Central European Initiative
Collective Security Treaty Organization
Common Fund for Commodities
Commonwealth of Independent States
Community of Portuguese-speaking Countries
Community of Sahelo-Saharan States
Conference on Interaction and Confidence-building Measures in Asia
Council of Europe
Customs Cooperation Council
East African Community
Economic Community of Central African States
Economic Communityof West African States
Economic Cooperation Organization
Energy Charter Conference
Eurasian Development Bank
Eurasian Economic Community
European Organization for Nuclear Research
Global Fund to Fight AIDS, Tuberculosis and Malaria
Global Green Growth Institute
GUUAM
Hague Conference on Private International Law
Ibero-American Conference
Indian Ocean Commission
Inter-American Development Bank
International Centre for Migration Policy Development
International Conference on the Great Lakes Region of Africa
International Fund for Saving the Aral Sea
International Humanitarian Fact-Finding Commission
International Hydrographic Organization
International Institute for the Unification of Private Law
Intergovernmental Authority on Development

International Anti-Corruption Academy
Islamic Development Bank Group
Italian-Latin American Institute
Latin American Economic System
Latin American Integration Association
Latin American Parliament
OPEC Fund for International Development
Organization for Economic Cooperation and Development
Organization for Security and Cooperation in Europe
Organization of American States
Organization of Eastern Caribbean States
Pacific Islands Forum
Pan African Intergovernmental Agency for Water and Sanitation for Africa
Permanent Court of Arbitration
Regional Centre on Small Arms and Light Weapons in the Great Lakes Region, the Horn of Africa and Bordering States
Shanghai Cooperation Organization
South Asian Association for Regional Cooperation
South Centre
Southern African Development Community
Union of South American Nations
West African Economic and Monetary Union

African Union

Address: Office of the Permanent Observer of the African Union to the United Nations
305 East 47th Street, 5th Floor
3 Dag Hammarskjöld Plaza
New York, N.Y. 10017

Telephone: (212) 319-5490

Telefax: (212) 319-7135, -6509

e-mail: aumission_ny@Yahoo.com
AU-NewYork@africa-union.org

website: www.africa-union.org

Ext. 22 — H.E. Mr. Téte **António***
Ambassador
Permanent Observer

Ext. 14 — Mrs. Louise Sharene **Bailey**
Adviser (Senior Political Affairs Officer)
Mr. Wesley Nathaniel Bailey

Mr. Adonia **Ayebare**
Adviser (Peacebuilding and Development)
Mrs. Ayebare Dorah Nampumuza

Mr. Ayoup Zaid **Elrashdi**
Adviser (Senior Economic Affairs Officer)
Mrs. Bushra Elkhzkhaz

Ext. 27 — Mr. Abdoulaye **Maiga**
Adviser (Conferences and Meetings)
Mrs. Habila Maiga

Ext. 26 — Mrs. Mirriam Auma **Omala-Gauvin**
Adviser (Conferences and Meetings)
Mr. Didier Jean-Félix Gauvin

Ext. 19 — Mr. Dinberu M. **Abebe**
Adviser (Administration and Finance)

Ext. 23 — Mr. Salem **Matug**
Adviser (Political Affairs Officer)
Mrs. Rehab Ali A. Awedan

Ext. 50 — Ms. Puseletso Adelinah **Molato**
Adviser (Economic and Social Affairs)

Mr. Simon **Yorou Raphael**
Adviser (Documentation Officer)
Mrs. Odette Tempe N'Dah

* See footnote on page 309

Ext. 18	Mr. Seshime **Dovlo** Attaché (Assistant Accountant) Mrs. Gisele Vedogbeton-Dovlo
Ext. 22	Mrs. Marie Cécile **Dembélé Boré** Attaché Mr. Bocar Boré
Ext.15	Mrs. Marieme **Kane** Attaché Mr. Mamadou Kane
	Mrs. Oumou **Daou** Attaché

Asian-African Legal Consultative Organization

Address: Office of the Permanent Observer of the Asian-African Legal Consultative Organization to the United Nations
188 East 76th Street, # 26B
New York, NY 10021

Telephone: (917) 623-2861

Telefax: (206) 426-5442

e-mail: aalco@un.int

Mr. Roy S. **Lee**
Permanent Observer

Caribbean Community (CARICOM)

Address:	Office of the Permanent Observer for the Caribbean Community (CARICOM) to the United Nations 71 Ocean Parkway, Suite #5L Brooklyn, NY 11218
Telephone:	(718) 438-1925
Telefax:	(718) 972-1254
e-mail:	Cari.per.obs.un@gmail.com; Missouri.shermanpeter@caricom.org
Website:	www.caricom.org

H.E. Ms. A. Missouri **Sherman-Peter***
Ambassador
Permanent Observer

* See footnote on page 309

Central American Integration System

Address: Office of the Permanent Observer for the Central American Integration System to the United Nations
320 West 75th Street, Suite 1A
New York, N.Y. 10023

Telephone: (212) 682-1550; -877-0946

Telefax: (212) 877-9021

e-mail: ccampos@sgsica-ny.org

Mr. Carlos **Campos**
Permanent Observer

Commonwealth

Address: Office of the Commonwealth
at the United Nations
800 Second Avenue, 4th Floor
New York, N.Y. 10017

Telephone: (212) 599-6190, 682-3658, 338-9410

Telefax: (212) 808-4975, 972-3970

e-mail: newyork@commonwealth.int

...
Permanent Observer

Mr. Michael **Mitchell**
Senior Adviser

Cooperation Council for the Arab States of the Gulf

Address: Office of the Permanent Observer for
the Cooperation Council for the Arab States of the Gulf
to the United Nations
One Dag Hammarskjöld Plaza
885 Second Avenue, 40th Floor
New York, N.Y. 10017

Telephone: (212) 319 3088, -3800

Telefax: (212) 319-3434

email: gccny@un.int

H.E. Mr. Abdulaziz Abdulrahman **Alammar***
Ambassador
Permanent Observer
Mrs. Asma Alshihah

Miss Farah Tawfeeq **AlMansoor**
Attaché

Mr. Bandar **Musa**
Attaché

* See footnote on page 309.

Economic Community of Western African States

Address: Office of the Permanent Observer for
the Economic Community of Western African States
to the United Nations
255 Huguenot Street, Apt. 2104
New Rochelle, N.Y. 10801

Telephone: (914) 738-0430

Telefax: (914) 738-0430

email: tanoukleon@yahoo.com
ecowasmission.ny@gmail.com

Website: www.ecowas.int

Mr. Tanou **Koné**
Permanent Observer

European Union

Address:	Delegation of the European Union to the United Nations 666 Third Avenue, 26th Floor New York, N.Y. 10017
Telephone:	(212) 292-8600
Telefax:	(212) 292-8680
e-mail:	delegation-new-york@eeas.europa.eu
website:	www.eu-un.europa.eu

292-8631	H.E. Mr. Thomas **Mayr-Harting*** Ambassador Head of the Delegation of the European Union Mrs. Elisabeth Mayr-Harting
401-0154	H.E. Mr. Ioannis **Vrailas** Ambassador Deputy Head of Delegation Ms. Christiane Bourloyannis
292-8621	Mr. Francesco **Presutti** Minister Counsellor Ms. Anna Lo Monaco
292-8634	Mr. Gilles **Marhic** Minister Counsellor Ms. Alice Forgac
292-8604	Mr. Jan Pirouz **Poulsen** Minister Counsellor
292-8612	Mr. Carl **Hallergard** Minister Counsellor Ms. Aurora De Bustos Garcia de los Salmones
292-8606	Mr. Eugeniusz **Szajbel** Minister Counsellor Mrs. Anna Szajbel
401-0109	Mr. John **Busuttil** First Counsellor Mrs. Jacqueline Busuttil Xuereb
292-8627	Ms. Carmel **Power** First Counsellor
401-0103	Mr. Predrag **Avramović** First Counsellor Ms. Sylvie Vanherberghen

* See footnote on page 309

401-0138	Mr. Americo **Beviglia Zampetti** First Counsellor
401-0150	Mr. Janusz **Wawrzyniuk** First Counsellor Mrs. Agnieszka Beldowska-Wawrzyniuk
401-0133	Ms. Eva Charlotta **Schlyter** Counsellor Mr. Brian Gorlick
292-8642	Mr. Rafael **de Bustamante** Counsellor Mr. Paul Frederick Geitner
401-0114	Mr. Filip **Vanden Bulcke** Counsellor
401-0136	Mr. Philippe **Latriche** Counsellor Ms. Shirley Latriche
292-8619	Mr. Roberto **Storaci** Counsellor Ms. Giuditta Scordino
292-8603	Mr. Pavel **Sustak** Counsellor Ms. Iva Sustakova
292-8602	Mr. Gerardus Antonius Wilhelmus **Van Den Akker** Counsellor Ms. Angelique Genevieve Gerritsen
401-4142	Mr. Omar Thomas Al-Amin **Bargawi** First Secretary Ms. Diana Jane Ewer
401-0107	Mr. Thibault **Devanlay** First Secretary
292-8645	Ms. Agnieszka **Klausa** First Secretary
292-8643	Mr. Pit **Köhler** First Secretary Ms. Mareike Köhler
401-0132	Ms. Eglantine **Cujo** First Secretary Mr. Mathias Forteau
401-0151	Mr. Jesús **Diaz Carazo** First Secretary
401-0119	Ms. Alexandra **Dedu** First Secretary

401-0124	Ms. Helen **Kaljulate** Second Secretary
292-8629	Ms. Anca Cristina **Mezdrea** Second Secretary
	Ms. Suvi Maria Pauliina **Seppäläinen** Second Secretary
401-0112	Mr. Bernard **Schelfaut** Attaché Ms. Nathalie Goossens
292-8615	Ms. Angela **Haeussler** Attaché Mr. IbrahimOzan
292-8633	Mr. Aurimas **Zabulis** Attaché Mr. Thomas Vershaeve
401-4141	Ms. Naomi **Benchaya** Assistant Attaché Mr. Lionel Busschaert

International Criminal Police Organization (INTERPOL)

Address: Office of the International Criminal Police Organization
(INTERPOL) Special Representative
to the United Nations
One United Nations Plaza, DC1, Suite 2610
New York, N.Y. 10017

Telephone: (917) 367-3463

Telefax: (917) 367-3476

e-mail: nyoffice@interpol.int

Mr. Joël **Sollier**
Acting Special Representative

---

(917) 367-3425 Mr. Chun Tung Tony **Ho**
Assistant Director

(917) 367-3456 Ms. Rowena **Lambert**
Policy Analyst

International Development Law Organization

Address: Office of the Permanent Observer for the International Development Law Organization to the United Nations
Uganda House
336 East 45th Street, 11th Floor
New York, N.Y. 10017

Telephone: (212) 867-9707 (Office)
(646) 229-0936 (Cellular)

Telefax: (212) 867-9719

e-mail: pcivili@idlo.int

website: www.idlo.int

Mr. Patrizio M. **Civili**
Permanent Observer
Mrs. Susan A. Civili

Ms. Judit **Arenas Licea**
Director, Communications and Public Affairs
Deputy Permanent Observer

International Institute for Democracy and Electoral Assistance

Address: Office of the Permanent Observer for the International Institute for Democracy and Electoral Assistance
to the United Nations
336 East 45th Street, 14th Floor
New York, N.Y. 10017

Telephone: (212) 286-1084

Telefax: (212) 286-0260

e-mail: unobserver@idea.int

Mr. Massimo **Tommasoli**
Permanent Observer
Mrs. Francesca Agneta Tommasoli

International Organization for Migration

Address:	Office of the Permanent Observer for the International Organization for Migration to the United Nations 122 East 42nd Street, 48th Floor, Suite 1610 New York, N.Y. 10168
Telephone:	(212) 681-7000, Ext. 264
Telefax:	(212) 867-5887
e-mail:	unobserver@iom.int
website:	www.iom.int/unobserver

Ext. 202	Mr. Ashraf Elnour Mustafa Mohamed **Nour** Permanent Observer
Ext. 203	Ms. Lea **Matheson** Deputy Permanent Observer
Ext. 212	Ms. Amy **Muedin** Programme Specialist Mr. Richard Fishler
Ext. 204	Mr. Christopher **Richter** Associate Migration Officer
Ext. 236	Mr. Kevin **Ritchie** Associate Migration Officer
Ext. 221	Ms. Olivia **Headon** Associate Migration Officer

International Organization of la Francophonie

Address: Office of the Permanent Observer for the International Organization of la Francophonie to the United Nations
801 Second Avenue, Suite 605
New York, N.Y. 10017

Telephone: (212) 867-6771

Telefax: (212) 867-3840

e-mail: reper.new-york@francophonie.org

website: www.francophonie.org

H.E. Mr. Paul **Tiendrebeogo***
Ambassador
Permanent Observer

Ms. Patricia **Herdt**
Deputy Permanent Observer

Ms. Emilienne Lionelle **Ngo-Samnick**
Programme Officer

Ms. Ange **Konan**
Administrative Assistant

Mrs. Carmelle **Cangé**
Managing Assistant

* See footnote on page 309

International Renewable Energy Agency

Address: Office of the Permanent Observer for the International Renewable Energy Agency to the United Nations
336 East 45th Street, 11th Floor
New York, N.Y. 10017

Telephone: (646) 738-2014

Telefax: (646) 738-5582

Website: www.irena.org

...
Permanent Observer

Ms. Yera **Ortiz de Urbina**
Deputy Permanent Observer

Mr. Christopher F. **Hackett**
Senior Adviser

International Union for Conservation of Nature

Address: Office of the Permanent Observer for the International Union for Conservation of Nature
to the United Nations
551 Fifth Avenue, Suites 800 A-B
New York, N.Y. 10176

Telephone: (212) 346-1163

Telefax: (212) 346-1046

e-mail: iucn@un.int

Website www.iucn.org

Mr. Narinder **Kakar**
Permanent Observer
Mrs. Neelam Kakar

Ms. Amy Parekh **Mehta**
Adviser (Programme Management)

League of Arab States

Address: Office of the Permanent Observer for the League of Arab States to the United Nations
866 United Nations Plaza, Suite 494
New York, N.Y. 10017

Telephone: (212) 838-8700

Telefax: (212) 355-3909, -8001

e-mail:: las.mail@un.int

H.E. Mr. Ahmed **Fathalla***
Ambassador
Permanent Observer

Mr. Abdelaziz **Enani**
First Counsellor
Deputy Permanent Observer

Ext. 207 Ms. Nasria Elardja **Flitti**
First Counsellor

Ext. 210 Mr. Ahmed M. **Nassouf**
Second Secretary

Ext. 211 Mr. Islam Abdullah Hassan **Al-Amri**
Third Secretary

Ext. 208 Mr. Yasser **Al-Shami**
Attaché
Mrs. Al-Shami

Mr. Ahmed Marii Zaid **Abdelgaber**
Attaché

Ext. 203 Mr. Mohammed **Morsi**
Adviser

Ext. 213 Mr. Bakri **Al-Khalifa**
Adviser

* See footnote on page 309.

Organization of Islamic Cooperation

Address: Office of the Permanent Observer for the Organization of Islamic Cooperation to the United Nations
320 East 51st Street
New York, N.Y. 10022

Telephone: (212) 883-0140

Telefax: (212) 883-0143

e-mail: oicny@un.int

website: www.oicun.org

H.E. Mr. Ufuk **Gokcen***
Ambassador
Permanent Observer

Mr. Shaher **Awawdeh**
Minister Counsellor
Deputy Permanent Observer

Ms. Amina **Kader**
Adviser

Mr. Mehmet **Kalyoncu**
Adviser

Ms. Amierah **Ismail**
Attaché

Ms. Satanaa **Eshak**
Attaché

* See footnote on page 309.

Parliamentary Assembly of the Mediterranean

Address: Office of the Permanent Observer for the Parliamentary Assembly of the Mediterranean to the United Nations
405 Lexington Avenue, Third Floor
New York, N.Y. 10174

Telephone: (646) 438-9440

Telefax: (646) 438-9228

e-mail: pam.unny@pam.int

Mr. Anton **Tabone**
Permanent Observer

Partners in Population and Development

Address: Office of the Permanent Observer for Partners in Population and Development to the United Nations
336 East 45th Street, 14th Floor
New York, N.Y. 10017

Telephone: (212) 286-1082

Telefax: (212) 286-0260

e-mail: nalam@ppdsec.org
rgarvey@ppdsec.org

website: www.partners-popdev.org

Mr. Mohammad Nurul **Alam**
Permanent Observer
Mrs. Rubaiyat Sadia Alam

Ms. Ruby **Garvey**
Assistant Attaché

University for Peace

Address:	Office of the Permanent Observer for the University for Peace 551 Fifth Avenue, Suites 800 A-B New York, N.Y. 10176
Telephone:	(212) 346-1163
Telefax:	(212) 346-1046
e-mail:	nyinfo@upeace.org
website:	www.upeace.org

Mr. Narinder **Kakar**
Permanent Observer
Mrs. Neelam Kakar

IV. Other entities having received a standing invitation to participate as observers in the sessions and the work of the General Assembly and maintaining permanent offices at Headquarters

International Committee of the Red Cross

Address: Delegation of the International Committee of the Red Cross to the United Nations
801 Second Avenue, 18th Floor
New York, N.Y. 10017-4706

Telephone: (212) 599-6021

Telefax: (212) 599-6009

e-mail: newyork@icrc.org

Mr. Philip **Spoerri**
Head of Delegation
Permanent Observer
Mrs. Lucy Morgan Edwards

Ms. Joy **Elyahou**
Deputy Head of Delegation
Mr. Sebastien Chessex

Mr. Stéphane **Bonamy**
Delegate
Mrs. Nancy Bonamy

Mrs. Véronique **Christory**
Adviser
Mr. Jean-François Christory

Mrs. Ann Kyung Un **Deer**
Adviser
Mr. Andrew Deer

Mr. Ernesto **Granillo**
Adviser

Mrs. Dolorosa **ArrummBrungs**
Administrator
Mr. Mark Brungs

Ms. Andrea **Cánepa**
Head of Chancery
Assistant to the Head of delegation

Mrs. Jessica Andre **Martinelli**
Administrative Assistant
Mr. Ricardo Martinelli

Mrs. Aude **Baldino**
Administrative Officer
Mr. James Baldino

Ms. Tandiwe **Maithya**
Programme Assistant

International Federation of Red Cross and Red Crescent Societies

Address: Delegation of the International Federation of Red Cross and Red Crescent Societies to the United Nations
420 Lexington Avenue, Suite 2811
New York, N.Y. 10170

Telephone: (212) 338-0161

Telefax: (212) 338-9832

e-mail: ifrcny@un.int

Ext. 201 — Mr. Marwan **Jilani**
Head of Delegation
Permanent Observer

Ext. 206 — Ms. Anne Bang **Christensen**
Senior Humanitarian Affairs Delegate

Ext. 204 — Mr. Ajay **Madiwale**
Adviser

International Olympic Committee

Address: Office of the Permanent Observer for the International Olympic Committee to the United Nations
708 Third Avenue, 6th Floor
New York, N.Y. 10017

Telephone: (212) 209 3952

Telefax: (212) 209 7100

e-mail: IOC-UNObserver@olympic.org

H.E. Mr. Mario **Pescante***
Permanent Observer

Ms. Lindsay **Glassco**
Deputy Permanent Observer

Ms. Margie **Kam**
Senior Adviser

* See footnote on page 309.

Inter-Parliamentary Union

Address: Office of the Permanent Observer for the Inter-Parliamentary Union to the United Nations
336 East 45th Street, Suite 10th Floor
New York, N.Y. 10017

Telephone: (212) 557-5880

Telefax: (212) 557-3954

e-mail: ny-office@mail.ipu.org

Ms. Patricia Ann **Torsney**
Permanent Observer

Mr. Alessandro **Motter**
Senior Adviser (Economic and Social Affairs)

Ms. Sandrine **Gigon**
Executive Assistant

Ms. Marilou **Delos Santos**
Administrative Assistant

Sovereign Military Order of Malta

Address: Office of the Permanent Observer for the Sovereign Military Order of Malta to the United Nations
216 East 47th Street, 8th Floor
New York, N.Y. 10017

Telephone: (212) 355-6213, -4601

Telefax: (212) 355-4014

e-mail: orderofmalta@un.int

H.E. Mr. Robert L. **Shafer***
Ambassador
Permanent Observer
Mrs. Ellen Schlafly Shafer

H.E. Mr. Oscar Rafael **de Rojas**
Ambassador
Deputy Permanent Observer
Mrs. Patricia Reyes de Rojas

Mr. Gian Luigi **Valenza**
Minister Counsellor
Mrs. Maria Barbara Valenza

Mr. Henry J. **Humphreys**
Counsellor
Mrs. Joanne Humphreys

Mrs. Fiamma **Arditi di Castelvetere Manzo**
Counsellor
Mr. Alessandro Manzo

Mr. Bertrand **de Looz Karageorgiades**
Counsellor
Mrs. Jacqueline de Looz

Mr. Philip Allen **Lacovara**
Counsellor
Legal Adviser
Ms. Madeleine Lacovara

Mr. James E. **Buckley**
Counsellor
Mrs. Francis Buckley

Mr. Michael **Espiritu**
Counsellor

Mr. Nicola **Tegoni**
Counsellor

* See footnote on page 309.

Mr. Hreinn P. **Lindal**
Attaché

Ms. Kara L. **DeDonato**
Attaché

V. Specialized agencies and related organizations maintaining liaison offices at Headquarters

International Labour Organization

Address:	ILO Office for the United Nations One Dag Hammarskjöld Plaza 885 Second Avenue, 30th Floor New York, N.Y. 10017
Telephone:	(212) 697-0150
Telefax:	(212) 697-5218
e-mail:	newyork@ilo.org

697-3030	Ms. Jane **Stewart** Special Representative to the United Nations and Director Mr. Henry Stolp
697-1196	Mr. Vinicius **Carvalho Pinheiro** Deputy Director Ms. Deise Leobet
Ext. 110	Mr. Kevin **Cassidy** Senior Communications and Public Information Specialist Mrs. Cheryl Cassidy
Ext. 106	Ms. Amber **Barth** Programme Analyst Mr. Abdellatif Bendaoud

Food and Agriculture Organization of the United Nations

Address: FAO Liaison Office with the United Nations
One United Nations Plaza, Room 1125
New York, N.Y. 10017

Telephone: (212) 963-6036

Telefax: (212) 963-5425

e-mail: lon-registry@un.org

963-0977 Mrs. Sharon **Brennen-Haylock**
Director
Mr. Claude Bromwell Fitzgerald Haylock

963-0994 Mrs. Marianna **Kovacs**
Senior Liaison Officer
Mr. Sandor Bolla

963-0985 Mr. Javier **Molina Cruz**
Liaison Officer

United Nations Educational, Scientific and Cultural Organization

Address:	UNESCO Office at the United Nations Two United Nations Plaza, Room 900 New York, N.Y. 10017
Telephone:	(212) 963-5995
Telefax:	(212) 963-8014
e-mail:	newyork@unesco.org

---

(917) 367-5224	Ms. Min Jeong **Kim** Officer-in-charge
963-5986	Mr. George **Papagiannis** External Relations and Information Officer
963-5985	Ms. Lily **Valtchanova** Liaison Officer Mr. Bradley Gray
963-4383	Mr. Ricardo **De Guimaraes-Pinto** Liaison Officer Mrs. Elisabetta Pollastri
963-2007	Ms. Ana **Persic** Programme Specialist
963-0186	Ms. Paulette **O'Sullivan** Senior Administrative Assisatnt

World Health Organization

Address: WHO Office at the United Nations
One Dag Hammarskjold Plaza
885 Second Avenue
26th floor
New York, N.Y. 10017

Telephone: (646) 626-6060

Telefax: (646) 626-6080

e-mail: wun@whoun.org

646-626-6045 Dr. Jacob **Kumaresan**
Executive Director
Mrs. Aruna Kumaresan

646-626-6046 Mr. Werner **Obermeyer**
Senior External Relations Officer
(Interagency Relations and UN Reform)
Mrs. Izel Obermeyer

646-626-6047 Ms. Fatima **Khan**
External Relations Officer

646-626-6050 Mrs. Angelica **Spraggins**
Communications Officer
Mr. Scott Spraggins

646-626-6043 Mr. Hervé **Verhoosel**
Manager, External Relations
Roll Back Malaria Partnership

646-626-6043 Mr. Geoffrey **So**
External Relations Officer
Roll Back Malaria Partnership

646-626-6054 Mr. Trey **Watkins**
External Relations Officer
Roll Back Malaria Partnership

World Bank

Address:	Office of the Special Representative of the World Bank to the United Nations One Dag Hammarskjöld Plaza 885 Second Avenue, 26th Floor New York, N.Y. 10017
Telephone:	(212) 317-4720
Telefax:	(212) 317-4733

317-4723	Mrs. Dominique **Bichara** Special Representative to the United Nations
317-4726	Ms. Veronica **Piatkov** Counsellor
317-4725	Ms. Clare **Gardoll** Counsellor
317-4722	Ms. Ana María **Arteaga** Office Manager

International Monetary Fund

Address: Office of the Special Representative of the International Monetary Fund to the United Nations
One Dag Hammarskjöld Plaza
885 Second Avenue, 26th Floor
New York, N.Y. 10017

Telephone: (212) 317-4720

Telefax: (212) 317-4733

e-mail: abertuchsamuels@imf.org
NSubramaniam@imf.org

317-4739	Mr. Axel **Bertuch-Samuels** Special Representative of the International Monetary Fund to the United Nations Mrs. Leslie Samuels
317-4738	Ms. Nritya **Subramaniam** Senior Liaison Officer

International Telecommunication Union

Address: ITU Liaison Office
at the United Nations
Two United Nations Plaza, Room 2524
New York, N.Y. 10017

Telephone: (212) 963-6121

Telefax: (917) 367-0801, -0802

e-mail: fowlie@un.org

Website: www.itu.int

Mr. Gary **Fowlie**
Director
Representative to the United Nations
Mrs. Karen Fowlie

Mrs. Kadiatou **Sall-Beye**
Project Officer

Ms. Sharon **London**
Administrative Assistant

World Meteorological Organization

Address: WMO Office at the United Nations
866 United Nations Plaza, Room A-302
New York, N.Y. 10017

Telephone: (212) 963-9444
(917) 367-9867

Telefax: (917) 367-9868

e-mail: pegerton@wmo.int

website: www.wmo.int

Mr. Paul D. **Egerton**
Representative and Coordinator to the United Nations and other international organizations in North America
Mrs. Tanja Naumovski-Egerton

World Intellectual Property Organization

Address: WIPO Coordination Office at the United Nations
Two United Nations Plaza, Room 2525
New York, N.Y. 10017

Telephone: (212) 963-6813

Telefax: (212) 963-4801

e-mail: wipo@un.org

Mrs. Lucinda **Longcroft**
Head
Mr. Dominic Longcroft

Ms. Rehana **Ariff**
Administrative Officer

International Fund for Agricultural Development

Address: IFAD Liaison Office with the United Nations
Two United Nations Plaza, Room 1128/1129
New York, N.Y. 10017

Telephone: (212) 963-0546

Telefax: (212) 963-2787

e-mail: z.bleicher@ifad.org

Mr. Zachary **Bleicher**
Head of the Office
Partnership Officer

United Nations Industrial Development Organization

Address: Office of the Representative of UNIDO
to the United Nations
One United Nations Plaza, Room 1110
New York, N.Y. 10017

Telephone: (212) 963-6890, -6891

Telefax: (212) 963-7904

e-mail: office.newyork@unido.org

website: www.unido.org/office/newyork

963-6890 Mr. Paul **Maseli**
Director and UNIDO Representative to the United Nations and other International Organizations

---

(917) 367-4884 Mr. Ralf **Bredel**
Senior Liaison Officer
Ms. Sonja Bredel

963-6887 Ms. Josieline **Berberabe Genio**
Administrative Assistant

World Tourism Organization

Address: Office of the Special Representative of the World Tourism Organization to the United Nations
220 East 42nd Street, Room DNB-1866
New York, N.Y. 10017

Telephone: (646) 781-4798

Telefax: (212) 682-5905

---

(646) 781-4794 Mr. Rafeeuddin **Ahmed**
Special Representative to the United Nations
Mrs. Nighat Ahmed

---

(646) 781-4797 Mr. Kazi Afzalur **Rahman**
Deputy Special Representative
Mrs. Shegufta Rahman

(646) 781-4796 Mr. Sarbuland **Khan**
Senior Counsellor
Mrs. Asma Khan

(646) 781-4798 Ms. Yanick **Calixte**
Senior Liaison Assistant

International Atomic Energy Agency

Address: IAEA Office at the United Nations
One United Nations Plaza, Room 1155
New York, N.Y. 10017

Telephone: (212) 963-6012

Telefax: (917) 367-4046

e-mail: IAEANY@un.org

Mr. Geoffrey **Shaw**
Representative of the Director General
to the United Nations and Director
Mrs. Gaynor Shaw

Ms. Tracy **Brown**
Liaison and Public Information Officer

Ms. Evelyn **Prinz-Ortiz**
Liaison Associate

Ms. Francine **Lontok**
Executive Assistant

International Criminal Court

Address:	Liaison Office of the International Criminal Court to the United Nations 866 United Nations Plaza, Suite 476 New York, N.Y. 10017
Telephone:	(212) 486-1362/1347
Telefax:	(212) 486-1361
e-mail:	liaisonofficeny@icc-cpi.int

486-1346 Ms. Karen Odaba **Mosoti**
Head of the Liaison Office

International Seabed Authority

Address: Office of the Permanent Observer for the International Seabed Authority to the United Nations
One United Nations Plaza, Room 1140
New York, N.Y. 10017

Telephone: (212) 963-6470, -6411

Telefax: (212) 963-0908

e-mail: seaun@un.org

H.E. Mr. Nii Allotey **Odunton***
Secretary-General
Permanent Observer

Mr. Michael **Lodge**
Deputy Permanent Observer

* See footnote on page 309.

International Tribunal for the Law of the Sea

Address: Office of the Permanent Observer for the International Tribunal for the Law of the Sea to the United Nations*
Two United Nations Plaza, Room 438
New York, N.Y. 10017

Telephone: (212) 963-6140

Telefax: (212) 963-5847

H.E. Mr. Vladimir **Golitsyn****
President of the Tribunal
Permanent Observer
Mrs. Olga Golitsyna

Mr. Philippe **Gautier**
Registrar
Deputy Permanent Observer
Mrs. Catherine Devresse

Correspondence should preferably be sent directly to the seat of the Tribunal in Hamburg. See footnote below for telephone and fax numbers, as well as the e-mail address.

* Address of the Headquarters:
International Tribunal for the Law of the Sea
Am Internationalen Seegerichtshof 1
D-22609 Hamburg
Germany
Telephone: 49 40 35607-0
Telefax: 49 40 35607-275
e-mail: gautier@itlos.org

** See footnote on page 309.

Annexes

1. **Members of the principal organs of the United Nations**
2. **Members of other standing organs at Headquarters**
3. **National holidays of Member States**

1. Members of the principal organs of the United Nations

General Assembly

President of the sixty-ninth session of the General Assembly:
H.E. Mr. Sam **Kutesa** (Uganda)

Vice-Presidents of the sixty-ninth session of the General Assembly:

Argentina
Burkina Faso
China
Cyprus
Democratic Republic of the Congo
France
Georgia
Grenada
Iceland
Kiribati
Libya
Niger
Oman
Pakistan
Portugal
Russian Federation
Saint Lucia
Swaziland
Tajikistan
United Kingdom of Great Britain and Northern Ireland
United States of America

Member States (193)

Afghanistan
Albania
Algeria
Andorra
Angola
Antigua and Barbuda
Argentina
Armenia
Australia
Austria
Azerbaijan
Bahamas
Bahrain
Bangladesh
Barbados
Belarus
Belgium
Belize
Benin
Bhutan
Bolivia (Plurinational State of)
Bosnia and Herzegovina
Botswana
Brazil
Brunei Darussalam
Bulgaria
Burkina Faso
Burundi
Cabo Verde
Cambodia
Cameroon
Canada
Central African Republic
Chad
Chile
China
Colombia
Comoros
Congo
Costa Rica
Côte d'Ivoire
Croatia
Cuba
Cyprus
Czech Republic
Democratic People's Republic of Korea
Democratic Republic of the Congo
Denmark
Djibouti
Dominica
Dominican Republic
Ecuador
Egypt
El Salvador
Equatorial Guinea
Eritrea
Estonia
Ethiopia
Fiji
Finland
France
France
Gabon
Gambia
Georgia
Germany
Ghana
Greece
Grenada
Guatemala
Guinea
Guinea-Bissau
Guyana
Haiti
Honduras
Hungary
Iceland
India
Indonesia
Iran (Islamic Republic of)
Iraq
Ireland
Israel
Italy
Jamaica

General Assembly [*continued*]

Japan
Jordan
Kazakhstan
Kenya
Kiribati
Kuwait
Kyrgyzstan
Lao People's Democratic Republic
Latvia
Lebanon
Lesotho
Liberia
Libya
Liechtenstein
Lithuania
Luxembourg
Madagascar
Malawi
Malaysia
Maldives
Mali
Malta
Marshall Islands
Mauritania
Mauritius
Mexico
Micronesia (Federated States of)
Monaco
Mongolia
Montenegro
Morocco
Mozambique
Myanmar
Namibia
Nauru
Nepal
Netherlands
New Zealand
Nicaragua
Niger
Nigeria
Norway
Oman
Pakistan
Palau
Panama
Papua New Guinea
Paraguay
Peru
Philippines
Poland
Portugal
Qatar
Republic of Korea
Republic of Moldova
Romania
Russian Federation
Rwanda
Saint Kitts and Nevis
Saint Lucia
Saint Vincent and the Grenadines
Samoa
San Marino
Sao Tome and Principe
Saudi Arabia
Senegal
Serbia
Seychelles
Sierra Leone
Singapore
Slovakia
Slovenia
Solomon Islands
Somalia
South Africa
South Sudan
Spain
Sri Lanka
Sudan
Suriname
Swaziland
Sweden
Switzerland
Syrian Arab Republic
Tajikistan
Thailand
The former Yugoslav Republic of Macedonia
Timor-Leste
Togo
Tonga
Trinidad and Tobago
Tunisia
Turkey
Turkmenistan
Tuvalu
Uganda
Ukraine
United Arab Emirates
United Kingdom of Great Britain and Northern Ireland
United Republic of Tanzania
United States of America
Uruguay
Uzbekistan
Vanuatu
Venezuela (Bolivarian Republic of)
Viet Nam
Yemen
Zambia
Zimbabwe

General Assembly [*continued*]

Office of the President of the sixty-ninth session of the General Assembly:

H.E. Mr. Arthur **Kafeero**
Ambassador
Chef de Cabinet

Mr. John Leonard **Mugerwa**
Deputy Chef de Cabinet
Sustainable Development

Ms. Alina **Padeanu**
Adviser
Post 2015 Development Agenda

...
Adviser
Climate Change

Ms. Aqeelah **Akbar**
Senior Adviser
Gender Equality and Empowerment of Women

Mr. Sipho **Seakamela**
Senior Adviser
Africa, Cooperation between UN and Regional Organizations

Mr. Robert B. **Mugimba**
Adviser
UN Security Council reform and GA Revitalizaton

...
Adviser
Mediation and Alliance of Civilizations

Mr. Steen Malthe **Hansen**
Senior Adviser
Conflict Prevention and Peacebuilding

Mr. Steven Nkayivu **Ssenabulya**
Special Assistant to PGA

Ms. Tala **Dowlatshahi**
Senior Adviser
Partnerships and Outreach

...
Adviser
First Committee

Ms. Li **Wen**
Adviser
Second Committee

General Assembly [*continued*]

Ms. Juliana Gaspar **Ruas**
Adviser
Second Committee

Ms. Santa Laker **Kinyera**
Adviser
Third Committee

Mrs. Melita **Gabrič**
Adviser
Third Committee

...
Adviser
Fourth Committee

Mr. Abdelghani **Merabet**
Senior Adviser
First Committee and Financing for Development

Ms. Veronica **Reeves**
Speechwriter

Mr. Jean Victor **Nkolo**
Spokesperson

Ms. Fanny **Langella**
Deputy Spokesperson
Deputy Speechwriter

Security Council

Presidents of the Security Council (2015):

January: Chile
February: China
March: France
April: Jordan
May: Lithuania
June: Malaysia
July: New Zealand
August: Nigeria
September: Russian Federation
October: Spain
November: United Kingdom of Great Britain and Northern Ireland
December: United States

Angola
Representative:
...

Deputy representative:
...

Alternate representatives:
...

Chad
Representative:
H.E. Mr. Chérif Mahamt **Zene**

Deputy representative:
Mr. Mangaral **Bante**

Alternate representative:
Ms. Alingue Madeleine **Andebeng Labeu**

Advisers:
Mr. Papouri Tchingombe **Patchanne**
Mr. Eric **Miangar**
Mr. Abdallah Bachar **Bong**
Mr. Ali Adoum **Ahmat**
Mr. Mahamat Adoum **Koulbou**
Mr. Makadjibeye **Letinan**
Mr. Amir Irdiss **Abderamane**
Mr. Mahamat Nourene **Abderamane**
Mr. Mahamat Zene **Ali**
Mr. Mohamed Mohamed **Kachallah**
Mr. Boukar **Doungous**
Mr. Hissein Oumar **Seidou**
Mr. Ahmat Absakine **Yerima**

Chile
Representative:
H.E. Mr. Cristian **Barros**

Deputy representative:
H.E. Mr. Carlos **Olguin**

Alternate representatives:
Mr. Ignacio **Llanos**
Ms. Belén **Sapag**
Mr. Patricio **Aguirre**
Mr. Juan Pablo **Espinoza**
Mr. Diego **Araya**
Mr. Fernando **Cabezas**
Mr. Alvaro **Arévalo**
Col. Gustav **Meyerholz**

Advisers:
Ms. Montserrat **Macuer**
Mr. Sang Yeob **Kim**
Mr. Ernesto **González**

Security Council [*continued*]

China
Representative:
H.E. Mr. **Liu** Jieyi

Deputy representative:
H.E. Mr. **Wang** Min

Alternate representatives:
Mr. **Shen** Bo
Mr. **Zhao** Yong
Mr. **Cai** Weiming
Ms. **Jiang** Hua
Mr. **Li** Yongsheng

Advisers:
Mr. **Wei** Zonglei
Ms.**Liu** Bing
Mr. **Yang** Zhiyu
Mr. **Zhu** Yanwei
Ms. **Xiao** Yue
Mr. **Xiang** Xin
Mr. **Jiang** Bo
Mr. **Wang** Yu
Mr. **Hong** Ming

France
Representative:
H.E. Mr. François **Delattre**

Deputy representative:
Mr. Alexis **Lamek**

Alternate representatives:
Mr. Philippe **Bertoux**
Mr. Tanguy **Stehelin**

Jordan
Representative:
H.R.H. Prince Zeid Ra'ad Zeid **Al Hussein**

Deputy representatives:
Mr. Mahmoud **Hmoud**
Mr. Eihab **Omaish**

Alternate representatives:
Mr. Samer **Naber**
Mr. Mohammad **Tal**
Mr. Salah **Suheimat**
Mr. Amjad **Al-Moumani**
Mr. Mohammad **Tarawneh**
Ms. Diana **Al-Hadid**
Mr. Adi **Khair**
Mr. Omar **Ababneh**
Mr. Mohammad **Albatayneh**
Mr. laith **Obeidat**
Mr. Faris **Al-Adwan**

Security Council [*continued*]

Lithuania
Representative:
H.E. Ms. Raimonda **Murmokaitė**

Deputy representatives:
Ms. Nida **Jakubonė**
Mr. Dainius **Baublys**

Alternate representatives:
Col. Darius **Petryla**
Mr. Aleksas **Dambrauskas**
Ms. Vaida **Hampe**
Ms. Rasma **Ramoškaitė**
Ms. Viktorija **Budreckaitė**
Ms. Agnė **Gleveckaitė**
Ms. Neringa **Juodkaitė-Putrimienė**
Mr. Aidas **Sunelaitis**
Mr. Dovydas **Špokauskas**
Ms. Rūta **Jazukevičiūtė**
Ms. Diana **Pranevičienė**

Advisers:
Mr. Vygintas **Čereška**
Ms. Solveiga **Vailionytė**
Ms. Erika **Prokofjeva**

Malaysia
Representative:
H.E. Mr. Hussein **Haniff**

Deputy representatives:
Ms. Siti Hajjar **Adnin**
Mr. Raja Reza Raja Zaib **Shah**

Alternate representatives:
Mr. Johan Ariff Abdul **Razak**
Col. Nazari Abd. **Hadi**
Mr. Hew Tse **Hou**
Ms. Murni Abdul **Hamid**
Mr. Ahmad Dzaffir Mohd **Yussof**
Mr. Riaz Abdul **Razak**
Ms. Rosfazidah Razi Varathau **Rajoo**
Ms. Shazana **Mokhtar**
Mr. Mustapha Kamal **Rosdi**
Mr. Mohd Ridzwan **Shahabudin**

New Zealand
Representative:
H.E. Mr. Gerardus Jacobus **van Bohemen**

Deputy representatives:
H.E. Ms. Carolyn **Schwaiger**
H.E. Mr. Phillip **Taula**

Alternate representatives:
Ms. Nicola **Hill**
Colonel David **Russell**
Ms. Angela **Hassan-Sharp**
Mr. Scott **Sheeran**
Ms. Felicity **Roxburgh**
Ms. Karena **Lyons**
Mr. Nicholas **Walbridge**
Mr. Bradley **Sawden**
Mr. Tom **Kennedy**
Lt. Col. Peter **Hall**
Mr. Ben **Steele**
Ms. Alex **Lennox-Marwick**
Mrs. Laura-Lee **Sage**
Mr. Paul **Ballantyne**
Mr. Peter **Wright**
Ms. Mette **Mikkelsen**
Ms. Nicola **Garvey**
Ms. Sarah **Bradley**

Nigeria
Representative:
H.E. Ms. Joy **Ogwu**

Deputy representative:
H.E. Mr. Usman **Sarki**

Alternate representatives:
Mr. Kayode **Laro**
Mr. Lawal **Hamidu**
Mr. Richards **Adejola**
Mr. Martin S. **Adamu**
Ms. Amina **Smaila**
Mr. Mohammed I. **Haidara**
Mr. Yakubu **Dadu**
Mr. Elias **Fatile**
Mrs. Mercy **Clement**

Security Council [*continued*]

Nigeria (cont'd)
Advisers:
Mr. Anthony **Bosah**
Maj. Gen. Jack **Ogunewe**
Mr. Ezenwa **Nwaobiala**
Mr. Emmanuel **Oguntuyi**
Mr. Magaji **Umar**
Mr. Mohammed **Aliyu**
Mr. Sunday **Edem**
Ms. Funmi **Olojo**
Mr. Ariyo **Ojagbamila**
Mr. Ginedu **Agorom**

Russian Federation
Representative:
H.E. Mr. Vitaly I. **Churkin**

Deputy representatives:
Mr. Petr V. **Iliichev**
Mr. Evgeny T. **Zagaynov**
Mr. Vladimir K. **Safronkov**

Alternate representatives:
Mr. Mikael V. **Agasandyan**
Mr. Maxim V. **Musikhin**
Mr. Andrey A. **Listov**
Mr. Alexander V. **Letoshnev**
Ms. Galina S. **Khvan**
Ms. Anna M. **Evstigneeva**
Mrs. Olga V. **Mozolina**
Mr. Alexander A. **Volgarev**
Mr. Roman O. **Katarskiy**
Mr. Evgeny A. **Ustinov**
Mr. Alexander V. **Repkin**
Ms. Elena S. **Mukhametzyanova**
Mr. Konstantin P. **Degtyarev**
Mr. Vadim Y. **Sergeev**
Mr. Oleg O. **Filimonov**
Mr. Dmitry I. **Nekrasov**
Mr. Roman G. **Bryulgart**
Mr. Sergey A. **Leonidchenko**
Ms. Elena A. **Melikbekyan**

Spain
Representative:
H.E. Mr. Román **Oyarzun**

Deputy representative:
H.E. Mr. Juan Manuel **González de Linares Palou**

Alternate representatives:
Mr. Fernando **Fernández-Arias Minuesa**
Mr. Ignacio **Díaz de la Guardia**
Mr. Javier **Gassó Matoses**
Mr. Jose Javier **Gutiérrez Blanco-Navarrete**
Mrs. María **Palacios**
Mr. Alberto Pablo **de la Calle García**
Mr. Luis Francisco **Martínez Montes**
Mr. Francisco Javier **García-Larrache Olalquiaga**
Mrs. Alejandra **del Río Novo**
Mr. Agustín **Rebollo**
Mrs. Carmen **Castiella Ruiz de Velasco**
Mr. Nicolás **Cimarra Etchenique**
Mrs. Victoria **Ortega Gutiérrez**
Mrs. Maria Luisa **Marteles Gutiérrez del Álamo**
Mr. Carlos **López Ortiz**

Advisers:
Mr. Luis **Viñas Casado**
Mr. Félix **Manjón Martín**
Mr. José Antonio **Latorre Remón**
Mr. Antonio **Sánchez Gil**
Mrs. Marta **Navarro Cuellas**
Mr. Juan Antonio **Ríos Reviejo**
Mr. Manuel **Pablos López**
Mrs. Mercedes **Negueruela Maldonado**
Mrs. Marina **Martínez Aboy**
Mr. Marco Alberto **Maceiras Pérez**
Mr. Jacobo **Tenacio Vara**

United Kingdom of Great Britain and Northern Ireland
Representative:
H.E. Sir Mark **Lyall Grant**

Deputy representative:
H.E. Mr. Peter **Wilson**

Security Council [*continued*]

United Kingdom of Great Britain and Northern Ireland (cont'd)
Alternate representatives:
H.E. Mr. Michael **Tatham**
Ms. Joanne **Neenan**
Mr. Simon **Day**
Mr. Mohammed Tahir **Khan**
Mr. Jesse **Clarke**
Mr. Neil **McKillop**
Mr. Douglas **Benedict**
Ms. Helen **Walker**
Ms. Grace **Pringle**
Mr. Philip Edward **Reed**
Mr. Martin **Shearman**
Mr. Mark **Maddick**
Ms. Corinne **Kitsell**
Ms. Iona **Thomas**
Mr. Nicholas **Conway**
Ms. Sally **Jobbins**
Mr. Yasser **Baki**
Ms. Alexandra **Davison**
Mr. Iain **Griffiths**
Mr. Alexander **Horne**
Mr. Mungo **Woodifield**
Mr. Simon **Cleobury**
Ms. Lisa **Maguire**
Mr. Simon **Billett**
Mr. James **Squire**
Mr. Thomas **Meek**
Mr. Matthew **Jackson**
Mr. Christopher **Hunter**
Ms. Fiona **Allan-Smith**
Mr. Steven **Hill**
Mrs. Senay **Bulbul**
Mr. Simon **Horner**
Ms. Helen **Mulvein**
Mr. Dan **Pilkington**
Mr. Jonathan **Dowdall**
Mr. Craig **Mills**
Mr. Mark **Power**
Ms. Catherine **Carr**

United States of America
Representative:
H.E. Ms. Samantha **Power**

Deputy representative:
H.E. Ms. Michele J. **Sison**

Alternate representatives:
H.E. Ms. Isobel **Coleman**
H.E. Mr. David **Pressman**
Mr. Stephen **Gee**
Mr. Christopher **Klein**
Mr. Curtis R. **Ried**
Mr. Mark A. **Simonoff**

Advisers:
Mr. Joshua **Black**
Mr. Shane **Chase**
Mr. Neil **DiBiase**
Mr. Hugh **Dugan**
Ms. Gail R. **Horak**
Mr. David **Lee**
Ms. Elizabeth **Lee**
Mr. Kevin **Lynch**
Ms. Kimberly M. **McClure**
Mr. Walter R. **Miller**
Mr. Tyler **Moselle**
Ms. Cynthia **Plath**
Ms. Rabia **Qureshi**
Mr. David N. **Richelsoph**
Ms. Dawn **Schrepel**
Mr. William **Wagner**
Mr. Christopher **Zimmer**

Venezuela (Bolivarian Republic of)
Representative:
H.E. Mr. Rafael Darío **Ramírez Carreño**

Deputy representatives:
H.E. Ms. María **Gabriela Chávez**
H.E. Mr. Henry **Suárez**

Security Council *[continued]*

Venezuela (cont'd)

Advisers:

Mr. Wilmer **Méndez**
Mr. Zael **Fernández**
Mr. Guillermo **Moreno**
Mr. Williams **Suárez**
Ms. Cristiane **Engelbrecht**
Mr. Alfredo **Toro**
Mr. Robert **Poveda**
Ms. Marisela **González**
Ms. Yaruma **Rodríguez**
Mr. Roberto **Bayley**
Ms. Liliana **Matos**
Ms. Yumaira **Rodríguez**
Mr. César **Chavarri**
Ms. Sau Ming **Chan**
Mr. Joaquín **Pérez**
Mr. Jhon **Guerra**
Mr. José Luis **Betancourt**
Mr. Adrian José **Graterol Clavier**

Economic and Social Council (2015)

President:
H.E. Mr. Martin **Sajdik** (Austria)*

Vice-Presidents:
H.E. Mr. Vladimir **Drobnjak** (Croatia)*
H.E. Mr. Carlos Enrique **García González** (El Salvador)*
H.E. Mr. Ibrahim O. A. **Dabbashi** (Libya)*
H.E. Mr. **Oh** Joon (Republic of Korea)*

Members:
Albania
Antigua and Barbuda
Austria
Bangladesh
Belarus
Benin
Bolivia (Plurinational State of)
Botswana
Brazil
Burkina Faso
Canada
China
Colombia
Congo
Croatia
Cuba
Democratic Republic of the Congo
Denmark
Dominican Republic
El Salvador
Ethiopia
France
Georgia
Germany
Greece
Guatemala
Haiti
India
Indonesia
Italy
Japan
Kazakhstan
Kuwait
Kyrgyzstan
Lesotho
Libya
Mauritius
Nepal
New Zealand
Nigeria
Panama
Portugal
Republic of Korea
Russian Federation
San Marino
Serbia
South Africa
Sudan
Sweden
Togo
Tunisia
Turkmenistan
United Kingdom of Great Britain and Northern Ireland
United States of America

* Member of permanent mission.

Trusteeship Council

President:
Mr. Alex **Lamek**
(France)

Vice-President:
H.E. Mr. Peter **Wilson**
(United Kingdom of Great Britain and Northern Ireland)

Members:
China
France
Russian Federation
United Kingdom of Great Britain and Northern Ireland
United States of America

International Court of Justice

President:
Mr. Peter **Tomka** (Slovakia) [*]

Vice-President:
Mr. Bernardo **Sepúlveda-Amor** (Mexico)[*]

Judges:
Mr. Hisadhi **Owada** (Japan) [*]
Mr. Ronny **Abraham** (France)[**]
Mr. Kenneth **Keith** (New Zealand)[**]
Mr. Mohamed **Bennouna** (Morocco)[**]
Mr. Leonid **Skotnikov** (Russian Federation)[**]
Mr. Antônio Augusto **Cançado Trindade** (Brazil)[***]
Mr. Abdulqawi Ahmed **Yusuf** (Somalia)[***]
Mr. Christopher **Greenwood** (United Kingdom)[***]
Ms. **Xue** Hanqin (China)[****]
Ms. Joan E. **Donoghue** (United States of America) [****]
Mr. Giorgio **Gaja** (Italy) [****]
Ms. Julia **Sebutinde** (Uganda) [****]

Registrar:
Mr. Philippe **Couvreur** (Belgium)[***]

[*] Term of office expires on 5 February 2015.

[**] Term of office expires on 5 February 2018.

[***] Term of office expires on 9 February 2014.

[****] Term of office expires on 5 February 2021

Secretariat

Address: United Nations Secretariat
New York, N.Y. 10017

Telephone: (212) 963-1234

Telefax: (212) 963-4879

2. Members of other standing organs at Headquarters

Military Staff Committee

Address: Military Staff Committee
United Nations, Room S-2462
New York, N.Y. 10017

Telephone: (212) 963-5278; (212) 963-9692

Telefax: (212) 963-4213

e-mail: easton@un.org
anderson6@un.org

Chairmen of the Military Staff Committee (2015):

January: China
February: France
March: Russian Federation
April: United Kingdom of Great Britain and Northern Ireland
May: United States of America
June: China
July: France
August: Russian Federation
September: United Kingdom of Great Britain and Northern Ireland
October: United States of America
November: China
December: France

Military Staff Committee Liaison Officer:
Colonel Mark **Easton** (Retired)

China
Head of Delegation:
Major General **Ming** Zhou

Army Representative:
Senior Colonel **Yin** Zhongliang

Deputy Army Representative and Secretariat:
Major **Gong** Guoxi

Navy Representative:
Senior Captain **Chen** Qingsong

Air Force Representative:
Senior Colonel **Su** Zhang

Deputy Air Force Representative:
Colonel **Bo** Feng

Assistants:
Major **Wang** Rui (Army)
Major **Guo** Dongliang (Army)

France
Head of Delegation:
Brigadier General Christian **Beau**

Military Adviser:
Colonel Christophe **Deherre** (Air Force)

Deputy Military Adviser:
Lt. Colonel Eudes **Ramadier** (Air Force)

France [continued]:
Assistant:
Chief Petty Officer Aurélien **Arnold** (Navy)

Russian Federation
Head of Delegation:
Captain, 1st Rank Evgeny V. **Senkin** (Navy)

Deputy Representatives:
Colonel Sergey V. **Tsygankov** (Army)
Captain Dmitry **Bogachev** (Navy)

Assistant Representatives:
Lt. Colonel A. **Chistyakov** (Navy)
Lt. Colonel Sergey **Dutov**
Major Grigory N. **Tushkanov** (Army)

Chief of Secretariat:
Colonel (Ret.) Sergey P. **Yakushev** (Army)

United Kingdom of Great Britain and Northern Ireland
Senior Representative and Head of Delegation:
Major General Buster **Howes**, OBE (Royal Marines)

Permanent Representative and Military Adviser:
Colonel Mark **Maddick** (Royal Marines)

Deputy Permanent Representative and Deputy Military Adviser:
Lt. Colonel Andy **Norris** (Army)

Secretariat:
Sergeant Sian **Brackett**, AGC (Army)

United States of America
Senior Representative and Head of Delegation:
Vice-Admiral Frank C. **Pandolfe** (Navy)

Deputy Representative:
Major General Anthony J. **Rock** (Air Force)

Alternate Deputy Representative:
Brigadier General Kenneth D. **Lewis** (Air Force)

Chief of Staff:
Colonel Michael **Vassalotti** (Army)

Deputy Chief of Staff:
Lt. Colonel Timothy **Monroe** (Air Force)

Army Representative:
Lt. Colonel David S. **Macdonald** (Army)

Deputy Army Representative:
Lt. Colonel Greg **Gimenez** (Army)

Secretariat:
Major Larry **Fonder** (Army)
Mr. Glenn J. **Sadowski**
Sergeant First Class Caesar **Smith** Jr. (Army)

Advisory Committee on Administrative and Budgetary Questions (2015)

Address: Advisory Committee on Administrative and Budgetary Questions
United Nations, Room CB-0163
New York, N.Y. 10017

Telephone: (212) 963-7456

Telefax: (212) 963-6943

Chairman:
Mr. Carlos **Ruiz Massieu** (Mexico)

Vice-Chairman:
Mr. Babou **Sene** (Senegal)

Members:
Ms. Jasminka **Dinić** (Croatia)
H.E. Mr. Richard **Moon** (United Kingdom)
Mr. David **Traystman** (United States of America)
Mr. Pavel **Chernikov** (Russian Federation)
Mr. Dietrich **Lingenthal** (Germany)
Mr. Mohanad **Al-Musawi** (Iraq)
H.E. Mr. Conrad **Hunte** (Antigua and Barbuda)
Mr. Tesfa Alem **Seyoum** (Eritrea)
Mr. Devesh **Uttam** (India)
Mr. Toshihiro **Aiki** (Japan)
Ms. Catherine **Vendat** (France)
Mr. **Ye** Xuenong (China)
Mr. Ali A. Ali **Kurer** (Libya)
Mr. Fernando de **Oliveira Sena** (Brazil)

Executive Secretary:
Ms. Shari **Klugman**

Deputy Executive Secretary:
Mr. Adrian **Hills**

* Member of permanent mission.

Committee on Contributions (2015)

Address: Committee on Contributions
304 East 45th Street
FF- Room 610
New York, N.Y. 10017

Telephone: (212) 963-5306

Telefax: (212) 963-1943

Chairman:
Mr. Bernardo **Greiver** (Uruguay)

Vice-Chairman:
Mr. Gordon **Eckersley** (Australia)

Members:
Mr. Pedro Luis **Pedroso Cuesta** (Cuba)
Mr. Nikolay **Lozinskiy** (Russian Federation)
Ms. Gönke **Roscher** (Germany)
Mr. Henrique da Silveira **Sardinha Pinto** (Brazil)
Mr. **Fu** Daopeng (China)
Mr. Kunal **Khatri** (United Kingdom)
Mr. **Yoo** Dae-jong (Republic of Korea)
Mr. Andrzej T. **Abraszewski** (Poland)
Mr. Syed Yawar **Ali** (Pakistan)
Mr. Ihor V. **Humennyi** (Ukraine)
Mr. Josiel Motumisi **Tawana** (South Africa)
Mr. Jean Pierre **Diawara** (Guinea)
Mr. Ali A. Ali **Kurer** (Libya)
Mr. Ugo **Sessi** (Italy)
Mr. Shigeki **Sumi** (Japan)
Mr. Edward **Faris** (United States of America)

Secretary:
Mr. Lionelito **Berridge**

United Nations Dispute Tribunal (2015)

Address: United Nations Dispute Tribunal
2 United Nations Plaza
Room DC-2-2440
New York, N.Y. 10017

Telephone: (917) 367-9883

Telefax: (212) 963-2525

e-mail: undt-newyork@un.org

Judges in New York:
Ms. Memooda **Ebrahim-Carstens** (Botswana)
Ms. Alessandra **Greceanu** (Romania)

Judges in Nairobi:
Mr. Vinod **Boolell** (Mauritius)
Ms. Nkemdilim Amelia **Izuako** (Nigeria)

Judges in Geneva:
Mr. Thomas **Laker** (Germany)
Mr. Jean-François **Cousin** (France)

Half-time Judges:
Mr. Goolam **Meeran** (United Kingdom)
Ms. Coral **Shaw** (New Zealand)

Registrar:
Ms. Hafida **Lahiouel**

Board of Auditors

Address: Board of Auditors
One United Nations Plaza, Room 2680
New York, N.Y. 10017

Telephone: (212) 963-5623

Telefax: (212) 963-3684

Chairman:
Sir Amyas C.E. **Morse**
Comptroller and Auditor General of the United Kingdom of Great Britain and Northern Ireland

Members:
Mr. Ludovick S.L. **Utouh**
Controller and Auditor General of the United Republic of Tanzania

Mr. Shashi Kant **Sharma**
Comptroller and Auditor General of India

Audit Operations Committee:
Mr. Hugh **O'Farrell** (Chairman)
Director of External Audit (United Kingdom of Great Britain and Northern Ireland)

Mr. Fransis **Kitauli**
Director of External Audit (United Republic of Tanzania)

Mr. Ranjan **Ghose**
Director of External Audit (India)

Secretariat:
Ms. Anjana **Das**
Executive Secretary
United Nations Board of Auditors
Panel of External Auditors of the United Nations, the specialized agencies and the International Atomic Energy Agency

International Civil Service Commission (2015)

Address: International Civil Service Commission
Two United Nations Plaza, 10th Floor
New York, N.Y. 10017

Telephone: (212) 963-8464, -8465, -2092

Telefax: (212) 963-0159, -1717

e-mail: icscmail@un.org

website: icsc.un.org

Chairman:
Mr. Kingston Papie **Rhodes** (Sierra Leone)

Vice-Chairman:
Mr. Wolfgang **Stoeckl** (Germany)

Members:
Ms. Marie-Françoise **Bechtel** (France)
Mr. Larbi **Djacta** (Algeria)
Mr. Minoru **Endo** (Japan)
Ms. Carleen **Gardner** (Jamaica)
Mr. Sergei V. **Garmonin** (Russian Federation)
Mr. Luis Mariano **Hermosillo** (Mexico)
Mr. Curtis **Smith** (United States of America)
Mr. Emmanuel **Oti Boateng** (Ghana)
Mr. Mohamed Mijarul **Quayes** (Bangladesh)
Mr. Aldo **Mantovani** (Italy)
Mr. **Wang** Xiaochu (China)
Mr. Eugeniusz **Wyzner** (Poland)
Mr. El Hassane **Zahid** (Morocco)

Executive Secretary:
Ms. Regina **Pawlik**

3. National holidays of Member States

Month	Day	Member State
January	1	Cuba, Haiti, Sudan
	4	Myanmar
	26	Australia, India
	31	Nauru
February	4	Sri Lanka
	6	New Zealand
	7	Grenada
	11	Iran (Islamic Republic of)
	15	Serbia
	16	Lithuania
	18	Gambia
	22	Saint Lucia
	23	Brunei Darussalam, Guyana
	24	Estonia
	25	Kuwait
	27	Dominican Republic
March	3	Bulgaria
	6	Ghana
	12	Mauritius
	13	Holy See
	17	Ireland
	20	Tunisia
	21	Namibia
	23	Pakistan
	25	Greece
	26	Bangladesh
April	4	Senegal
	16	Denmark
	17	Syrian Arab Republic
	18	Zimbabwe
	23	Israel (2015)
	26	United Republic of Tanzania
	27	Netherlands, Sierra Leone, South Africa, Togo
May	1	Marshall Islands
	3	Poland
	15	Paraguay
	17	Norway
[*May*]	20	Cameroon, Timor-Leste
	22	Yemen
	24	Eritrea
	25	Argentina, Jordan
	26	Georgia
	28	Azerbaijan, Ethiopia Nepal
June	1	Samoa
	2	Italy
	6	Sweden
	10	Portugal
	12	Philippines, Russian Federation
	13	United Kingdom of Great Britain and Northern Ireland (2015)
	17	Iceland
	18	Seychelles,
	23	Luxembourg
	25	Croatia, Mozambique, Slovenia
	26	Madagascar
	27	Djibouti
	30	Democratic Republic of the Congo
July	1	Burundi, Canada, Rwanda Somalia
	3	Belarus
	4	United States of America
	5	Cabo Verde, Venezuela (Bolivarian Republic of)
	6	Comoros, Malawi
	7	Solomon Islands

[*July*]	9	South Sudan
	10	Bahamas
	11	Mongolia
	12	Kiribati, Sao Tome and Principe
	13	Montenegro
	14	France
	20	Colombia
	21	Belgium
	23	Egypt
	26	Liberia, Maldives
	28	Peru
	30	Morocco, Vanuatu
August	1	Benin, Switzerland
	2	The former Yugoslav Republic of Macedonia
	6	Bolivia (Plurinational State of) Jamaica
	7	Côte d'Ivoire
	9	Singapore
	10	Ecuador
	11	Chad
	15	Congo, Liechtenstein,
	17	Gabon, Indonesia
	19	Afghanistan
	20	Hungary
	24	Ukraine
	25	Uruguay
	27	Republic of Moldova
	31	Kyrgyzstan, Malaysia, Trinidad and Tobago
September	1	Slovakia, Uzbekistan
	2	Viet Nam
	3	San Marino
	6	Swaziland
	7	Brazil
	8	Andorra
[*September*]	9	Democratic People's Republic of Korea, Tajikistan
	15	Costa Rica, El Salvador, Guatemala, Honduras, Nicaragua
	16	Mexico, Papua New Guinea
	18	Chile
	19	Saint Kitts and Nevis
	21	Armenia, Belize, Malta
	22	Mali
	23	Saudi Arabia
	24	Guinea-Bissau
	30	Botswana
October	1	China, Cyprus, Nigeria, Palau, Tuvalu
	2	Guinea
	3	Germany Republic of Korea
	4	Lesotho
	9	Uganda
	10	Fiji
	12	Equatorial Guinea, Spain
	24	Zambia
	26	Austria
	27	Saint Vincent and the Grenadines, Turkmenistan
	28	Czech Republic
	29	Turkey
November	1	Algeria, Antigua and Barbuda
	3	Dominica Micronesia Panama
	4	Tonga
	9	Cambodia
	11	Angola
	15	State of Palestine
	18	Latvia, Oman

[*November*]	19	Monaco	[*December*]	5	Thailand
	22	Lebanon		6	Finland
	25	Suriname		11	Burkina Faso
	28	Albania, Mauritania		12	Kenya
	30	Barbados		16	Bahrain, Kazakhstan
December	1	Central African Republic, Romania		17	Bhutan
	2	Lao People's Democratic Republic, United Arab Emirates		18	Niger Qatar
				23	Japan
				24	Libya